SHANGHAI FUTURE

D1605818

ANNA GREENSPAN

Shanghai Future

Modernity Remade

OXFORD
UNIVERSITY PRESS

OXFORD
UNIVERSITY PRESS

Oxford University Press, Inc., publishes works that further Oxford University's
objective of excellence in research, scholarship, and education.

Oxford New York

Auckland   Cape Town   Dar es Salaam   Hong Kong   Karachi
Kuala Lumpur   Madrid   Melbourne   Mexico City   Nairobi
New Delhi   Shanghai   Taipei   Toronto

With offices in

Argentina   Austria   Brazil   Chile   Czech Republic   France   Greece
Guatemala   Hungary   Italy   Japan   Poland   Portugal   Singapore
South Korea   Switzerland   Thailand   Turkey   Ukraine   Vietnam

Copyright © 2014 Anna Greenspan

Oxford is a registered trade mark of Oxford University Press in the UK
and certain other countries.

Published by Oxford University Press, Inc
198 Madison Avenue, New York, New York 10016

Published in the United Kingdom in 2014 by C. Hurst & Co. (Publishers) Ltd.

www.oup.com

Oxford is a registered trademark of Oxford University Press

Library of Congress Cataloging-in-Publication Data is available for this title
Anna Greenspan
Shanghai Future
Modernity Remade
ISBN 978-0-19-020-669-7 (paperback)
978-0-19-020-668-0 (hardback)

Printed in India

To Max and Zoe, my future.

CONTENTS

Acknowledgements   ix
Preface   xi

Introduction   1

PART I

1. Master and Disciple   17
2. The Road Versus the Street   29
3. The Power of Spectacle   53

PART 2

4. Gothic Futurism   69
5. Created in China   87
6. Neo-haipai   111

PART 3

7. Dreams from the Edges   131
8. The Floating City   155
9. Shadow Markets   181
Conclusion   207

Notes   211
Index   237

ACKNOWLEDGEMENTS

The idea for this book came many years ago while standing in the Toronto subway, engaged in a conversation about Shanghai with my brother Jeremy Greenspan. So, my first thanks go to my family in Canada who are both my support as well as my inspiration. Much of the writing and research for this book took place in conjunction with my course 'Shanghai: Global Connections', which I have taught at NYU Shanghai since 2009 when first invited by Mingzheng Shi, whom I warmly thank for his welcome of me to NYU, and for his leadership which helped establish the Shanghai Studies Society and make the NYU Shanghai Study Away Site such a supportive and stimulating environment. In addition, I am grateful to Diane Geng and Joyce Ge for their amazing administrative support over the years, to Lisa Weir for help getting that first 'Global Connections' off the ground, and to all the wonderful students who have taken the course since it first launched. I also want to thank some of my long-term colleagues who have contributed to my knowledge of the city: David Perry, Duncan Hewitt, Dan Guttman, Jianjun Zhang, Barbara Edelson, Andrew Field and, especially, Shaoyi Sun. I would like to express my gratitude to some of the faculty and administrators at the newly launched NYU Shanghai portal site who have been particularly supportive of my work: Lucia Pierce, Joanna Waley-Cohen, John Robertson, Marianne Petit and Matthew Belanger. Finally, at NYU Shanghai, I am especially thankful to my colleagues and friends Amy Goldman and Francesca Tarocco, who enrich both my work and my life.

A host of people in Shanghai assisted me in various ways. To them, too, I would like to express my gratitude. From an early stage of the writing process fellow writers Sara Naumann and Kathryn Pauli offered encouragement, advice, and sometimes much needed breaks. Xinlei Wang helped with many of the early interviews. A number of old Shanghailanders—Anne Warr, Peter Hibbard and the late Michelle Blumenthal—led me on explorations of their beloved city. More recently, I have learnt much from walks and rides around town with Clare Jacobson. My insights into Shanghai were tested and improved from many long, enjoyable conversations with Chen Weihua (and our fellow diners Barry Porter and Jenny Laing-Peach), Vivian Shi and her family, Ding Haijiao, Xiong Wei and Chen Hangfeng. Rebecca Catching is my guide to the two most important aspects of city life: art and food. I am also deeply indebted to her for introducing me to a network of amazing women, all of whom have taught me much about Shanghai: Lisa Movius, Mary Bergstrom, Mara Hvistendahl, Christina Shmigel and Monika Lin, who helped design this book's cover. Also in Shanghai, I wish to thank the fellow founders of Hacked Matter, David Li and Silvia Lindtner, who are pushing my thoughts of the future onto new ground.

This book owes much to a number of frequent visitors who have helped me think and see the city in new ways. I have especially enjoyed my photographic tours with Tong Lam, research explorations with Xin Gu, and stimulating conversations with Justin O'Connor and James Farrer. My ideas have been tuned and reconfigured by intense and stimulating conversations with Steve Goodman, Peggy Rawes and Suzanne Livingston whenever they pass through town. I am particularly indebted to Jeffrey Wasserstrom and wish to thank him for his friendship and his scholarship on Shanghai's past as well as its future.

To some dear friends old and new who have fed the writing of this book in one way or another, I also wish to extend my thanks: Michelle Murphy, Matt Price, Deepti Gupta, Beth Chichakian, Laura Turcotte, Nunzia Carbone, Valerie Ransom, Suzanne Freeman, and Nuong Tran.

I owe most, as always, to Nick Land. Thank you for the adventure.

PREFACE

THE FUTURE IS NOT DATED

Is Shanghai the twenty-first century's New York?[1]

Shanghai World Expo 2010

Upon entering the auditorium of the Shanghai Automotive Industry Corporation-General Motors (SAIC-GM) pavilion, visitors were strapped into moving seats. The main show took place on a wraparound screen and the combined technologies created a flyover effect. The story was painfully schmaltzy, but it served only as a backdrop. The central attraction was a depiction of the city twenty years in the future. The portrayal of Shanghai in 2030 had none of the looming horrors that come from China's massive automobile boom. Congestion, pollution, accidents have all been eliminated. Instead, future citizens float through a vast sci-fi cityscape of spectacular skyscrapers and highway overpasses in intelligent, battery-powered pods. There is no need to drive and passengers spend their journeys interacting with the giant windowpane, which functions as a networked, holographic screen. Outside the view is of green parks, blue skies, clean beaches and giant wind farms. The pods approach their final destination and enter great external elevators that traverse the city's towers on both the vertical and horizontal plane. After depositing their 'drivers' at the entrance to their sky-pads, the pods steer themselves into parking positions on giant wheel landing stations, which then roll off out of view.

The SAIC-GM pavilion shows a world that will not arrive for decades, but its futurism is rooted in the past. What was on view at Shanghai's Expo 2010 was explicitly designed to recall GM's wildly popular 'Futurama' pavilion at the New York World Fair of 1939. Like its Shanghai counter-point, the central feature of 'Futurama' was a ride depicting a world that was twenty years away. Visitors were invited to 'travel into the future' and take a glimpse at the 'greater and better world of tomorrow that we in America are building today'. Once buckled into their seats they were treated to a detailed diorama that portrayed the 'Wondrous World of 1960'. The model featured farms 'made efficient by scientific progress', amusement parks and the 'great highways and motorways of the future' that connected rural life to urban civilisation. The radically zoned city, governed by what the voiceover described as 'modern and efficient city planning', consisted of 'beautiful landscaped parks around the banks of the river', elevated pavements and 'quarter mile high skyscraper towers equipped with landing decks for heli-copters and autogyros'. When the ride was over, guests were given a blue and white button that read: 'I have seen the future'.

The theme of the 1939 fair was 'The World of Tomorrow'. Today, few traces of it remain. Yet, while time has erased all physical evidence, GM's Futurama pavilion has re-emerged in cyberspace. The video of the 'Wondrous World of 1960' is now available on YouTube.[2] It is a dramatic testament to how far yesterday's futurism has slipped away. Click play and a syrupy father-knows-best narration captures the explicit ideology of the times. We are making 'progress on all the highways of improvement', it exalts. 'Mentally and physically we are progressing towards new horizons', it continues in a voice emboldened with all the confidence of the age. 'Man continuously strives to replace the old with the new ... We are heading towards a future that can be imagined, shaped and continues to get better.'[3]

Today, in the developed world at least, this progressive optimism strikes many as archaic, absurd and shockingly naïve. It is not so much that GM's vision of the 1960s is outmoded—after all the Futurama pavilion foreshad-owed the immensely transformative US interstate highway system, which was built under Eisenhower in the mid-1950s, a couple of decades after it was first presented at the World Fair. Rather, it is the spirit of futurism itself that seems so remarkably out of date. The progressive presumptions embod-ied by Futurama induce—together with images of jetpacks and robot maids—a wistful, tragi-comic nostalgia for a future that never arrived. Autogyros, in particular, seem to taunt us as a broken promise. 'Where are the flying cars?' ask writers disappointed by the dreams left unfulfilled.[4] 'A rich legacy of failed predictions has accumulated over a century (or more) of science fiction, futurology and popular expectations of progress, covering topics from space colonisation, undersea cities, extravagant urban designs, advanced transportation systems, humanoid domestic robots and ray-guns, to jumpsuit clothing and meal pills,'[5] writes Nick Land in his blog on Shanghai time.[6] This apparent gap between what is and what we once thought might be has left us wracked with doubt about the world to come. 'We don't have the same relation to progress as we used to,' claims author Michael Specter. 'We talk about it ambivalently. We talk about it with ironic little quotes around it—"progress".'[7] In our cynical, postmodern age, 'retro-futurism' is the only form of futurism that survives.

'Touch the Future'[8]

Everything new in Shanghai was produced in the past two decades. Residents have been forced to adapt to massive, high-speed urban change. In my own time here, since 2002, I have witnessed, in addition to the frequent churn of shops, restaurants and bars, the emergence of parks, skyscrapers, and multiple subway lines—all this in my neighbourhood alone. The long-standing joke that the construction crane is the national 'bird' of China arises out of the enormous mutations that have been occurring in the urban landscape of Shanghai. 'The speed and efficiency with which the Communist authorities would move Shanghai from mothballed relic of the past to stunning vision of the future would rattle the world,' writes Daniel Brook, author of *A History of Future Cities*. 'In just 20 years, the city's people would go from commuting to run-down factories by bicycle to riding to the city's new international airport on the fastest train on earth. Makeshift huts would be replaced by a high-rise cityscape boasting more skyscrapers than Manhattan.'[9] Shanghai, remarks designer Greg Yager, 'is the greatest transformation of a piece of earth in history'.[10]

Still, the intensity of urban redevelopment that occurred in the lead up to Expo astounded even those who have grown accustomed to Shanghai's rapid-fire pace. In the run up to Expo 2010 the entire city got a spruce up. Teams of migrant workers were everywhere—hanging from ladders, dangling from ropes. Brick by brick, they replaced almost every sidewalk, painted almost every wall and fence, recovered every grid, retouched every façade. Along the iconic Bund, lanes of traffic were buried and a dozen historic buildings were restored. The subway underwent an astonishingly vast expansion. Everywhere you looked transport hubs, super-towers and parks seemed to magically appear. True to Shanghai style, the 2010 World Expo dwarfed all other World Fairs in every conceivable way. It had an unprecedented budget, the largest area, the most participants and—at over

PREFACE

seventy million people—the biggest audience. Its clear and conscious aim was to reanimate the World Fairs of a previous age. In hosting the 2010 World Expo, Shanghai deliberately sought to revive the progressive optimism of an earlier age.

Outside Shanghai, however, few had even heard of Expo. Fewer still believed it had any importance. Don't World Fairs with their overt celebration of modernism, science and technological progress belong to the past? Isn't the dream of a future metropolis over? 'Hosting the World Expo with grand pavilions and futuristic displays, Shanghai can barely contain its brimming pride,' wrote scholars Jeffrey Wasserstrom and Maura Cunningham in an article comparing the World Expo with the Beijing Olympics of 2008. 'But for all the razzle-dazzle, the Chinese government must feel some disappointment that this "second Olympics" is barely registering in world opinion.'[11] World Fairs have long ago 'been consigned to the toy box of history', concurs futurist philosopher Virginia Postrel. 'Like Space Food Sticks and Jonny Quest, they are fondly remembered—at least by those over 50—but a bit ridiculous.'[12] Patti Waldmeir in an article for the *Financial Times* expressed the same sentiment with a question. 'Is the [Shanghai] Expo about imagining the future, or just redreaming the past?'[13]

There is, then, a widespread belief that Shanghai's attempts to fashion a 'World of Tomorrow' are an ironic testament to the city's backwardness. Rather than forging ahead, beyond the realm of the known, Shanghai is simply recapitulating a previous era, destined to repeat a process that elsewhere, has already played itself out. Modernity, writes the scholar Ananya Roy 'is too often interpreted as emerging from the West and spreading to the rest. So it is with urbanism. It is thus that the modernity and globality of Southern cities is studied in the valence of surprise and dismay; they are seen to be weak copies of a Western urbanism.'[14]

According to this line of thought, as China follows the well-laid path of development, it will eventually outgrow its naïve faith in the future—just as the Western world has done. Shanghai's dreams of building the City of Tomorrow will thus traverse a predictable and well-travelled course. 'The Chinese', writes Postrel in a post entitled 'The Lost Glamour of the World's Fairs', 'can't figure out why we don't love their World's Fair. They'll learn.'[15]

This idea, however, that Shanghai's present is based on mimicry; that its current futurism is inevitably reminiscent of the past; that its attempts to press ahead only reveal the fact that it still lies far behind implies, as we will see, a very particular understanding of both the future and of time. Most fundamentally, it entails thinking of the future relatively, as a specific place on a line; a point that lies ahead of us in time. This book questions this notion of temporality and argues that Shanghai's continuing rise involves an alternative to this, now dominant, form of time-consciousness. Shanghai's ambition—to emerge as the great metropolis of the twenty-first century— requires not only that it impact what is *in* the future but also, more fundamentally, that it transform the very idea of what the future might mean.

Historically, modern time was produced through a synthesis of clock and calendar. The first of these technologies, the mechanical clock, served to sever time from the events that occurred inside it. Clocks unhinged temporality from the movements of the planets and the cyclic repetition of seasons upon which traditional time-consciousness was based. With the invention and subsequent dissemination of the clock, time was released from its implicit spatial bias and became empty of all qualitative distinctions. Time, thus, became pure, absolute duration, conforming perfectly, as Nick Land has written 'to its mathematical idealization (as the real number line)'.[16]

Clocks were invented in China in the eleventh century but their true power was not unleashed until three hundred years later when the technology was rediscovered in Europe. As a result of this tremendously powerful historical contingency, the pure, empty and abstract method of subdividing minutes and hours (clock time) was fused with the Gregorian calendar when it came to counting the days. The time of modernity thus became intertwined with the Christian calendar. The Gregorian calendar originated in 1582, at the dawn of capitalism, when Pope Gregory XIII introduced modifications into the Julian calendar. It was adopted by the protestant German states in 1699, England and its colonies in 1752, Sweden and Japan in 1873, and China in 1912. Today, Pope Gregory's calendric reforms have become the basis for an unchallenged time marker that has spread across the world and the Gregorian calendar is now considered to be the (almost) undisputed calendar of globalisation. 'It is an intriguing and ineluctable paradox of globalized modernity,' continues Land in a blog post entitled 'Calendric Dominion', 'that its approximation to universality remains fundamentally structured by ethno-geographical peculiarities of a distinctly pre-modern type'.[17] A culture's rhythms, history and aspirations are rooted in their calendars. This is why calendars have always been so important to both rulers and revolutionary groups. Calendars are the surest means through which a culture can separate itself both from their immediate past and from their existing surroundings. Thus, calendric change has frequently been recognised as a culture's first and most crucial step in establishing their autonomy and solidifying their traditions. As author William Burroughs noted, if you want to change a culture, you have to change its calendar.

The numeracy of the Gregorian calendar (particularly the lack of a year zero), and the rituals and rhythms that are embedded in its count, fix modern time within a very particular cultural matrix. At its core, this culture is shaped by the idea of temporal progression. The Judeo-Christian tradition has a built-in eschatology. Time itself is infused with a forward momentum and a strong directional pull. Following the scholar Norman Cohn, we can trace the ancient roots of this sense of evolutionary time to Zoroaster, who broke from an older temporal mode, which was governed by an ongoing and unresolvable struggle between the forces of chaos and order. Zoroaster, claims Cohn, introduced the conception of 'time advancing towards a single, final consummation through incessant conflict, towards a conflictless state'.[18] After Zoroaster, not only history, but time itself could be viewed as progressing towards a final destination. Within this eschatological time-consciousness, the future became synonymous with a point waiting for us on the road up ahead. The revolutionary shift in time, which began with Zoroaster, was inherited by the culture of ancient Greece (note the progressive advance towards civilisation inherent in the *Theogony* or the *Oresteia* for example). It was also adopted, and, ultimately strengthened, by monotheistic traditions. This progressive understanding of a time encoded with both a beginning and an end has been enormously influential and its impact is still felt today. From Marxism 'with its quasi-millenarian elements',[19] to the utopian visions of the City of Tomorrow, modernity, and the futurism it invokes, still largely expresses this same conception of time.

Western culture has thus been exceedingly effective at coding modern time with its own cultural narratives. It has been terrifically successful at branding modernity its own. Indeed, many of China's most enthusiastic modernisers—from the intelligentsia of the May Fourth movement, through the Marxist revolutionaries, to the technocratic planners of today—have largely accepted this narrative, advocating that China rid itself of its backward traditions and adopt a forward-looking chronology.

This book maintains that Shanghai futurism ultimately depends on breaking free from this now common assumption about the nature of time. It senses in contemporary Shanghai the possibility of an altogether different future that is not relative but rather real and absolute. This absolute futurism does not belong to linear history. It is not a temporal destination that can be defined relationally. Rather, the absolute future exists today precisely as it has existed before, as an atemporal presence, a virtual realm that 'infuses the present retroactively with its effects'.[20] Viewed in this manner, Shanghai's recollection of yesterday's modernity is not being driven by a compulsion to repeat. Rather, the city is attempting to reanimate a lost futurism that is just as unpredictable today as it was in the past. What will ultimately emerge is impossible to predict, plan or project, since, by definition, it is utterly unforeseen. We do not yet know what China's most future-oriented city will be like or what future this city will create.

The world of tomorrow

In order to map the city of the future as it returns in a new time and place, we must first examine its disappearance. What happened to the futurism of the recent past? How did the idea of a relative future become so discredited? Why, today, is the World of Tomorrow so firmly identified with an era now gone by?

The 1939 World Fair was built on the site of an old ash heap in Flushing Meadows, Queens, New York. The entire site, the largest ever used for a World Fair, was cleaned up and paved over. By the time the Fair opened all traces of industrial wreckage were cleared away and the site had been neatly divided into colour-coded sections each with its own theme. The Fair's architecture provided a grand showcase of this peak moment of modernity, combining Streamlined Moderne, examples of what would later be known as Art Deco, as well as the still-rising International Style.

The most prominent structures—the key symbols of the Fair—were a gleaming white tower and dome, named in the imaginative spirit of the age, the 'Trylon' and the 'Perisphere'. Visitors entered the giant dome through the largest escalator ever built. Inside was the Expo's second most popular exhibit, 'Democracity', a diorama of a utopian metropolis circa 2039.

The spirit of frenzied optimism was most dramatically embodied by the 'Westinghouse Time Capsule' which consisted of a tube filled with cultural objects—everything from Einstein's writings to a Mickey Mouse watch— that was sealed and buried underground, where it was meant to remain for 5000 years, at which time it would be dug up and studied by future histori- ans. This cultural impulse to predict a world thousands of years away con- verged with the growing popularity of science fiction as a cultural form. The First World Science Fiction conference, which was attended by such notable writers as Isaac Asimov and Ray Bradbury, took place in conjunction with New York's 1939 World Fair.

Alongside this fantastic speculation were displays of technological innovations that would shape everyday life in the twentieth century. Nylon, 3D
movies and fluorescent light were all introduced at the Fair. Inside the
Carrier Corporation's 'Eskimo Igloo of Tomorrow' many visitors had their
first experience of air conditioning. The Westinghouse pavilion, in addition
to their regular demonstrations of 'Electro the Motor Man', featured compe-
titions between 'Ms. Drudge' who washed dishes by hand the old-fashioned
way and 'Ms. Modern' who used the new modern convenience of the wash-
ing machine. President Franklin Roosevelt's opening address was the first
mass event to be broadcast on television. 'The eyes of the United States,' he
told the world, 'are fixed on the future.'[21]

This celebration of the future was intrinsic to the spirit of the Fair, which,
since its inception with the Great Exhibition of 1851 had always been a
festival of global modernity. In the beginning, at the end of the nineteenth
and early twentieth century, World Expositions were massive, momentous
events. In an era before television they were the most important of global
spectacles by far. The Exhibitions far overshadowed the Olympics, for
example, and in fact, both at the turn of the century in Paris and in St Louis
in 1904, the Olympics were just an auxiliary performance to the World Fair.

The Fair began as a giant trade show, initially designed to celebrate the
modern wonders of the world. Many of the greatest technological achievements including the steam engine, the elevator, the typewriter, telephones,
films and robots were first exhibited at Expo. Charlotte Bronte, after visiting
the Crystal Palace, which housed the Great Exhibition of 1851, expressed
the widespread awe that visitors experienced:

Its grandeur does not consist in one thing, but in the unique assemblage of all things.
Whatever human industry has created you find there, from the great compartments
filled with railway engines and boilers, with mill machinery in full work, with splen-
did carriages of all kinds, with harness of every description, to the glass-covered and
velvet-spread stands loaded with the most gorgeous work of the goldsmith and sil-
versmith, and the carefully guarded caskets full of real diamonds and pearls worth
hundreds of thousands of pounds. It may be called a bazaar or a fair, but it is such a
bazaar or fair as Eastern genii might have created. It seems as if only magic could
have gathered this mass of wealth from the ends of the earth—as if none but supernatural hands could have arranged it thus, with such a blaze and contrast of colours
and marvellous power of effect.[22]

For cities like London, Paris and New York, playing host to these events,
commonly considered the timekeepers of progress, was a crucial contribution as well as a pivotal rite of passage to their status as global cities.

Yet, almost from the start, there were inklings of contradictions inherent in the Fair, tensions that would, eventually, lead to its demise. With the onset of the First World War, the optimism of modernity was hit with the first, in what would become a terrible series of cataclysmic blows. 'The first great wave of global modernity, along with its attendant illusions reached its zenith in the early summer of 1914. Then came apocalypse,' writes Land in a condensed summary of twentieth century horrors, written for *Urbanatomy's Shanghai Expo Guide*. 'Over the course of three decades, Europe self-destructed, as war on a previously unimagined scale tore the continent to pieces, followed by plague, economic collapse, totalitarian revolutions, and war again, this time infernalized by systematic genocide, even greater global expansion, and science fiction weaponry of cosmic potency.'[23] Even still, the global calamities were slow to impact the utopianism embodied by the Fair. In 1933 Chicago held an enormously successful Expo themed 'A Century of Progress' that drew forty-eight million visitors.

Opening six years later, the 1939 World Fair had spectacularly bad timing. It took place during the brief hiatus between the miseries of the Great Depression and the horrors of the Second World War. Conceived of as an event to counter the darkness of the period, it was meant to show a downtrodden world that even in the face of the food lines and mass unemployment, the best was still to come. The futurism on show at the Fair expressed the hopeful culture of America. Yet, it also revealed—at least with hindsight—the inadequacy of imagination. To take but one simple yet revealing example, the documents that were buried in Westinghouse's Time Capsule, which were meant to be preserved and read only in the year 6939, were printed on microfilm, a technology that was, at that very moment, in the process of being rendered obsolete by the advent of digital technology. More ominously still, sovereign countries represented in 1939 suffered invasion and defeat before the Fair had even drawn to an end. On Japan day, less than two years before Pearl Harbor, US officials went to the Japan pavilion to receive the 'torch of eternal friendship'. Clearly, the vision of global modernity on display at the World Fair was becoming unhinged from reality. The World of Tomorrow was not conforming to well-laid plans since, beneath the fantasies, a real world was coming into being. 'The predictions', says Jason Robards narrating a wonderfully nostalgic documentary about the 1939 Fair, 'were both too insufficient and too outlandish, as predictions always are.'[24]

Nevertheless, the Fair's brand of optimistic futurism was successfully promoted for another twenty years. Both the 1964 World Fair in New York

PREFACE

and the 1967 World Fair in Montreal, Canada were grand celebrations of the dawn of the space age. By the close of the 1960s, however, it had become starkly apparent that the rosy ideology embodied in the Fair was being undermined by unanticipated events. Social, cultural and technological revolutions, neither predicted nor planned, made a mockery of GM's conjuring, which envisioned a 'Wondrous World of 1960', that had no place for feminism, civil rights or the Vietnam War. The measured blueprint of progress advanced by the World Fairs, writes Virginia Postrel, 'started to seem both socially obnoxious and empirically false. In the 1960s, the New Left and the Goldwater Right, hippies and hackers, personal liberation movements and historic preservationists, all rebelled against the tyranny of expertise.'[25]

A collapsing faith in the future can be dated as far back as 1962, the year that Hanna-Barbera launched the TV cartoon *The Jetsons*, which, still today, is considered the quintessential example of retro-futurism in popular culture. 'I've been monitoring the way that we talk about the future for years,' states Matt Novak on his blog *Paleofuture*. 'And no point of reference has been more popular and varied as a symbol of tomorrowism than "The Jetsons".'[26] *The Jetsons* tapped into a popular celebration of the space age. True to its times, as Novak notes, it merged techno-utopianism with Cold War fears. Yet, what was most vital about *The Jetsons* was its subversive humour. Set in a futuristic utopia of 2062, the show featured a family that lived in a sky-pad, drove aerocars and had a robot maid named Rosy. In spite of this setting, however, the cartoon, like the other Hanna-Barbera classic *The Flintstones* (which was set in prehistoric times), joked about the stereotypical suburban life of the 1950s. While on the one hand it offered a comforting 'projection of the model American family into the future',[27] *The Jetsons* also poked fun at social structures that wanted to be considered eternal but were already in the process of being revolutionised. In setting this retrogressive 1950s culture in a fantasy model of a far distant time, it created at this early date what Novak calls the 'nostalgia for the futurism of yesteryear'.[28] '*The Jetsons* first aired in 1962', writes Land, 'the Golden Age had ended, and the laughter had begun.'[29]

Raygun Gothic

Twenty years later, in the early 1980s, with the emergence of cyberpunk, the science fiction vision of the future imploded. The clean, glistening projection of a future that was 'far, far away' was dismissed as absurd. In its place cyberpunk sought to depict a future that was up close and dirty, pushing up against us at the edge of tomorrow. 'The future has already arrived,' William Gibson, cyberpunk's most celebrated spokesman famously wrote, 'it's just not evenly distributed.'[30] In this new, darker, more gothic futurism, the socio-technological mutations wrought by capitalism still existed—the pace of change was not only not stopping, it was speeding up—yet, the emergent transformations that were just around the corner could no longer be planned, predicted or controlled.

In his 1981 short story *The Gernsback Continuum*, Gibson tracks this transition in how the future was perceived. The story is named after Hugo Gernsback who, as the founder of the pulp magazine *Amazing Stories*, is widely considered to be the father of traditional science fiction. In 1911, Gernsback wrote a novel, called *Ralph 124c41+*, typical of the kind of science fiction his magazine was to represent. The story gave detailed descriptions of the world in 2660, still more than 600 years away.

Gibson's story is set today. In it, the sterile utopian visions of traditional sci-fi gives way to the dystopian imaginings of a messy future that is difficult to envision and impossible to master. Gibson mocks the utopian visions of Gernsback stories by contrasting them with the scarred experiences of the twentieth century. 'The Thirties dreamed white marble and slipstream immortal crystal and burnished bronze chrome,' he writes, 'but the rockets on the covers of the Gernsback pulps had fallen on London in the dead of the night, screaming. After the war, everyone had a car—no wings for it—and the promised superhighway to drive it down, so that the sky itself darkened, and the fumes ate the marble and pitted the miracle crystal.'[31]

The Gernsback Continuum begins with a photographer sent on assignment to shoot photos for a book entitled *The Airstream Futuropolis: The Tomorrow that Never Was*. The job involves immersing himself in the architecture and design of American Streamlined Moderne, a style Gibson calls 'Raygun Gothic' for its intrinsic temporal complexity. Surrounded by these relics of a future that never arrived, the protagonist slips through the 'thin membrane of possibility' over 'the Edge' and into the futuristic world of the 1930s and 1940s. He finds himself lost in a replica of precisely the type of future city he had been researching. It looked like 'sketches of an idealized city that drew on *Metropolis* and *Things to Come* but squared everything, soaring up through an architect's perfect clouds to zeppelin docks and mad neon spires'. The photographer finds this 'fantasy stage set' deeply unnerving, a 'plastic world' filled with 'plastic people' in which everyone is wearing loose white clothing, has blond hair and 'probably has blue eyes'. Here, muses the protagonist, people lived 'on and on in a dream logic that knew nothing of pollution, the finite bounds of fossil fuel, or foreign wars it was possible to lose'. They were 'smug, happy and utterly content with themselves and their world'.[32] In this picture-perfect realm, the photographer senses a grotesque blindness and the terror of a totalitarian nightmare. 'Searchlights swept the sky for the sheer joy of it. I imagined them thronging plazas of white marble, orderly and alert, their bright eyes shining with enthusiasm for their floodlit avenues and silver cars. It had all the sinister fruitiness of Hitler Youth propaganda.'[33]

Horrified by his immersion in this science fiction utopia, Gibson's main character seeks salvation in the gritty world of cyberpunk. Escape comes from submergence in 'condensed catastrophe'. Watch as much TV as you can, he is advised; porn and news clips of our 'near dystopia' are most effective. Towards the end of the story the photographer visits a newsstand to stock up on stories of war and ecological disaster. '"Hell of a world we live in. But it could be worse, huh?"' remarks the vendor. '"That's right", I said,' writes Gibson voicing one of the key sentiments of the genre he helped invent, '"or even worse, it could be perfect."'[34]

Shanghai's retro-futurism

Future visions of the twentieth century collapsed slowly over a period of decades. Bombarded by a reality that wasn't foreseen, a weary culture came to progressively distrust modernity's forward momentum. Schooled in the sinister consequences of utopian visions, people gradually grew suspicious of any future plans. Postmodern distrust, however, which assumes that faith in the future belongs to an age that once was, arises out of a very specific culture and history.

Modern Shanghai did not suffer a slow and cumulative eclipse. Rather, the city's early heyday was suddenly, violently and instantaneously interrupted. At the beginning of the twentieth century, Shanghai was a crucial site of global modernity. During the 1920s and 1930s, in the city's golden age, the cosmopolitan metropolis hosted Jews, Russians, French, American, British and Japanese. The city was also a gathering place for Chinese migrants from all over the country as revolutionary writers, early communists, gangsters and tycoons fled the dangers of their native places searching for new opportunities. 1920s Shanghai was one of the great hubs of Art Deco architecture and was a centre of the Jazz Age.[35] In addition, almost all modern technologies came to Asia via Shanghai. Gaslights were introduced in 1865, the telephone in 1881, electricity in 1882, running water in 1884, and the tram in 1901. Marie-Claire Bergère puts it in her wonderfully authoritative history, Shanghai was 'China's Gateway to Modernity'.[36] Known alternatively as the 'Whore of the Orient', and the 'Paris of the East', it was, as the native writer J. G. Ballard puts it, 'an electric and lurid city more exciting than any in the world'…

This history was interrupted by the sudden intensity of unexpected events. The brutality of the Japanese invasion was followed by a regime committed to instantaneous utopia. Influenced perhaps by the tradition of 'sudden awakening' advocated by Chan philosophy, Mao rejected Marx's gradual theory of progress (the stages of a dialectic history), offering instead an immediate revolution led by those who were 'pure and blank'. Mao, of course, was driven by his own grand visions of surging forth into the the future, which, as the historian Jeff Wasserstrom points out, newspaper columnists like to reanimate when writing about the futurism of today. 'China's Great Leap Upwards' has been used as a title for reports for everything from China's space-race to the rise of its celebratory architecture.[37] Yet the fast-forward eschatology of the communist ideal, rooted in the rural peasantry, couldn't be more different from the urban futurism of Shanghai. The future that had seemed 'inevitable to the globalising, technophilic, piratical capitalist Shanghai of the 1920s–1930s went *missing*, writes Land, as the momentum accumulated over a century of accelerating modernisation was untracked by aerial destruction, invasion, revolution, and agrarian-oriented national integration.'[38] China's most cosmopolitan, modern and commercial metropolis was left in a state of frozen shock.

'Sometimes it feels as if time itself is suspended in the city today,' wrote Lynn Pan, who returned to the city of her birth in the 1980s in search of old Shanghai. 'The only changes to have occurred are the ones wrought by dereliction and decay. The city has been hardly touched by that destroyer of history's relics the dark angel of Development, but nor has it profited much from careful preservation. The grime of years lies so thick upon its facades that it is almost as if the place is pickled in history.'[39] This sense of a city pickled and preserved lasted until the early 1990s. It was only then that the cranes converged on Shanghai and the moment of suspended animation lifted. Shanghai, as Jeffrey Wasserstrom notes in his book *Global Shanghai*, has a strong affinity with the *Sleeping Beauty* myth.[40]

In 1978 when Deng Xiaoping introduced the revolutionary policies of *gaige kaifang* (reform and opening), Shanghai was deliberately left out of the loop. The commercial centre was judged too important to be at the forefront of experimentation. Instead, Deng began by establishing Special

Economic Zones, intended to pry open the economy in less central places like Shenzhen and Xiamen. It was not until the winter of 1992, after
his famous 'tour of the South', that Shanghai was finally, belatedly, let off
the leash.

The first big building to rise in the era of the 'new China' was the Oriental
Pearl Tower, symbol of the upcoming financial district of Pudong.
Construction began in 1990 and took four years to complete. At 468m (1,535
feet), the Oriental Pearl, was the tallest structure in China from 1994 until
2007, and remains today the most iconic structure in the city. The building
is impossible to miss. It stands near the river's edge on an enormous tripod
base that supports a series of eleven bright pink and steel silver balls. Its
deliberately archaic sci-fi design recalls Toronto's CN Tower, which was
built in the 1970s, Berlin's Television Tower, which was completed in 1969
and the Seattle Space Tower, which was constructed for the 1962 World Fair.
By the mid-1990s the landmark already seemed, at least to outsiders, an
apparition from a future that had already passed by. The Oriental Pearl is 'a
monstrous tower … all legs and bulbs and pods and needles … a mongrel of
a thing', wrote author Simon Winchester in his 1996 book *River at the
Center of the World*. It is 'a high technology fantasy by an architect who was
commissioned merely to build something that was defiantly and symboli-
cally twenty-first century'.[41] The Oriental Pearl, agrees Seng Kuan in his
influential book on Shanghai urbanism, is 'visually provocative, but it is a
dated interpretation of futurism'.[42] Much of the city's subsequent architecture revels in this same sentiment. Look up retro-futurism on *Wikipedia* and
what you find is an image of Shanghai. The highlighted building is the
Radisson Hotel, one of the older high-rises that borders People's Square.
The skyscraper plays off the city's love for rooftop follies with a huge
revolving restaurant at the top that looks, from the outside, like a giant UFO
has landed in the centre of town. From the start, then, Shanghai's rebirth
wholeheartedly embraced a futurism that the city felt had passed it by. 'The
virtual future inherent in its "Golden Age" continued to haunt it,' writes
Land, 'surviving spectrally as an obscure intuition of urban destiny. Upon
re-opening, in the early 1990s, this alternative fate flooded back.'[43] Expo
2010 exalted in the embodiment of this retro-futurist spirit. As Wasserstrom
notes, the city's Expo dreams date back over a century, to 1902 when Liang
Qichao penned 'The Future of New China,' which prophesied that Shanghai
would one day host the World's Fair.[44] In Shanghai, then, Expo 2010 was
perceived as the fulfilment of a long awaited destiny. The city's unapologetic
embrace of the World of Tomorrow was particularly acute at the 'Pavilion

of the Future', which was housed in a refashioned power plant, one of the few remnants from an industrial complex that included the old Jiangnan shipyard that once existed on the site.[45] The shell of the old structure was left visible in its retrofitted steam punk décor—old pipes and metal walls now transformed by hanging gardens of green. A massive sculpture of recycled rubbish hung in the hallway upstairs. Visitors entered the pavilion through a tunnel whose walls were converted into massive film screens. The words 'Yesterday's Dreams of Tomorrow' introduced a montage of classic sci-fi visions—from Fritz Lang's *Metropolis* to the manga classic *Ghost in the Shell*. At the end of the tunnel was a room dedicated to the modern masters of urban planning: Ebenezer Howard, Le Corbusier and Frank Lloyd Wright.[46] The next room displayed contemporary projects both real and imagined including David Fisher's 'dynamic skyscraper' with its rotating floors, Soleri's Solare: The Lean Linear City, the Seoul Commune 2026 and, of course, Gensler's Shanghai Tower, the city's super-tall skyscraper, due for completion in 2014. A little further in, the architectural plans gave way to utopian imaginings. Vast screens took up a giant wall, depicting cartoon children in an intelligent eco city frolicking with deer, then in an orbiting city floating deep in space and, finally, in an underwater metropolis where everyone dons scuba gear to venture outside. In the pavilion's final room existent technologies, a 3DTV, a networked fridge and an intelligent toilet, were exhibited, as if to say, that all these future fantasies were just around the corner.

This audacious futurism is, for many, the most unnerving aspect of China's current rise. The coming 'China Century', which Beijing celebrated so exuberantly at the Olympics of 2008, was further accelerated by the financial crisis that broke later that year. The crisis left Europe and America deeply scarred, with profound doubts about what the world of tomorrow might bring. As the decade came to a close, opinion makers, especially in America, looked to China with a gathering sense of unease. A widely publicised survey put out by *Global Language Monitor* in 2009 showed that the biggest story of the decade, by far, was China's economic rise, outdistancing the number two internet story—the Iraq war—by 400 per cent. People throughout the developed world began to worry about their ability to compete with the country's vast tech-savvy population and its ability to suddenly embrace whole new industries (taking the lead in green tech, for example).[47] China's seemingly miraculous capacity to lay down vast tracts of infrastructure with astonishing speed was of particular concern. Yet, even more troubling is that these physical manifestations were accompanied by a palpable optimistic energy. *The Economist* magazine reported on this as 'a redistribution of hope'.[48] According to the ever-deepening narratives of global rebalancing, China now seems to possess, more than anywhere else in the world, what columnist David Brooks called in a column entitled 'The Nation of Futurity' an 'eschatological faith in the future'. This faith, argues Brooks is the 'molten core of a country's dynamism'.[49] Once this seemed to define America. Today it is easier to find in Shanghai. 'If one wants to understand what "embrace the future" means in practice,' concurs scholar Martin Jacques, 'then there is no better vantage point than China.'[50] This palpable future orientation is embedded everywhere in the urban landscape. Even 'before the event had begun,' Wasserstrom observed in his book *Global Shanghai,* 'the city looked more like a metropolis that had already held an Expo than like one that was gearing up for one.'[51] It is no accident that Hollywood films that seek to depict the future in general are increasingly being set in Shanghai (see for example *Code 46, Looper*, and *Her*). 'Perhaps more than any city in the world,' writes Wasserstrom, 'Shanghai already resembles a futuristic fairground even when no circus is in town.'[52]

Postrel, whose writing is more cyberpunk than science fiction, argues that the West's widespread disenchantment with 'tomorrowism' proves only that a particular type of futurism is in decline. She urges us to celebrate future's unplanned dynamism over and against the type of staged futurism presented at the World Fair:

Whether one considers the spread of Japanese manufacturing practices, the generation upon generation of Silicon Valley startups, the fresh-food revolution that migrated east from Alice Waters's Chez Panisse, or the logistical innovations of Wal-Mart, the creative destruction of the late 20th century showed that the old experts, public and private, didn't know as much about either technological possibility or consumer desires as they'd imagined. Progress was far from over, but it would be more disruptive and surprising than any World's Fair exhibit could depict.[53]

The problem, however, is that the recognition of a future that is out of control has been concurrent with a paralysing sense of doubt. The rightful disillusion of utopian imaginings has arisen alongside a deeper loss of the future itself. It is not only the ability to plan that now seems missing in much of the Western world, but also—more importantly—the boldness to envision what tomorrow might bring. 'The future as such,' says theorist Mark Fisher, 'has succumbed to retrospection.'[54] As Postrel herself writes, it is 'our cynical culture' that is 'done with World's Fairs'.[55] In the introduction to *The Shock of the New*, his great book on modernist art, Robert Hughes laments all that has disappeared in the century between 1898 and 1989, the year the book was written. What has been lost, he writes is 'ebullience, idealism, confidence, the sense that there was plenty of territory to explore'.[56] At their best, the futurism of World Fairs should not be simply dismissed as the choreographed presentation of a preplanned tomorrow. Instead, in their excited celebration of that which is just about to emerge, they act for the cities which host them, whether in 1939 or in 2010, as an affirmation of the future itself. This spirit of absolute futurism can never go out of date.

INTRODUCTION

THE FUTURE IS ALWAYS MODERN

An era of creation is about to commence.

Le Corbusier

The way of the Creative works through change and transformation.

Yijing

Contemporary Shanghai is best viewed from those zones of the city that are still incomplete. Downtown, in People's Square, Shanghai's Urban Planning Museum showcases a miniature model of the city that corresponds to a future date. Structures that are already standing are modelled in white, while those that are as yet unfinished are left transparent. Residents are said to come here before buying property to check if their houses will soon be torn down. In the model, the giant towers that are to come dwarf even the city's brand new skyscrapers.

Shanghai is a city hungry for the future. To get a taste, head to the heights of the financial district in Pudong's Lujiazui. At dusk, the view from the ninety-first floor of the Shanghai World Financial Center is fantastically alien. Outside the enormous windows, the metropolis stretches out like an off-world fantasy; a film apparition of a science-fiction city. Across the road is the pagoda-inspired Jinmao tower, the oldest of a planned trio of skyscrapers. At only eighty-eight stories the Jinmao now seems oddly comforting. What shocks is the building surfacing outside. The hole for the Shanghai Tower was dug in 2011. At that time, peering down, deep within the chasm, one could glimpse the fiery light of workers and their heavy machines as

1

they prepared the ground for a building that will, once complete, spiral 128-stories high, far above the expansive landscape.

Everywhere there is the sense that the city is more process than place. In vast newly constructed satellite towns on the urban periphery the landscaping is done, the paint is dry and most of the units are sold. Hotels, stores and bars display signs reading 'Open All Day', but there is nothing behind the façade. The film set effect is a little creepy in a city of twenty million people—like a ghost town haunted by those who have yet to arrive.

Nearby, surrounding rural villages have been swallowed by this incessant urban growth. Here the suburbs have the feel of a frontier settlement. Though the canals, old houses and fields still remain, the farmers are mostly gone. Their homes have been carved up and rented to migrant workers who take over the village's main street. Teenage boys with dyed orange hair and tight black jeans stroll past stalls selling street food, plastic buckets, cheap motorbikes, pirated cell phones and the other tidbits necessary for a new urban life.

Shanghai's economy of anticipation is equally transformative closer to the urban core, where long abandoned industrial zones are being gutted, stripped and then restored. These empty shells of a bygone era—brick and concrete factories and warehouses now wrapped in glass—architecturally express the city's fervent desire to awaken its latent potential. Though still mostly vacant, these new 'clusters' seek to unlock a creativity buried in the urban unconscious. The intent is that by reanimating what now lies dormant, Shanghai will finally be able to fulfil its ambition, recapture its lost destiny and re-emerge as the future city that it once promised to become.

Implicit in the futurism so palpable in twenty-first century Shanghai is a rebirth of modernity. As it looks forward, Shanghai is forever harking back. Its current rise is based on a deep nostalgic memory of an 'urban golden age' that peaked in the 1920s and 1930s. To use Ackbar Abbas' formulation, Shanghai today is 'not Back to the Future, but Forward to the Past.'[1] Throughout the city, heritage architecture—villas, lane houses, factories, banks, churches and hotels—are being preserved and restored. What lies behind this architectural revival is an attempt to revivify the lost spirit of the modern age. In bars, cafes, teahouses, parks and boutiques, urban inhabitants play out their roles in this time-travel fantasy. Through its architecture, design, self-image and style, contemporary Shanghai strives to remember, and to reinvent, the creative flourishing it once—too briefly—hosted. Driven by this fractured destiny, it is embedded in a spiral of time, actively trying to splice together its imminent future with a past futurism that never had the chance to play itself out.

In its current embrace of the modern, however, Shanghai does more than recall its own particular history. It has also, more crucially, revived the much wider modern project of building a future city. With its super-tall towers, elevated highways and suburban 'garden towns', Shanghai today, increasingly resembles yesterday's dreams of the metropolis of tomorrow.

Modernity is a notoriously difficult concept to define. Inextricably bound to the interlocking and revolutionary processes of globalisation, urbanisation and mechanisation, it also encompasses the cultural impulse to express, process and understand these vast material transformations. Yet, in addition to these socio-economic and cultural conditions, modernity can also be apprehended philosophically, as a particular conception of time. Martin Jacques, in his book on China's rise, adheres to this definition. Modernity, he writes, quoting the sociologist Goran Therborn, marks 'the arrival of an epoch turned to the future'.[2] To be modern, according to this understanding, is to be in the present just on the cusp of its erasure, to be necessarily and always, at the most urgent edge of now. In a piece entitled 'Neomodernity', Shanghai-based philosopher Nick Land elaborates on this conception:

Modernity dates awkwardly, and intriguingly, because it positions itself upon the leading edge of time expressing an infusion from the future. In its vital, colloquial sense, the 'modern' is an indexical term that describes what is happening now, or recently. It is in this sense that modernization remains irrepressibly up-to-date, anchored, indexically, to the contemporary. To slip unanchored from the 'now' into the dead waters of history is thus to forsake the claim to modernity. What is distinctively past cannot be modern, and the modern cannot be simply past.[3]

Modernity, understood as a mode of time oriented to the future, occurs at the level of the production of time itself, and is in this (transcendental) sense beyond or before history. Nevertheless, the modern time-consciousness manifested itself most intensely at a specific historical moment. The sense that one was living in modern times, though it tracks its roots back centuries, reached an apex in the early decades of the twentieth century when the world was infused with an aura of anticipation. Time itself seemed to be propelling forward, rushing towards a destination. Everywhere was an intuition that the future was about to arrive.

Only decades later, as we have seen, this sense of momentum was lost, and the very notion of a time oriented to the future was treated with scepticism and disbelief. Modernity, it is now widely maintained, belongs to history and we have entered (or perhaps, by now, even surpassed) a postmodern age. 'Many people think the modernist laboratory is now over,' wrote Robert Hughes in 1980. 'It has become less an arena for significant experiment and more like a period room in a museum, a historical space that we can enter, look at, but no longer be a part of ... We are at the end of the modern era.'⁴

In twenty-first century Shanghai, however, this temporality of anticipation, the sense of an immanent future, has returned. Today in China's largest, richest, fastest growing metropolis a second, regenerated modernity—modernity 2.0—is currently underway. In positing this recapitulation, this book rejects the notion that the modern now belongs to the past. Instead, due to its future orientation, the modern should not be comprehended chronologically as a moment easily plotted in time and thus cannot be superseded. Modernity, as Land writes:

resists absorption into accomplished history, because it relates to an absolute future. The dynamized now of modernity is irreducible to a period or moment in time. What modernity discovered, and perpetually recalls, was not just the next thing up the road, but the road ahead in general, and perhaps even the road.

Though it mirrors an earlier age, then, the modernity Shanghai is calling upon, and being called towards, does not, at least in any straightforward sense, imply an imitation of something that already has been. Shanghai today must, necessarily, be based on more than mere mimicry. Rather, the city's continued re-emergence rests on the 'atemporal' eruptions of an absolute futurism (which Nietzsche called the *untimely*) that produces all that is radically and unpredictably new. Shanghai, in other words, must summon and unleash the creativity inherent in modernity, out of which the future has always been forged.

An outline and a map

Two seemingly contradictory forces combine to produce the future city. On the one hand there is the authoritarian will, governed by a controlling desire, that sets out to master the revolutionary transformations taking place on the ground; to envision what is to come, and to shape and plan its course. Inevitably, this is disrupted by a countercurrent that is produced by the spontaneous innovations that emerge, unexpectedly, from the everyday culture of the street. This fundamental tension, between the desire to plan for the future and the knowledge that the future is, by its very nature, impossible to foresee or control, is at the very heart of the modern metropolis. The pages that follow will map this dichotomy—between the planned and the unplanned—as it plays itself out in contemporary Shanghai. In these discussions, there is particular attention to the realm of urban architecture. This

4

focus is perhaps best justified by the theorist Fredric Jameson in his famous treatise on postmodernism. 'It is in the realm of architecture,' writes Jameson, 'that modifications in aesthetic production are most dramatically visible, and that their theoretical problems have been most centrally raised and articulated.'[5] Thus it is through the construction of a modernist urban landscape—that is, the attempt to create the dream of the modern city—that the culture and ideals of modernity have been most clearly expressed.

We begin in Pudong on the eastern shore of the river that bisects the city. If the supercharged pace of China's recent rise has a pure expression, it is Pudong. Only twenty years ago the area was all farmland and factories. Today, it is the site of one of the densest clusters of skyscrapers anywhere in the world. When people want a symbol of Sinofuturism, this is where they come. The urbanism of Pudong, however, with its broad boulevards, super-dense high-rise housing and landscaped parks is a deliberate reanimation of earlier visions of the modern metropolis. In the case of the Shanghai World Financial Center, the city's tallest tower, this echo of a previous dream is particularly explicit, since Minoru Mori, the developer of the building, is an ardent admirer of the arch-modernist Le Corbusier. Part 1 zooms in on Pudong's super-tall towers, in order to explore the ways in which Le Corbusier's ideas for a contemporary city—elsewhere dismissed and reviled—are being reborn in twenty-first century Shanghai. This rebirth, however, is not simply an instantiation of a plan made long ago. Rather, Pudong's neo-modernism seeks to access one of the abstract solutions to hyper-urbanism: decongestion through density, a strategy that famously seeks to leave space for nature by building up high (Le Corbusier's 'tower in the park'). In Pudong, then, Shanghai aims to invent a skyscraper city that fuses modernist imaginings with the high-speed intensity of Asian urbanisation.

Pudong has plenty of critics. Many view it as exemplifying the unchecked power of China's authoritarian regime, which operates from on high developing cities with little thought about how they are actually going to be used. Pudong might look good from afar, say its detractors, but with its windswept plazas and long empty roads, it is more a place for looking at than for living in. Others, however, see in Pudong's miraculous rise evidence of the positive side of authoritarianism; a snapshot portrait of a regime that can build infrastructure with a speed and efficiency that now seems impossible in the democracies of the developed world. Part 1 explores the tension, so evident in Pudong, between the top-down tendencies and bottom-up realities that are at play in China's new urban landscape. It does so by referring back to the famous conflict between master builder Robert Moses and acclaimed urbanist Jane Jacobs. This clash, so crucial to the formation of the modern metropolis of the twentieth century, pitted a car-based culture, with its cities of high-speed motorways against the everyday rhythms of the street. Embedded in this tension, between the road and the street, is the modern production (or manifestation) of a progressive historical time that aims (however disastrously) to pave over the old in order to make way for the new.

It can appear that Pudong has wholeheartedly embraced the road-based urbanism and the underlying modern timeline that this implies. Yet, underneath the surface, Shanghai's enormous mutation is being powered by conditions that are singularly its own. Take, for example, the idea of the spectacle, which is of crucial importance to the Chinese conception of power and strength. Westerners tend to see the spectacle cynically, as a means of hiding the truth. Chinese culture, however, with its yin/yang rotation of darkness and light, and its positive emphasis on the culture of 'face' does not share the notion that everything must be made visible. Instead, it accepts a distinction between what appears on the surface and a shadowy world that lies beneath. This recognition, that part of urban life occurs in back alleys, behind closed doors, hidden from view, is precisely what the penetrating, totalising control of the modernist plan could never allow. Thus, by accepting the shallowness of spectacle, and obsessing on façade, Shanghai can, at least sometimes, enable a far more messy, flexible and pragmatic reality to thrive in a realm that is hidden from view.

The flow of this book follows a course from light to darkness. Beginning with the showy exhibition of Pudong's skyscrapers, it moves through the more occulted modernity of Puxi to end in the shadowy realms at the edges that exist largely out of sight. Here, as we will see in the book's final section, Shanghai's newest and most dynamic population, the undocumented migrant workers, have created an informal or grey economy capable of massive, disruptive change.

If Pudong reinvents the high modernism of the international style, Puxi, the older part of the city on the western side of the river, is more attuned to the 'alternative modernisms' of art deco and expressionism. Part 2 begins by looking at these 'other modernities', that were flourishing during Shanghai's lost golden age in order to show how these darker inventions of the future metropolis—in cinema, literature and architecture—run counter to the temporal linearity celebrated by the modernists of the May Fourth movement. Understood in this way, the future nostalgia for Shanghai's 'golden age' seeks to recall and reconstruct a conception of 'Shanghai Modern' that is based on the singular twisting of a 'gothic futurism', which does not, and never has, followed the straight order of time.

In the early decades of the twentieth century the streets of Puxi created a singular style, which must be imaginatively reawakened before the city can truly revive. Part 2 examines Shanghai's creative ambitions, beginning with a tour through the architectural remnants of the city's modern industrial heritage. Shanghai factories and warehouses are being converted into hyper-designed 'clusters' aimed at attracting a new 'creative class'. This vast urban transformation (there are now close to 200 of these 'clusters' in Shanghai) is meant to help propel China's largest and most prosperous city beyond its current status as factory of the world into an innovative centre of the global economy. Yet, while the spaces themselves, with their complex temporal layering, are at the cutting edge of a neo-modern aesthetic, many—even most—still lie empty and unused. The failure of these clusters challenges China's strategy of 'build it and they will come', serving instead as a stark illustration of the oft-repeated opinion that China's hardware is far in advance of its software. 'Building a tower is easy,' says hip-hop entrepreneur Gary Wang, 'it's changing people's minds that is hard'.[6] In trying to engineer creativity, Shanghai is discovering the limits of its projections and plans. The problem facing the city is how to embrace the intrinsic 'drift of innovation'—to borrow Jane Jacobs' phrase—where there are no clear goals and 'no one knows what is going to happen next'.[7]

Alongside the conversion of these industrial spaces are numerous attempts to restore and revivify Shanghai's distinctive lane-house architecture. It was in these dense residential communities, with their intense micro-commercial activity, that Shanghai's hybrid urban culture—known as *haipai*—was born. Today, this old urban fabric is coming to life in a myriad of ways. This architectural revival, which recollects at the same time that it transforms, is based on the knowledge, however unconscious, that Shanghai's hope of transitioning from imitation to true creativity depends upon plugging into the city's lost futurism; a possibility that now permeates city life. Yet, Shanghai's attempts to produce a neo-*haipai* culture faces many forces—the censorship of the authoritarian regime, the prevalence of piracy, the rigidity of the education system, the brutal erasures of recent history—that serve to stifle what the city is so desperately trying to become.

Resolving these tensions has implications that extend far beyond the city limits. In a book entitled *Cities in Civilization*—a vast tome which runs to over 1,000 pages—the great urban historian Peter Hall offers a complex history of the world as told through the creative potential of its cities. Hall zooms in on particular times and places where an intense eruption of innovation has occurred. These disruptive moments, whether in arts, technology or methods of social organisation have always occurred in cities. 'Every great burst of human creativity in history,' Hall writes, 'is an urban phenomenon.'[8] His book, which tells of Athens in the fifth century, Florence in the fourteenth, Victorian London, Paris at the end of the nineteenth and New York in the mid-twentieth century among many others, shows that it is these urban 'golden ages' that revolutionise the course of history. In these singular instants, Hall contends, a city becomes not so much a place but an epoch, that is at once both fully global and, simultaneously, hyper-local. Cities at the height of their golden age, writes Hall embrace 'everyone who enters with a power that cannot be resisted'. 'To become a Berliner—that came quickly, if one only breathed in the air of Berlin with a deep breath,' Hall writes quoting a resident of Weimar Berlin, 'Berlin tasted of the future.'[9] Reading Hall in contemporary Shanghai one cannot help but wonder, might we, here, too be on the cusp of such a golden age? Is Shanghai capable of a creative flourishing influential enough to impact the world? Are we nearing a threshold in which it is no longer modernisation that is changing China but rather China that is changing what it is to be modern? Though the answers to these questions are still unknown it is the contention of this book that the continuing rise of Shanghai—and indeed China—rests upon this type of deep and far-reaching urban creativity.

Part 3, the final section, moves away from the core in order to explore the urban periphery. Shanghai's edges are a complex jumble of gated communities, relocated factories, apartment high-rises, foreign-themed satellite towns, remnants of the countryside and new migrant communities. In this heterogeneous mix all the clashes and contradictions of Shanghai's current futurism are in play. The city's master plan involves utopian dreams for the suburbs. Drawing on the modern imaginary, it envisions a series of garden satellite new towns with quiet streets, elaborate villas and landscaped lawns whose function is to de-intensify the city centre. Yet, so far at least, there is little evidence that Shanghai's upwardly mobile middle class is mimicking the North American love of suburbia. Despite frequent allusions to the 'villafication of Chinese cities' and 'the spread of Western suburbs', the peripheries of Asia's urban centers, as Ananya Roy says, embody 'much more than the American suburb'.[10]

Instead, peripheral development has flourished primarily due to a frothy property market, with its ties to the practice of land leasing, which underpin the country's quasi-communist economy. Yet, despite this primarily commercial motivation, outlandish experiments have taken place on the borders of town and the strange complexes built on the city's edges provide an interesting test-ground for the idea of 'Shanghai as remake'.[11]

More important than any outward trend towards suburbia, however, is the flow of population coming in. The underlying reality of Shanghai's suburbs, despite the idealised fantasies of planners and government officials, lies in the great migration that is currently reshaping both China and the world. We are, at the beginning of the millennium, in the midst of the greatest wave of urbanisation the planet has ever known. Author Doug Saunders calls it 'the final great human migration'.[12] 'A third of the world's population is on the move this century,' he writes, 'this time in the developing world.' Throughout Asia, Africa, Latin America and the Middle East, the villages of the countryside are emptying out. In 2007 the threshold was crossed. For the first time in history 50 per cent of the world's population became urban dwellers. Megacities are mushrooming everywhere. *National Geographic* reports that in 1950 New York was the only city in the world with a population over ten million, by 2015 there will be twenty-one of these giant cities—almost all in the developing world.[13] Saunders writes:

What will be remembered about the twenty-first century, more than anything else is the great, and final, shift of human populations out of rural, agriculture life and into cities. We will end this century as a wholly urban species. This movement engages an unprecedented number of people—two or three billion humans, perhaps a third of the world's population—and will affect almost everyone in tangible ways.[14]

'The age of nations is over,' concurs Parag Khanna writing for *Foreign Policy* magazine in their 2010 special *Metropolis Now*. 'The new urban age has begun.'[15]

Nowhere is the global transformation from rural to urban life more intense than in China. Here urbanisation is faster and larger than ever before. In 1980 under 20 per cent of China's population lived in its cities. Today it is over 40 per cent. This explosive trend shows no sign of abating. Intense high-speed urbanisation is a central tenant of the Xi Jinping/Li Keqiang regime. Government officials predict that the urban population will surpass 700 million in the next five years, exceeding the number of rural dwellers for the first time. McKinsey Global forecasts that by the year 2030 there will be a billion people living in Chinese cities.[16] Once a year the country gets a sense of this monumental human flow when urban migrants return to their villages to celebrate the New Year. Throughout China, every spring festival, people flood onto trains and buses to participate in this annual ritual.

Together this 'floating population' rhythmically repeats the largest human migration in history.

Part 3 explores the lives of Shanghai's newest migrants focusing on the immense impact of the *hukou* (or household registration) system, a bureaucratic policy that—more than anything else—makes urbanisation in China unique. Shanghai's singular migrant communities exist mostly on the city's borders. Yet these frontier settlements, where the new metropolis meets the countryside, are very different from the 'planet of slums' proliferating elsewhere in the developing world. Shanghai's new migrants have not yet fully urbanised. Instead they 'float' between the villages where their birth is registered and the emerging metropolis, which they are helping to build. This precarious in-betweeness is reshaping the very process of urbanisation itself. Like the population it hosts, the city has in turn become more fluid and, therefore, can no longer be understood simply as a clear destination at the end of the line.

Migrant workers build Shanghai's high-rises and fill its factory floors. They are also among the city's most dynamic entrepreneurs. Urban residents know this from their everyday dealings with the vast informal economy, a shadowy realm of street food, recyclers, DIY electronics and makeshift markets that infiltrates everywhere, just under the surface, despite—and beyond—all urban plans. Operating outside state control, this intensely vibrant and dynamic grey zone makes a vital contribution to the urban economy. It also manages to possess many of the qualities Shanghai is often accused of lacking. Risk taking, flexibility and the entrepreneurial spirit, which is often missing in the clever but cautious Shanghainese, are found in abundance among the micro-commercial activities of the unplanned economy. The exciting and spontaneous street life, with its noodle stands and high-tech gadgets, has huge disruptive potential. Shanghai's future aspirations—its quest to find a new modernity—rests not only in the glossy skyscrapers of Pudong, but, also here in the unexpected innovations that arise through the unplanned, unpredictable, out of control and everyday culture of the street.

China Time

The most prominent social thinkers of the nineteenth and twentieth century, theorists like Karl Marx and Max Weber, held that Chinese modernity could never be of its own making. China, they believed, was held in a state of perpetual stasis by the conservative traditions of its culture and by the stagnant forces of the 'Asiatic mode of production'. The internal momentum of historical progress, therefore, would, inevitably, have to arrive from elsewhere. China could only break free from its endless cycle of stagnation and participate in the advances of the modern world when cultural evolution was imposed on it from outside. This book offers itself as a guide to contemporary Shanghai in order to show that its neo-modernity is not—or at least not simply—an imposition from the West. Rather, modernity 2.0 unfolds out of another philosophical matrix, with an altogether different understanding of time.

From a Western point of view, the radical otherness of China's temporal traditions is revealed through the difficulty of grasping the most basic of time words. Westerners tend to think of the passage of time 'as an upward line of growth and accumulation'. This conception of a rising temporal order is represented most iconically, as Land notes, in the popular image of Darwinian evolution, which is 'characterized as a process of ascent that shows an ape creature erecting itself in stages to a climactic state of proud human verticality'.[17] In China, on the other hand, the course of time is depicted as a descent. Unlike English, Mandarin uses time words, rather than grammatical components as temporal markers. The two most basic of these are *shang* (up) and *xia* (down), which stand for the past and future respectively. This mode of measuring time as a 'descent into the future' is based undoubtedly on the water clock, a technology that dates as far back as 4,000 BC in China. The lasting impact of this ancient technology enables the Chinese, as is evident in their language, to think of 'time tangibly as a continuous fluid,' which flows forever downward. This no doubt helps explain the country's huge enthusiasm for countdowns (which was particularly evident in Shanghai in the lead up to Expo 2010). Indeed, in Shanghai eagerness for the future is so palpable that, as Jeff Wasserstrom notes, even the countdowns are high speed. In 1999 'millennial countdown clocks in both Beijing and Shanghai were ticking away the time until the new century and the new millennium began ... The difference,' Wasserstrom observed, 'is that those I saw in the capital were set to go off on 1 January 2001, but those in Shanghai, a city impatient to enter the twenty-first century and the start the new millennium before its northern rival, were programmed to hit zero a full year earlier, on 1 January 2000.'[18]

This conception of a downstream temporal flow, however, becomes twisted in Shanghai due to the city's complex relation to its own history. Today, the era of 'Old Shanghai', is constantly being revived as a futuristic memory. Everywhere a past modernity is evoked, not as a time that once was, but as an immanent possibility. This sense that contemporary modernisation was anticipated in a former era has the effect of folding time in on itself, opening the possibility of an echo that does not simply repeat. In his essay 'Introductions to the Afterlife', Land elaborates on the temporal riddle of 'a repetition always in advance of the repeated. If we can speak of the recapitulation of the past in the present,' he writes, 'we must also speak of the repetition of the future through the invocation of the past.'[19]

Shanghai's desire to return to the future finds expression through a myriad of time-travel performances, which recur incessantly in the city's cafes, hotels, shops, restaurants and bars. Through this insistent future nostalgia, the culture of the contemporary metropolis coils time in on itself, breaking free from both the linear model of Western modernity as well as the looped cyclic stagnation of traditional Chinese time. 'Neomodernity is at once more modernity, and modernity again. By synthesizing (accelerating) progressive change with cyclic recurrence, it produces a distinctive schema or figure: the time spiral.'[20]

This idea of a spiral of time has a long history in China.[21] Its underlying and deeply paradoxical thought—that return brings with it the production of the new—is, as commentator Wonsuk Chang writes, embedded in the *Yijing*, China's most ancient text:

Time in the *Yijing* may serve a conservative purpose—namely, restoring the past. But it also serves the creative purpose of producing novelty. These two aspects of time do not contradict each other. Many passages in the *Yijing*, if not all, express that which restores the past simultaneously involves some element of novel creation. The process begins from its incipient movement and finally reaches the point where creative novelty emerges. This evolutionary process is that of an advancing spiral, which ever produces novelty while simultaneously returning again and again to the nascent sources.[22]

At the beginning of Chinese recorded history, there is already a gesture exceeding the boundaries of linear causality, with the use of the *Yijing* to gain insight into the future. According to translator Jing Nuan Wu, the text crosses these temporal chasms by accessing a virtual temporality that is simultaneous to the present, although it is often concealed. The rituals encoded in the *Yijing* are designed to open a wondrous door (*qi men*) to a hidden time (*dun jia*) that exists in a 'realm outside the senses but that very much influences the here and now.'[23]

This notion of an exterior, atemporal zone that is always—at least virtually— available, can also be found in Chan Buddhism, one of the most indigenous and innovative adaptations that has emerged from China's long and fruitful encounter with Indian Buddhism. Chan's most famous techniques, its intentionally incomprehensible poems (*gong'an* or *koan*) and the physical (sometimes violent) teachings of its masters, stem from a philosophical rejection of 'gradualism'; the belief that enlightenment is a destination that one slowly progresses towards. The 'subitists' counter the idea of a 'gradual cultivation' with the conception of 'sudden awakening'. Enlightenment is not a future goal that one systematically approaches, incrementally, in time. Rather, awakening comes suddenly, in an instant, not because it is easy to attain, but, because time itself works this way.

In its rhythmic repetition of renewal and renaissance, Confucianism, too, is productive of a time-spiral that cannot be comprehended as a straightforward linear order. Confucius spoke of his own work as the restoration of an older tradition, a move that is repeated by the Song-Ming Neo-Confucians, and then once again by the New Confucians active in the twentieth century. This recurrent Confucian return to an older tradition (which is itself always a process of recreation), is evoked, however, in the service of creating the new. This is especially apparent in new Confucianism (whose most fascinating proponent is Mou Zongsan), which arose as a 'conservative' counter to the May Fourth movement and as a direct engagement with the novelty of modernity.

Chinese philosophy, then, offers some hints about how we might conceive a modernity outside the straight line of time. It gestures towards a future that is exterior to the chronological order no longer imagined as an eschatological end. This reconceptualisation of modern time is, for now, only suggestive. Since as a project it is still (and perhaps necessarily) incomplete. Nevertheless, the importance of what is at stake cannot be overemphasised. In an op-ed in the *New York Times* author Anand Giridharadas asks about the soul of Asia's emerging giants. 'What kind of world will they summon?' he asks. 'What will be, when the hot growth cools and the deeper reckoning comes, the meaning of their rise?'[24] Modernity 1.0 may still mutate and grow. Yet the basic culture, values and thought generated by the rise of both Europe and America is more or less known. We may debate concepts like freedom, democracy and individualism but we still understand, at least more or less, what they mean. The neo-modernity still brewing in Shanghai, on the other hand, is largely unknown. If it is to truly become the global hub of the twenty-first century, for that is what it wishes, Shanghai will need to produce a new modernity as creative and revolutionary as the first. In this project, Shanghai, of course will not act alone. It has always been impacted by the flows of the region, the country and the world. But as one of Asia's most vast, dynamic and cosmopolitan metropolises, Shanghai, no doubt, has a special role to play. Modernity 2.0 is not just a copy of Modernity 1.0. China's great city is not only influencing what will take place in the future, it is also transforming the very idea of the future itself. As it modernises, Shanghai is necessarily recreating what it is to be modern.

PART 1

1

MASTER AND DISCIPLE

Suppose we are entering the city by way of the Great Park. Our fast car takes the special elevated motor park between the majestic skyscrapers ... Here, bathed in light, stands the modern city ... As twilight falls the glass skyscrapers seem to flame. At the feet of the first skyscraper is not a meager shaft of sunlight. The whole city is a park.

Le Corbusier

Asia is different from the United States and Europe. We dream of more vertical cities. In fact, the only choice here is to go up and use the sky.

Minoru Mori

There is a 'before and after' photograph of Shanghai, taken twenty years apart, that periodically circulates through cyberspace.[1] The contrasting images zoom in on the shores of the Huangpu, the city's main river. By fast forwarding through time, they maximise the impact of the recent urban mutation. The result is a visceral illustration of the shocking intensity of Shanghai's high-speed rise. In the sepia-toned image from 1990, the Huangpu acts as a sharp divide, the line separating urban density from rural sprawl. While the western shore (Puxi) is dominated by the colonial architecture of a once modern metropolis, the Pudong district, in the east, is nothing but a nondescript flatland of factories, shanty-town housing and farmland. Zhao Qizheng, then deputy mayor charged with the development of Pudong, bemoaned the imbalance, describing 1990s Shanghai as a 'mal-developed cripple'.[2]

The contrasting picture, of Shanghai 2010, is taken at night, when the city is awash with neon and LED lights. Pudong, by then home to one of the densest clusters of skyscrapers in the world, dominates the urban landscape. In this image, the city resembles the backdrop of a future fantasy with whole buildings metamorphosing into massive screens. Here, in these illuminated high-rises with their garish explosion of colour, China's economic miracle receives its most vivid and concrete manifestation. This awe-inspiring view of Pudong has become the quintessential icon of twenty-first century Shanghai. It is the face of China's development, the window onto the country's current modernisation. This image of Pudong's skyline accompanies almost all stories of China's rise.

In 2012 the Shanghai World Financial Center (SWFC) was the tallest tower in Pudong. Though completed in 2008, the tower is a modernist masterpiece. In its simplicity of form and engagement with the spectator, it recalls the paintings of abstract expressionism and the clean lines of minimalist sculpture. The giant structure lacks all ornamentation, yet its appearance mutates depending upon the angle from which it is seen. Get up close and walk around and it seems like a giant shape-shifter, transforming itself before your eyes. The effect is particularly dramatic at night when the tower's contours are illuminated in an electric blue.

Plans for the SWFC began as early as 1993, when Pudong's science fiction skyline was still only a dream. In 1997 the foundations were laid. For the next ten years, construction was plagued with difficulty. Almost as soon as it began the project was halted by the Asian economic crisis. On at least two occasions the blueprints were changed, first in response to the terrorist attacks on 11 September 2001, and then, later, to accommodate cultural sensitivities on the ground. Initial designs featured a giant circular hole at the top of the tower complete with a working Ferris wheel. The hole was intended as a 'moon-gate', a common motif in traditional Chinese landscaping, but prickly locals viewed the circle as a rising sun, the national symbol of Japan. The idea of a super-tall building resembling the Japanese flag rising over the Chinese metropolis was deemed politically unacceptable and the top cavity had to be changed into a rectangle (which many believe gives the building the appearance of a giant bottle opener). In the end, the SWFC took more than ten years to complete and cost over $1bn. Yet, when it was finally finished, it was widely heralded as a triumph. The SWFC was originally conceived as the tallest building in the world and, when judged by roof and not spires, it achieved this, however briefly. In its ambition, innovative engineering, height and form, it has made a singular contribution to the skyscraper renaissance currently taking place in Asia. The Council on Tall Buildings and Urban Habitat named the SWFC the best building of 2008, and in the same year, *Fortune Magazine* awarded the building's developer, Minoru Mori, the title of 'businessman of the year'.[3]

The SWFC is Mori's brainchild and stands as an expression of his particular vision of Asia's urban future. William Pedersen, design partner at the New York firm Kohn Pedersen Fox (KPF), the architects of the tower, stressed this point in a talk he gave in 2009 as part of the *China Prophecy* show at the Skyscraper Museum in Manhattan. 'To discuss Shanghai and its tall buildings, one must talk about the urbanism that these tall towers create,' Pedersen began, 'and to talk about urbanism in Asia one must talk about one man—Minoru Mori.'[4]

In the initial discussions over the SWFC, KPF dealt exclusively with Minoru's father, Taikichiro. Already in his nineties at the time, Mori Sr. would meet the American designers dressed in a traditional kimono. His son, when present, sat on the sidelines without saying a word. Taikichiro Mori had become, through his investments in the Tokyo property market, one of Asia's most important real estate tycoons. By the time he died in 1993, he had amassed a fortune of thirteen billion dollars, making him the richest man in the world. His sons carried forth his legacy. In 2004 *Time* ran a story featuring the Moris entitled 'The Families that Own Asia'.[5]

As a young man, Minoru Mori did not immediately join his family's real estate empire. He sought instead to pursue a literary life as a novelist and philosopher. These earlier intellectual interests stayed with him in his work as a developer. 'It was a smooth transition,' Mori says of his career path. 'I started with an interest in writing novels about people's lives as they were and moved to an interest in writing prescriptions for how their lives should be.'[6] Initially Mori viewed the job of property development as nothing more than building and leasing office buildings. Before long, however, he saw the potential to make a much greater impact and began to consider new urban forms and experiences. What eventually emerged was a development strategy steeped in a futurist philosophy. 'I am drawn more to the unknown than to the past with its established reputations,' Mori is quoted as saying, 'and I yearn to continually create things that are new'.[7] This impulse draws him to projects that are daring, visionary and extremely high-risk. Eventually this approach, which invariably requires amassing huge amounts of debt, caused a parting of ways with his younger and more cautious brother, Akira, who started his own real estate company, Mori Trust. The two are said to be on amicable terms, though occasionally their differences surface in interviews.

'My brother,' says Minoru, 'is more interested in creating a good company with a high valuation than in creating cities.'[8]

Due to his work in Tokyo and Shanghai, Minoru Mori has become one of the most influential developers of the twenty-first century Asian metropolis. Pedersen calls him 'the most brilliant urbanist I've ever met'.[9] Mori's futurism, however, is firmly rooted in the past. He is deeply inspired by the ideas of arch modernist Le Corbusier, whose work he has been collecting for over twenty years. In his gallery, The Mori Art Museum, located on the top floor of Roppongi Hills in Tokyo, there are 300 paintings and sketches by the master on display. 'Le Corbusier is my great teacher, and also a presence that I feel I must strive to exceed,' says Mori. 'Even today, there are many discoveries that I can make by looking at his art and urban planning.' While he works in an entirely different time and place, Minoru Mori is one of Le Corbusier's most faithful, as well as most contemporary, disciples.

In evoking Le Corbusier, Mori's supertowers enact a twist in time and place, as ideas that belong to a modernist past are revived in the futuristic buildings of today. Many urban theorists—noting Le Corbusier's ongoing influence in China—treat this as a sign of backwardness, since there is perhaps no modern architect that has been more widely criticised than Le Corbusier. Conceptions about urban design that have elsewhere been rejected are today being reanimated in the growing megacities of Asia. Yet, Mori's modernism is not simply a naïve rehashing of ideas that have already been tried and found wanting. Instead, what Mori is attempting to tap into is an abstract solution to the problem of urbanisation itself, and in so doing to engineer a return that still holds innovative potential. His ambition is to build urban landscapes that surpass what even Le Corbusier imagined. 'My improved Le Corbusier model,' he calls it.[10] Though it harks back to an earlier age, the skyscraper City of Tomorrow is as 'future oriented' today as it was when Le Corbusier first dreamed it in the early decades of the twentieth century.

The contemporary city

Charles-Édouard Jeanneret (the man who came to be known by his pseudonym Le Corbusier) was born in 1887 to an artisan family in a town in Switzerland near the border with France. His father was a watchmaker and Le Corbusier himself was trained in the elite craft of watch case engraving. Yet, by the turn of the century the processes of industrialisation were already beginning to overwhelm this specialised artisan trade. Le Corbusier watched as what was once a skill requiring patient training became easy to imitate and cheap to mass-produce. According to the urban historian Robert Fishman, Le Corbusier's early years were thus dominated by the crisis and decline in his way of life brought on by modernisation.[11]

Observing the destruction of his family's traditional craft, the young Jeanneret did not withdraw in defeat, but, instead, sought a rebirth through the full embrace of the modern future he sensed was about to arrive. He was, as Fishman notes, both a witness and a product of modernity. This conflicting dynamic, so formative in his early life compelled a creation of the self. The transformation occurred in Paris, a city that became his liberation. Paris, writes Fishman, was 'not just his home but his obsession.'[12] Once settled in the metropolis, Charles—now refashioned as Le Corbusier—quickly hooked up with the metropolitan avant-garde. Yet, while deeply inspired by the energy and inventiveness of the modern city, he also reacted with disgust and horror at the chaos and disorder of urban life. These two contradictory forces—creativity and revulsion—propelled him forward on a singularly inventive path.

Le Corbusier rejected the craftsmanship of his childhood as a dying trade. In its place he was committed to the discovery of an 'art of the future' that was true to his age. For Le Corbusier, 'reviving the arts of the past was impossible'. Fishman explains, 'because creativity depends on the mastery of the most advanced ideals and technology of one's own time'.[13] For creativity to be true, it had to be modern. 'Le Corbusier's art of the future must be an art of the Machine Age or it would not exist at all.'[14]

In this quest, Le Corbusier experimented with a variety of artistic forms. In painting, along with artist Amédée Ozenfant, he pioneered an offshoot of Cubism called 'Purism' that rejected ornamentation and embraced, instead, the basic, 'pure' forms of the modern machine. Purism was launched with a document entitled *After Cubism*, which was filled with Le Corbusier's characteristic, slogan-dense, manifesto-style prose. These concise, highly provocative statements—most famously 'a house is a machine for living in'—are, in many ways, Le Corbusier's most important legacy. It was in architecture and especially in the new realm of urban planning, however, that Le Corbusier ultimately found his 'art of the future'. The destruction wrought by modern machines that he had witnessed from childhood could also, he believed, lead to salvation. Yet, for this to occur, it was imperative that, as Fishman writes, they be 'mastered at its controlling point—the great city'.[15] Le Corbusier thus sought a solution to the problems of urbanisation and modernisation in the creation of the metropolis of the Machine Age.

Le Corbusier's vision, so the story goes, came to him in 1922, when he was invited to participate in a salon on urbanism. He was asked to enter a design competition that was looking for a comprehensive street art 'for stores, signs and the like', and was to include 'such things as ornamental glass knobs on railings'.[16] 'Fine', Le Corbusier is said to have replied, 'I shall design a great fountain and behind it place a city for three million people.'[17]

Le Corbusier's City of Tomorrow[18] sprang straight from the mind, perfectly complete from the moment of inception. As an ideal product uncontaminated by empirical reality, it was deeply philosophical in nature. 'ARCHITECTURE,' Le Corbusier insisted, 'is the art above all others that achieves a state of platonic grandeur.'[19] The purity demands a blank slate. Modern urban planning, as dreamed up by Le Corbusier, needs a perfectly flat plain, a tabula rasa that was uncontaminated by the mess of any particular city. Anything else would get in the way. 'The planner needed open spaces in which he was free to create his own urban order,' writes Fishman. 'He must be master of the whole environment. Nothing can be undertaken properly without a view of the whole.'[20] 'A level site is the ideal,' declared Le Corbusier. 'WE MUST BUILD IN THE OPEN.'[21]

Pudong and the Modern Metropolis

Zhao Qizheng recalls that when Minoru Mori first heard of the proposals for Pudong, his 'eyes lit up'. Energised by the area's potential, Mori called for an on-the-spot investigation and decided there and then to invest. As soon as the word was out that the district's designs included a trio of skyscrapers, Mori asserted his interest. 'We talked for about two hours,' Zhao Qizheng is quoted as saying. 'I told him we wanted to build three large commercial towers in the centre of the new area. We would build the first one, but the other two were undecided. Mr. Mori replied immediately, "Let me build the second one."'[22]

It is easy to see why Mori was so excited by the prospect of building in Shanghai. In the early 1990s Shanghai's new district promised what all modern urbanists dream of: an empty canvas on which to create. In the hinterlands, on the other side of the river, Shanghai found a way to flee the dense, winding chaos of its older streets and alleys and recreate at least a part of itself as the ideal modern city. 'Pudong,' as urban theorist Thomas Campanella writes, 'was now the blank slate on which the future of Shanghai would be written.'[23]

Plans for the Pudong New Area were drawn up in the late 1980s and early 1990s, precisely the time that postmodernism in the West—with its culture of scepticism and irony—was at its height. Untouched by this spirit of disillusion, Shanghai embarked on a project whose scale, speed and ambition would prove just as radical as anything attempted in modern times. The district's design reflected this reanimation of yesterday's futurism. With its neat rows of hyper-dense towers surrounded by landscaped green-spaces, broad boulevards and pedestrian overpasses, Pudong follows a blueprint long abandoned elsewhere. Intended as a contemporary city for the twenty-first century, it—more than anywhere else in Shanghai—overtly recalls the high modernist imaginings of a future metropolis. The resemblance is no accident. Pudong is best understood—alongside Le Corbusier's City of Tomorrow, Baron Haussmann's Paris and Robert Moses' New York—as one of the great projects of modern urbanisation.

Density and decongestion

> *The park is not in the city; the city is in the park.*[24]
>
> Sir John Summerson (referring to Le Corbusier's designs)

At the core of Mori's vision of the modern city is the contradictory postulate—essential to Le Corbusier's thought—that to decongest the city it is necessary to increase the density of the urban core. This seemingly paradoxical idea is best understood in contrast to the opposite inclination: decentralisation. Faced with the pollution, squalor and chaos of newly-industrialised cities, governments and planners tend to support a strategy of fleeing outwards, believing that spreading people out into small suburban towns or 'garden cities' that are built on the urban edge could deintensify the city and make mass urbanisation more manageable. Le Corbusier vilified this impulse with characteristic ferocity, attacking decentralisation as an 'illusion', 'falsehood' and deceptive 'mirage'.[25] Garden cities with their 'mock nature' should be banned, he proclaimed. Suburbs should be eliminated. Instead, Le Corbusier advocated for compact cities that cram people tightly together, rather than extending ever outward. In the Metropolis of the Machine Age, we should 'pile the city on top of itself'.[26]

Central to Le Corbusier's argument is that as a consequence of this intense urban density the city can be made green. Urban dwellers have no need to escape into the false nature of suburbia, he insisted. Instead, nature could be 'brought into the cities themselves'.[27] The key to this dense but decongested metropolis infused with the natural world is the skyscraper. When work, leisure and housing are packed inside mega-towers, Le Corbusier maintained, plenty of room can be left for trees, flowers and open spaces. His sketches show clusters of high rises set within large areas of green. In his plans for a 'contemporary city' the 'skyscraper in the park' would replace the unruly chaos of urban sprawl. The 'Contemporary City', wrote Le Corbusier is a 'Green City'. 'Not one inhabitant occupies a room without sunlight; everyone looks on trees and skies'.[28]

The skyscraper is a purely urban form. Where there is a skyscraper there is necessarily a city. The very scale of these super-tall towers highlights the artificiality of the urban experience. To many, they are profoundly—even terrifyingly—alien. In Shanghai, the tallest skyscrapers like to play with this disturbing subversion of gravity. The most awesome feature of the Jinmao Tower is a giant atrium that extends from the fifty-sixth to the eighty-eighth floor, which makes peering down the interior of the building even more unnerving than gazing at the view outside. When it first opened, the SWFC pushed this play on heights to an even more provocative extreme, constructing the floor of the one hundredth story observation deck entirely out of glass. Many visitors couldn't bear the vertigo, however, and now only a few glass panels remain allowing those who dare to peer down over 400 metres at the traffic flowing below. By defying the mass of gravity, skyscrapers demand human mutation. To work and live so far above ground requires deep mammalian rewiring. Nevertheless, by occupying this profoundly unnatural space, skyscrapers can, paradoxically, offer urban citizens a powerful connection with the natural world.

The ability to build up depends, of course, on the elevator. Le Corbusier called this invention the 'keystone of all modernisation'.[29] Architect Rem Koolhaas names this machine of vertical transportation, which can lift mass and allow urban citizens to occupy the sky the 'great emancipator'. The elevator opens up a new dimension of the city, and thereby reintroduces an element of the natural world that street-level existence has obliterated. Skyscrapers, wrote Le Corbusier, 'provide a sublime expression (the mature fruit of machine-age evolution) of this century's strength. To bring back the sky. To restore a clear vision of things. Air, light, joy.'[30] Koolhaas concurs: 'The greater the distance from the earth, the closer the communication with what remains of nature (that is, light and air)'.[31]

This idealised vision of the skyscraper—enormous towers that would make way for nature—is a recurrent theme in the work of modern urbanists.

Even Frank Lloyd Wright, who is famous for his 'organic architecture', which sought to harmoniously integrate buildings with their surrounding environment, designed a skyscraper that soared a mile high. The 528-storey high-rise, known as The Illinois, converted Wright's architecture 'conceived for the horizontal plane, and translated it into the vertical dimension'.[32] Wright imagined The Illinois as a 'city within a city' that would contain 100,000 people. Its purpose was to restrict the density of urban life into a single building, which could thereby preserve vast tracks of open land and wilderness.

This idea, that human civilisation be contained in vast structures, which can leave room for an untamed countryside finds a most bizarre and fascinating expression in the diagrammatic writings of Wright's one-time apprentice Paolo Soleri. Soleri's work is based on the idea of 'Arcologies', a hybrid term invented to express the melding of architecture with ecology. 'Arcologies', he explains, are compact settlements with a definite boundary somewhat analogous to ocean liners. Their construction is meant to precipitate the 'radical reorganisation of the sprawling urban landscape into hyperdense, integrated, three-dimensional cities'.[33] By creating environments of extreme density, Arcologies minimise the use of energy, raw materials and land; reduce waste and environmental pollution; and allow interaction with a surrounding uncontaminated wilderness. In this way, they offer a solution to both the problem of suburbia and to what Soleri calls 'megalopoly', a term used to describe the flat megacities of today. Soleri sketches these massive structures, conceived as self-contained organisms, orbiting the earth, submerged under ground, rising like giant pods from the desert sand.[34]

Vertical garden cities

The skyscraper as the quintessential form of urban modernity is an American invention. 'Tall buildings became possible in the 19th century,' writes urbanist Edward Glaeser, 'when American innovators solved the twin problems of safely moving people up and down and creating tall buildings without enormously thick lower walls.'[35] The modern skyscraper emerged first in the fantastic vertical metropolises that arose in early twentieth century New York and Chicago. Today, however, few super-talls are built on American soil. Instead, the great American export is transforming the urban landscapes of Asia. According to the 2009 *China Prophecy* exhibit at the Skyscraper Museum, Hong Kong, with 7,200 high-rises, holds the title for most vertically intense city. Yet, buildings of an unprecedented height are sprouting throughout the mainland, particularly, the curators note, in the still 'ascending' urban landscape of Shanghai.

In his talk at the Skyscraper Museum, William Pedersen showed an image of Minoru Mori peering over a detailed model of Tokyo. The model was built, Pedersen says, with the express purpose of comparing the sprawl of the Japanese metropolis with the compact concentration of Manhattan. To Mori a successful city is a dense city and Tokyo is simply not dense enough. 'If Manhattan were to be described as a vertically oriented city,' reads the text on Mori's official company website, 'Tokyo would, in contrast, be aptly described as a planar city. Because land usage in central Tokyo is highly inefficient, factors such as overpopulation and the flow of industry to the suburbs has created an expansion of urban areas, resulting in a huge, sprawling metropolis.'[36] Mori's stated aim is to 'replace Tokyo's chaotic, low-rise industrial-era neighbourhoods with a more modern and convenient urban environment'. In Japan the instantiation of this vision would inevitably require widespread destruction. Pudong thus promised something that had eluded Mori in his hometown—the wholesale replacement of low-rise urban sprawl.

Mori's urbanism seeks to counter the congestion of decentralisation through the development of 'Vertical Garden Cities', a concept he inherited from Le Corbusier. These mixed-use ultrahigh-rise structures are designed to house super dense populations and function as 'cities within a city', integrating work, residences, entertainment, education and commerce in such a way that everything can be reached on foot. 'When you look at Le Corbusier's architecture, it was truly mixed-use,' Mori notes with admiration. 'Take one building with many different functions that a city needs, for example, a post office. The rooftops were covered by gardens; the building had other functions, commercial shops and even kindergartens'.[37] By diminishing the need to commute, Vertical Garden Cities can reduce urban congestion and increase the amount of open, green spaces. Cities, says Mori, reflecting the influence of his master, 'should be built around several high-rises that would be able to liberate the foothold for nature. The idea of building vertically and having ample green spaces is better for both nature and people.'[38] Mori's most accomplished Vertical Garden City to date is Roppongi Hills in Tokyo, an inner-city mega-complex that encompasses a museum, a cinema, a public arena, a sculpted garden and a plaza filled with high-end shops. The SWFC is modelled after Roppongi Hills.

The Vertical Garden City, then, is an old idea made new. The question is, what type of temporality is at work in this revival? Is this a case of history repeating itself; of development as backtrack in which concepts once tried but now forgotten are destined to play themselves over until they are abandoned once again? Or, alternatively, is the return to modernity the result of a time spiral in which recollection is combined with innovative production? In this latter case the future need no longer be defined relationally as a temporal moment but, instead, can be reconceived as a qualitative condition of time that is always, at least virtually, accessible.

The green metropolis

In the current debates over urbanisation, the modernist idea of dense but green skyscraper cities is converging with environmental concerns. Contemporary theorists like David Owen and Edward Glaeser defend the ecological merits of high-density urban environments. Compact and crowded cities, where people mostly walk instead of drive, live in energy-efficient apartment blocks and generally leave wilderness alone, they contend, are far more sustainable than small towns and suburbs with lots of green. 'A Thoreau-like existence in the great outdoors isn't green,' writes Owen, author of the book *Green Metropolis*, 'density is green:'

Dense urban centers offer one of the few plausible remedies for some of the world's most discouraging environmental ills ... Manhattan is the greenest community in the world ... New Yorkers, individually, drive, pollute, consume, and throw away much less than do the average residents of the surrounding suburbs, exurbs, small towns, and farms, because the tightly circumscribed space in which they live creates efficiencies and reduces the possibilities for reckless consumption.[39]

This contention that sustainable futurism rests not on 'solar-powered mountainside cabins or quaint old New England towns'[40] but rather on super-dense vertical cities like Manhattan, or Shanghai, is increasingly being advocated by economists, architects and planners worried about the effects of China's high-speed urban growth. In a report entitled 'Preparing for China's Urban Billion', McKinsey Global urged the country to counter the trend towards urban sprawl and opt for policies tailored to concentrated urbanisation. 'By adopting policies of concentrated urban growth,' the report argues, 'China could produce 20 per cent higher per capita GDP, be more energy efficient and contain the loss of arable land.'[41]

This idea of a dense, green, compact and vertical city featured heavily at Expo 2010. Sustainable design was showcased everywhere: e-buses traversed the site, solar panels powered many of the pavilions and developments in urban farming—rooftop gardens, 'hydro-plants' and 'green walls'—were all prominently on display. Indeed, if there was one technology on show at Shanghai's Expo, it was the 'living wall', which was a highlight at the Alsace Pavilion, the Canadian Pavilion, The Future Pavilion and The Shanghai City Pavilion among others. The massive green wall on the exterior of the 'Theme Pavilion' covered 5,000 square metres and was the largest in the world.

Shanghai's most cutting edge experiment in sustainable design, however, is taking place back in Lujiazui, next door to the SWFC at the site of Pudong's third giant skyscraper, The Shanghai Tower, which at 128 storeys high will soar above the landscape of Pudong and become—at least for an instant—the second tallest building in the world.[42] Super-tall skyscrapers, due to their exorbitant cost, operate as singular showcase buildings, and are thus uniquely positioned to pioneer practices in engineering design. The Shanghai Tower is 'Leadership in Energy and Environmental Design'-certified, and blueprints have been lauded for pioneering environmental construction. 'We hope,' says Art Gensler, chairman of Gensler, the firm that is in charge of construction, 'that Shanghai Tower inspires new ideas about what sustainable tall buildings can be.'[43] The massive edifice has a cylindrical core that is wrapped in a transparent outer skin that twists up to the sky. This double-skin façade will act as a 'thermos bottle', insulating the building and increasing its energy efficiency. The structure will also harvest rainwater, recycle grey water and use wind turbines to generate power. Between its two curtain walls are nine indoor gardens each with a fourteen-storey atrium. These sky gardens will separate the buildings into 'vertical neighbourhoods' which will be open to the public and are meant to function as city parks with space for leisure, exercise and play.[44] The tower is conceived of, according to Gensler's Dan Winey, as 'a vertical sustainable city'.[45] The influence of Mori, and of Le Corbusier, is clear. 'One is almost on top of the greenery, one sees a sea of trees; and here or there are those majestic crystals, pure prisms, limpid and gigantic [the skyscrapers]. Majesty, serenity, joy.'[46]

The modern vision of the 'Contemporary City' is not tied to any particular place and time. Instead, it is produced on an empty, abstract plain. It is precisely this abstraction that makes the modern metropolis continually futuristic. Its time, writes Robert Fishman, was 'the time of the present, not any calendar day or year, but that revolutionary 'here and now where the hopes of the present are finally realized'. 'It is called contemporary,' Le Corbusier insists, 'because tomorrow belongs to nobody.'[47] In much of the world the Contemporary City may be a relic, but in Shanghai dreams of the future metropolis live on.

2

THE ROAD VERSUS THE STREET

The plan must rule ... the street must disappear.

Le Corbusier

The street finds its own use for things.

William Gibson

Great cities are made of great streets. In Shanghai the long, narrow, tree-lined streets encompass and delight in all the impossible contradictions of the rising metropolis. On Ulumuqi Lu, Fuxing Lu, Xiangyang Lu, Changle Lu and the other main avenues of the former French Concession, colonial-style garden villas and art deco apartments look out onto glistening high-rises of concrete and glass. Gourmet restaurants and trendy boutiques intermingle with noodle stands, fruit sellers and tiny stalls stuffed with cheap plastic tchotchkes. Stylish pedestrians walk past the hubbub of street vendors with their mobile carts selling stockings, fresh vegetables, house-plants and pirated DVDs. Closer to the Bund, the city's most mythical and majestic of boulevards, the streets become increasingly grandiose. Here, nearer to the city centre, markets cluster in formations that have sedimented over for decades. On touristy Nanjing Lu stand the giant department stores; on Fuzhou Lu, once at the heart of the red-light district, tiny shops and giant malls stock an enormous variety of stationery and books; under the arcades of Jingling Lu stores selling musical instruments mix with those trading in buttons, ribbons and lace. In Shanghai when you ask someone what they did at the weekend, where they are going on a date, what they do in their spare time, often they will answer *guang jie* (strolling the streets). Shanghai's best

29

streets are full of life and rich in commerce and culture. All the best ones are located in Puxi.

Pudong is built around main arteries. Its capillaries are hard to find. Chief among the straight, wide roads is Century Avenue, which serves as the district's vast diagonal spine. Shiji Dadao, as it is called in Chinese, runs from the heart of the financial core in Lujiazui, past the area's cultural centres (the Science and Technology Museum and the Centre for Performing Arts) and ends in the pedestrianised entrance to one of Shanghai's largest parks. French architect Jean-Marie Charpentier designed Century Avenue with the explicit intent to make it exactly one metre wider than the Champs-Élysées. The enormous boulevard has eight car lanes, four bike lanes, green islands and vast pavements. Yet, though it was modelled after one of the world's most famous landmarks, and has generous walkways lined with leafy trees and benches, Century Avenue is not a place that many come for a stroll. Its huge blocks are filled with enormous towers that do not face the street (as Charpentier proposed), but instead run perpendicular to the avenue due to the Chinese insistence on south-facing rooms. There are almost no shops and pavements contain little commercial activity. Century Avenue was built for cars, not for people. It is most certainly a road, not a street.

The modern metropolis was conceived of as a city of roads, designed for the new technology of the car. Planners dreamt of a city made of straight lines that would accommodate the fast and shining machines. From the start this road-based urbanism was suffused with utopian tendencies. It is no accident that GM's model of 'The World of Tomorrow' was produced in order to promote the highway and motor vehicle.

In designing car-based cities, modern urban planners envisioned 'avenues of progress' that would lead, inevitability, to a future destination waiting for us on the road up ahead. The linear mode of temporality is encoded ferociously in the road-based imperative of creation: destroy the old to pave the way for the new. This master plan of the modern metropolis conceived of as a city of roads, however, is and has always been contested. There is another, alternative and more messy vision of the future city, which emerges bottom-up, out of the continuously disruptive and enormously innovative culture of the street.

Shifting allegiances

The writings and sketches that comprise Le Corbusier's designs for the modern metropolis are compiled in English under the title *The City of Tomorrow and its Planning*. The book begins at the start of autumn as Le

Corbusier finds himself, after the quiet lull of the summer, suddenly over-whelmed by the madness of the traffic on the Champs-Élysées. Immersed in the swarm of cars, he mourns the loss of a more peaceful age:

After the emptiness of summer, the traffic was more furious than ever. Day by day the fury of the traffic grew. To leave your house meant that once you had crossed your threshold you were a possible sacrifice to death in the shape of innumerable motors. I think back twenty years, when I was a student; the roads belonged to us then.[1]

Within the space of a single paragraph, however, Le Corbusier undergoes a remarkable transformation. The fearful lament is replaced by euphoric celebration. Seduced by the intensity of the machine, Le Corbusier switches sides. No longer identifying himself with the pedestrian that once owned the street—*the roads belonged to us then*—Le Corbusier now claims allegiance to the power and speed of the car. 'An enthusiastic rapture filled me,' he exalts, 'the rapture of power. The simple and indigenous pleasure of being in the centre of so much power, so much speed.' In his tome *All that is Solid Melts Into Air*, author Marshall Berman elaborates on the monumental sig-nificance of Le Corbusier's conversion. 'Le Corbusier's modern man will make one big move that will make further moves unnecessary,' he writes in his description of this paragraph, 'one great leap that will be the last. The man in the street will incorporate himself into the new power by becoming the man in the car.'[2]

By the end of the preface, *The City of Tomorrow* has determined the battle lines. From now on, a hard, and often-brutal, dichotomy will govern the making of the modern city. The road had become the enemy of the street. To Le Corbusier this difference is fundamental. In his models of the future city there are no snaking streets, only 'sane and noble' roads that do not curve and bend. The determined linearity of the metropolis complies with the ordered rationality of the modern mind. 'Man walks in a straight line,' Le Corbusier asserts, 'because he has a goal and knows where he is going... The modern city lives by the straight line.'[3]

Le Corbusier's reverence for sharp angles is rooted in his veneration of geometry, which he honours as the highest art. 'We struggle against chance, against disorder, against a policy of drift and against the idleness which brings death,' Le Corbusier proclaims with typical dramatic fervour: 'we strive for order, which can be achieved only by appealing to what is the fundamental basis on which our minds can work: geometry.'[4] The prejudice is drawn from deep within Western thought. The inscription on the door to Plato's ancient academy: 'No one may enter here that does not know geometry', could equally be written at the entrance to Le Corbusier's *City of Tomorrow*. 'The modern sentiment is a spirit of geometry, a spirit of construction and synthesis, exactitude and order are its essential condition.'[5]

In *The City of Tomorrow* Le Corbusier contrasts the dignified rationality of the straight line to the directionless meanderings of a pack donkey. The winding streets that host this aimless rambling animal embody a backwardness that the determined, forward-looking creative spirit of modernity abhors. 'The winding road is the result of happy-go-lucky heedlessness, of looseness, a lack of concentration and animality,'[6] he insists with a palpable revulsion. Cities based on the pack donkey trail are tangled and inefficient. They are badly formed organisms, 'all capillaries, no arteries', riddled with disease. For Le Corbusier the older, outdated town with its 'passion for twisted streets and twisted roofs' must be banished, conquered and placed under control. The task is fiercely urgent. Without geometry, and the self-mastery it entails, the chaotic web of the old organic city looms as a menacing presence, waiting to engulf.

Baron Haussmann and the making of Paris

Le Corbusier viewed himself as the rightful successor to Paris' other illustrious urbanist, Georges-Eugène Haussmann. Haussmann's work, Le Corbusier believed, was still incomplete. A great task remained; to bring Haussmann into alignment with the new age of the tower and the car.[7]

Baron Haussmann was hired in 1852 by Napoleon III to 'modernise' Paris. Today, he is widely credited as being the city's master builder—the person responsible for transforming Paris into the earliest showcase of a modern metropolis. The scale of the urban change he engendered was tremendous. 'No one in the entire history of urbanism,' writes Peter Hall, had 'ever transformed a city as profoundly during such a short period of time.'[8]

In the years before Haussmann, Paris was collapsing under the weight of a vast flow of immigrants, all participating in the massive wave of urbanisation that was revolutionising Europe at the time. At the beginning of the nineteenth century, France's capital—with a population of a little over half a million—was still quite small. But, as the century progressed a 'sea of humanity poured into Paris'. By 1850 there were 1.3 million living in the city; fifty years later, by 1900, 3.3 million called Paris home.[9] The urban infrastructure simply could not keep up with this explosive growth. Water shortages were particularly acute. Before Haussmann, 'fewer than 150 houses in the whole of Paris had running water'.[10] Sewers were massively inadequate and poorer districts had nothing but open cesspools. The entire city was dark, squalid and overcrowded, streets gave off a revolting stench and disease was rampant. The cholera epidemic of 1832, to take but one grim example, killed 20,000 people in Paris. Another 19,000 died in the epidemic of 1849. Haussmann transformed the city by building underground infrastructure. Hidden below the surface, he created a system that could provide safe water and treat the city's sewage.[11] Yet, his fame lies with what he built above ground not with what he did underneath. The reconstruction of Paris rested on Haussmann's most celebrated innovation—the great new boulevards; the first modern roads.

Pre-Haussmann Paris was cramped and impossibly congested. 'The centre of the city was a maze of narrow streets, barely more than alleyways, in which traffic found it almost impossible to move.'[12] Haussmann cut through this dark, dank labyrinth of dingy lanes by building long, straight roads— wider than any that were previously known. The boulevards made Paris into a singular whole. It united the disparate parts of the city together by accommodating modernity's most vital force—speed. 'When Haussmann's work on the boulevards began, no one understood why he wanted them so wide,' writes Berman in his history of modernity: 'from a hundred feet to a hundred yards across. It was only when the job was done that people began to see that these roads, immensely wide, straight as arrows, running on for miles, would be ideal speedways for heavy traffic.'[13]

The boulevards were planned to accommodate a rapid movement from place to place. Yet, they were also built for leisurely walks. Haussmann lined them with a new type of housing—grand downtown apartments—that lured the growing bourgeoisie to settle in the centre of town. Would-be residents were enticed by a stimulating urban environment that could now be accessed right outside their front doors. The boulevard's pavements were wide and lined with trees and benches. On each corner, they hosted restaurants and terraced cafes. Avenues had built-in pedestrian islands that allowed for easier crossings and rewarded the walker with novel ways to see and sense the city. Monumental vistas were included in the very planning of the boulevards. Haussmann, Hall tells us, 'never thought of a new route, above all a principal route, without considering how it would offer a new point of view'.[14]

By creating a space in the city for people to come and wander, the boulevards engineered an unprecedented zone that was both public and also, through the anonymity it offered, still strangely private. This experimental sphere became the key to a freedom that was unknown prior to city life. The boulevards became the subject of poetry and painting, as well as the new arts of film and photography. People began to walk the city simply to soak in its atmosphere and—especially with the coming of electricity—be transformed by the excitement of its sights and sounds. As Jean-Louis Cohen writes in his essay on the history of the modern street, 'For walkers the experience of the street founded a new sensibility, a new language.'[15] The poet Baudelaire and the literary critic Walter Benjamin gave a name to these strollers; they called them 'flaneurs' and argued that through their participation and portrayal of the city, these urban wanderers were central to the experience of modernity. The boulevards thus became the stage upon which the modern urbanite was born.

Robert Moses and the making of New York

Haussmann's twentieth century counterpart emerged not in Paris but across the Atlantic—in what many consider the true archetype of the modern metropolis—New York. Robert Moses consciously modelled his career on Paris' master builder. Berman calls him Haussmann's most 'illustrious and notorious successor'.[16] Moses' astonishing power over the urban planning of New York lasted over four decades. During this period he not only reshaped the city and its sprawling suburbs but also 'influenced the destiny of all the cities of twentieth century America'.[17] Robert Caro, who immortalised Moses in the epic biography *The Power Broker*, calls him 'America's greatest builder'.[18] His visionary work impacted New York in a myriad of ways. Moses opened up the beaches of Long Island, built seventeen state parks and dotted the city with playgrounds and pools. Miles of high-rise housing was erected under his watch. He constructed monumental buildings—the Lincoln Center, Shea Stadium and the headquarters of the UN—and was also in charge of New York as it hosted two World Fairs.

Yet, like Haussmann what Moses is remembered for most are his roads. During his tenure he created a vast network of tunnels, bridges and highways that, for the first time, linked New York's disparate boroughs into one coherent whole. In tying together a set of distinct islands, Moses constructed the roads that fashioned New York into a single, unified urban entity. In addition to this intra-city network he also developed a series of parkways that extended deep into the suburbs. 'Lump together all the superhighways in existence in all the cities on earth in 1945,' writes Caro 'and their mileage would not add up to as many miles as Robert Moses was planning in 1945 to build in one city.'[19] Moses, was 'the most influential single architect of the system over which rolled the wheels of America's cars'.[20]

Haussmann's boulevards already embodied the modern fascination with traffic. Yet, as Caro points out, though Haussmann's boulevards were impressive, they were nonetheless 'designed for the carriage rather than the car'.[21] Moses, on the other hand, was attuned to the spread of the automobile, modernity's most influential machine. 'Cities,' he said provocatively, 'are created by and for traffic'. It was time, he believed, for the pedestrian to give way to the car. Under Moses, then, the boulevards of Europe mutated into the highways of America and the precarious balance between the road and the street was destroyed. 'The automobile age created in the twentieth century a need for roads of a new dimension,' Caro explains with a vivid, horrifying clarity. 'Roads a hundred feet or more across, roads with underpasses and overpasses and with interchanges so immense that to create them hundreds of acres of earth must be covered over with concrete—gigantic roads, not highways, but superhighways.'[22] Under the sway of the car, the modern metropolis became a place not for people but for their vehicles. Marshall Berman writes starkly of the transition, 'The distinctive sign of nineteenth century urbanism was the boulevard, a medium for bringing explosive material and human forces together; the hallmark of twentieth century urbanism has been a highway, a means for putting them asunder.'[23]

Destruction and control

In their creation of the modern city, Le Corbusier, Haussmann and Moses shared the conviction that the older urban centres that had stood in their way had to be destroyed. They viewed the pre-modern city as riddled with slums that needed to be cleared away. Small, dense, crowded lanes were condemned as a cumbersome relic, unsuitable for the coming new age. In this lineage of modern urban planning, the bulldozer has always been the most important tool in the creation of the future.

Haussmann's reconstruction of Paris was founded on a vast destruction of what had come before. He demolished nearly three-quarters of the Cite to create his wide-open boulevards. 'Between 1853 and 1870, [Haussmann] removed more than half the buildings in Paris,'[24] reports Edward Glaeser in his book *Triumph of the City*. 'He evicted vast numbers of the poor, turning their homes into wide boulevards that made Paris monumental. He lopped off a good chunk of the Luxembourg Gardens to create city streets. He tore down ancient landmarks.'[25] Critics derided him as an urban vandal, arguing that the creation of a new Paris rested on the destruction of the old. Yet, as Peter Hall writes, 'Haussmann had little concern for the heritage of the past; it simply got in the way.'[26]

Demolitions under Moses were equally severe. From 1949 to 1960 Moses acted as chairman of the mayor's committee for slum clearance. During that time he oversaw the nation's largest urban renewal programme—a model of the raze-and-replace urbanisation that was promoted at the time. His projects and roads rammed through neighbourhoods, dislocating hundreds of thousands of people, obliterating much of the existing urban fabric. Seemingly oblivious to the destructive path that lay in the wake of his developments, Moses appeared to delight in his particular form of 'creative destruction'. 'When you operate in an overbuilt metropolis,' he notoriously maintained, 'you have to slash your way through with a meat axe.'[27]

Le Corbusier expresses this sentiment with an even sharper intensity. The pure creative impulse inherent in the progressive instinct of modern time required a break from all that came before. The organic city, which emerged slowly, piece by piece, driven by the contingencies of events, was outmoded. Le Corbusier's famous call for the destruction of much of central Paris is treated in his writings as an obvious and practical solution to the city's problems—a necessary clearing away. 'Our modern culture, acquired by the West, has its roots set deep in the invasions which extinguished antique culture… Man's own immanent death in the Great city has been replaced by *the death of the street*. An Improvement!'[28]

Le Corbusier's imagined metropolis was never actually constructed. It exists today, as it did at its inception, as pure abstraction. This is how it should be. What mattered most to Le Corbusier was not any empirical actuality but rather the integrity of the plan. It was this, rather than any of its specific components, that was the crucial element separating the old organic town from the new modern city. 'The Plan is the generator,'[29] he wrote. The grandiose scale of his ambition extended far beyond the construction of any particular building, neighbourhood or town. What Le Corbusier sought to create was not a specific city but the axioms of a brand new urbanism. His aim was to formulate 'the fundamental principles of urbanism' to create 'the rule according to which the game can be played.'[30] 'Modern life,' Le Corbusier declared, 'demands, and is waiting for, a new kind of plan.'[31]

For these plans to be implemented the modern architect required absolute power, total access to resources and complete control. Le Corbusier was notoriously hostile to democracy, believing instead that industrial society should be hierarchically organised and administered from on high. In the Machine Age, 'what was necessary was a rigorous theory implemented from above'.[32] Le Corbusier's dramatic prose crystallised the authoritarian impulse of the modern planner. Yet, all successful builders of modern cities have demanded, and received, a high degree of centralised control. Large-scale urban development requires firm leadership. Haussmann, the prototype modern urban planner, acted on behalf of Louis Napoleon III, and his power to transform Paris was intimately tied to the emperor's reign. 'If you want to rebuild a city,' states Glaeser pragmatically, 'it helps to have an autocrat behind you.'[33] 'Paris is unified', he continues, 'because it was the planned product of a single master builder, whose imperial overlord gave them a free hand. Haussmann did things that would be unthinkable in a modern democrat age.'[34] The key to Haussmann's success, concurs Peter Hall, lay in his relationship with the king, with whom he was in almost daily contact. 'Paris was built through the bond between planner and autocrat. It arose as an ordered whole.'[35]

Robert Moses also famously sought, and ultimately achieved, a vast degree of unconditioned power. Moses recognised early on that he would be unable to fulfil his dreams without executive control of the city. He therefore dedicated himself, as Robert Caro so persuasively details, to carving out niches that allowed an authority that was above and beyond that of any elected official. A master of the political game, Moses managed to seize property, mobilise vast sums of money and create a web of public authorities that were answerable to him alone. For decades nothing happened in New York without his approval. At the height of his career, Moses' word functioned as dictatorial fiat, forceful enough to reshape New York.

Le Corbusier, Haussmann and Moses sought to mastermind the City of Tomorrow through the building of roads. This project, and projection, expressed and also helped create the idea that modernity was inextricably tied to a linear and progressive time. In wiping away the old to make way for the new, modern urban planners aimed to construct the future as a utopian destination (the end point in history). In town planning no less than religion, this has involved an alliance with authoritarian rule and a faith that the future can be mastered.

A woman of the streets

In 1961 the self-taught urbanist Jane Jacobs published her most famous work *The Death and Life of Great American Cities*, which presented itself as a critique of the thinking surrounding modern cities. 'This book,' it begins, 'is an attack on current city planning and rebuilding.'[36] Despite the fact that Jacobs was a self-taught housewife when she wrote it, *Death and Life* contained a powerful, ultimately devastating blow to modern planners in the tradition of Le Corbusier, Haussmann and Moses. Instead of starting from a Platonic ideal of what a future city should be, Jacobs presented a view of the city that was grounded in the material reality of the street. *Death and Life* looked to real cities to find what worked. 'I shall be writing about how cities work in real life,' Jacobs states from the start, 'because this is the only way to learn what principles of planning and what practices in rebuilding can promote social and economic vitality in cities, and what practices and principles will deaden these attributes.'[37] By looking, listening and learning from the street, Jacobs discovered that the most vibrant urban neighbourhoods were precisely those that the modernists were eagerly clearing away. In the messiness of older urban neighbourhoods Jacobs saw the successful workings of a complex and diverse system, which assembled itself from the ground up, and was thus totally at odds with the planners' desire for total control. In replacing the chaos of the streets with the pristine organisation of well-planned high-rises and parks, modern urban planners were, Jacobs maintained, guilty of a deep anti-urbanism; 'anti-city planning' she called it. Blind to the 'street dance' made from the intimate rhythms of everyday life, the modernists were destroying the productivity, innovation and human interaction so crucial to urban innovation. Their reverence for imposed order was creating vast tracks of desolate spaces empty of life. 'This is not the rebuilding of cities,' she wrote emphatically. 'This is the sacking of cities.'[38]

According to the high modernist tradition, urban development needs to be mastered through the implementation of top-down plans. Jacobs' critique rested on the counterargument; cities are too complex to be comprehended from on high. She railed against the arrogance—and impossibility—of imposing a single abstract ideal on the diverse multiplicity that was essential to urban innovation and growth. The cities' complexity meant that unforeseen consequences would always, invariably, upset the plan. Tear down slums and build new public housing and what you ultimately end up with are projects so derelict and dangerous that the only solution is to blow them up. Build more roads and, rather than solving the problem of congestion, all you do is attract more traffic. These unfortunate consequences are not accidental. Plans go wrong because planners do not think on a neighbourhood scale. Instead, they view the city as a whole, try to comprehend it from on high and seek to impose order from above. Jacobs, who was attentive to and immersed in the micro-rhythms of daily life, argued for bottom-up emergence, or order from below. Cities are built from the emergent order of individuals not the oversight of all-powerful planners. They work, not because they adhere to the neat lines of a well-ordered plan, but rather due to the vital everyday entrepreneurialism of the street.

The road versus the street

The battle between the road and the street has always been about more than urban planning. Cities and their traffic flows are as crucial to the workings of power as the geopolitics of nation states. When Napoleon III hired Haussmann he did so, in part, to deal with the cramped squalor and chaos brought by Paris' high-speed urbanisation. Haussmann's reconstruction brought safer streets, comfortable housing, better sanitation and smoother traffic. Yet, the boulevards were also created as an attempt to rid Paris of the revolutionary potential of the streets, which in just sixty years starting in 1789, had succeeded in toppling three monarchs. Haussmann's straight, long arterial boulevards were consciously designed to be too wide to blockade. They were intended to be inhospitable to urban rebels and designed instead to accommodate the easy circulation of cavalry, artillery and troops.[39]

The street as crucible of rebellion is a potential that haunts all urban centres. 'Take to the streets' is the familiar call of revolutionaries everywhere. In China, where all politics is under Party control, street protest plays a vital, if often virtual, role. This became apparent in Shanghai in 2008, when NIMBY middle class homeowners joined in 'collective walks' to protest against the extension of the maglev train.[40] Since then, the strategy of protest as informal gathering has gained increasing strength. 'In the past three years,' wrote *The New Yorker*'s Evan Osnos in 2011, 'people in Xiamen, Shanghai, Chengdu, and probably elsewhere, have taken to "strolling" as a wry form of protest that toys with the official definition of, and prohibition against, demonstrating.'[41] Today, even the hint of a 'stroll' is enough to bring the police out in force. In 2011 provocateurs inspired by the Arab Spring called for urban citizens to stroll in the name of a 'Jasmine Revolution'. Urbanites were urged to gather at central corners (in Shanghai it was at the corner of Nanjing Lu and Fuzhou Lu in People's Square). They were told not to carry placards or shout slogans so that they could blend indistinguishably into the crowded street. Due to the zealousness of internet censorship few locals had even heard of the campaign. Nevertheless the rumour of a street protest was enough to bring the police (and the Western media) out in full force.

The modern city, then, is produced by two tendencies that are locked in a dialectical duel. These opposing forces, which Berman deftly describes as the 'world of the expressway' and 'the modernity of the street' are continuously poised as on the brink of battle.[42] The master builders of roads, the lovers of traffic and speed, have sought to hack their way through an older, unruly chaos. Their goal, writes Berman, is to 'silence the shouts and wipe the streets off the map'. Yet the streets, which run alongside and between the roads are stubborn in their persistence and refuse to be erased.

In mid-twentieth century New York, these two faces of urban modernity—the planning of roads and the celebration of the street—clashed decisively in a fight which pitted the immense political power of Robert Moses against the neighbourhood activism of Jane Jacobs. The conflict was enormously influential and, ultimately, provoked a profound change in how people think about the cities of the future and how, or even if, they should or could be planned. The spark came with Moses' desire to extend his road building projects through New York's urban core, first with the extension of Fifth Avenue and then with construction of the Lower Manhattan Expressway. Had he got his way motorists would have been able to speed through the heart of the city, driving straight across Washington Square Park, and much of Greenwich Village would have been demolished.

Moses' campaign was long and protracted, but eventually Jacobs' brand of local activism and neighbourhood resistance proved victorious. Puncturing the unquestioned authority of Moses created a ripple effect throughout the planning world that has lasted for decades. 'Moses' fall from power signaled the end of a paradigm of the modern city based on automobile access, high rise housing and top down planning.'[43] The grandiose project of modern planning has been widely denounced. 'Modernist urbanism,' proclaimed the theorist Fredric Jameson in his essay 'Future City', 'is at a dead end.'[44] Rem Koolhaas, in his seminal text *S, M, X, XL*, echoes and elaborates the death knell: 'Modernism's alchemistic promise has been a failure, a hoax: magic that didn't work. Its ideas, aesthetics, strategies are finished. Together, all attempts to make a new beginning have only discredited the idea of a new beginning.'

In his searing critique of a Le Corbusier retrospective held in 2009, critic Theodore Dalrymple captures, with a scathing humour, the many reasons high modernism has been so thoroughly rejected. 'Le Corbusier was to architecture what Pol Pot was to social reform,' Dalrymple writes with rebuke. 'Like Pol Pot, he wanted to start from Year Zero: before me, nothing; after me, everything ... He does not belong so much to the history of architecture as to that of totalitarianism.'[45] Le Corbusier, 'wanted to be to the city what pasteurization is to cheese.'[46] As evidence, Dalrymple points with scorn to a 1920s film clip that 'shows Le Corbusier in front of a map of the center of Paris, a large part of which he proceeds to scrub out with a thick black crayon with all the enthusiasm of Bomber Harris planning the annihilation of a German city during World War II.'[47] This palpable pleasure in destruction makes clear the architect's total disdain for the people he was supposedly planning for. Le Corbusier's deep anti-humanism was apparent, argues Dalrymple, throughout his sketches of buildings and parks, all of which are empty of human life. People were where they should be, 'out of sight and out of mind (the architect's mind, anyway), in their machines for living in (as he so charmingly termed houses), sitting on machines for sitting on (as he defined chairs)'.[48] Out of this deep inhumanity stems the modernist love of roads as well as their hatred of streets. 'Roads were impressive thoroughfares for rushing along at the highest possible speed … which therefore had a defined purpose and gave rise to no disorderly human interactions. The street, by contrast, was unpredictable, incalculable, and deeply social.'[49]

Modern planning was condemned for being anti-people, and it has not recovered from this rebuke. Today, the modernists' preference for wholesale clearance and superblock urbanism has been largely abandoned and a 'new renewal strategy and model of street-based urbanism has taken hold. Instead of trying to impose their plans on everyone else, many urbanists have come to celebrate a "renaissance of the street"'.[50] There has been a turn to more organic, bottom-up processes that won't destroy the internal fabric of city neighbourhoods from on high. Though the battles between suburb and city are still being fought, many planners now consider sustainability, heritage and localism—even in the car-based peripheries—as the key factors for urban growth.

Pudong and the modern master plan

One of Shanghai's most persistent myths is that before its redevelopment in the early 1990s, Pudong was virtually vacant. Yet the truth is that it took a lot of work to empty Shanghai's eastern shore. Though taken as a whole, the district was sparsely populated and largely rural, the urbanised strip of Pudong, along the Huangpu waterfront was one of Shanghai's densest neighbourhoods. At the start of the 1990s, there were over one million residents living in Pudong, mostly in the zone by the river's edge. Before its redevelopment Pudong was home to a heavy concentration of the city's grimmest factories.[51] In 1990 about 1bn yuan, approximately 8 per cent of Shanghai's GDP, was generated by the district's low-tech industries.

Creating Pudong's apparent emptiness required a mass relocation of industry, businesses and homes. Yawei Chen, who has carried out detailed research on the district, claims that 22,214 households and 136 blocks of flats were relocated in the making of Pudong. To create the central zone of Lujiazui alone, 27,000 houses had to be moved.[52] The speed and efficiency of this mass relocation was eased by the fact that few held any sentimental attachment to the area. 'Better a bed in Puxi, than a house in Pudong,' was the commonly heard refrain. There are few if any stories of Pudong's lost old-worldly charms. Nevertheless, for Shanghai to modernise, an older urban district had to be wiped away.

Pudong's density, like Paris in the years before Haussmann, was made worse by neglect. To engineer the district's rise required an enormous investment in infrastructure. There was no airport or railway in the area, public utilities—including water, sewage treatment and telecommunication—were vastly inadequate and the only land-link to the rest of the city was an old two-lane tunnel that—by 1990—was carrying over 17,000 cars a day. The insufficiency of transport links became horrifically clear in 1987 when crowds trying to get to work in Puxi caused a deadly stampede on a ferry from Pudong that killed eleven people.

To remake Pudong as futurist fantasy required not only that basic infrastructure be developed to meet existing needs but also that the area be geared towards servicing all that was imagined would come. From the start, plans for Pudong included the creation of sixteen passenger ferries, four car ferries, a deep water port, an airport, a rail network, a metro system, an urban highway system with numerous bridges and tunnels, a modern water and sewage system, and a proper telecommunication network. In the decade between 1990 and 2001, an investment of more than 93bn yuan ($11.23 bn) was made in the infrastructure of Pudong. By 2010 basically all that had been planned was complete.[53]

It appears, considering the intensive, high-speed mutation of the district, that Pudong, reanimates the high modernist, road-based urbanism of an earlier age. The impact of Jacobs' street activism seems negligible. Elsewhere, perhaps, modernist planning with its heavy authoritarian streak, abstract idealism and demand for top-down centralised control, has been renounced, but Pudong gives the impression that it is enjoying a grand revival.

There are those that celebrate this resurgence. Impressed by China's incredible speed and efficiency in laying down infrastructure, some have begun to rethink the merits of top-down autocratic rule. Unlike in a democratic society, say these increasingly vocal opinion makers, if China wants to build a road, a bridge or a skyscraper, the decision is not subject to endless rounds of negotiation and debate. Multiple new subway lines, vast tracks of high-speed trains, glossy new communities and luxury shopping malls, the vast Expo Site and whole new satellite towns are seemingly made possible by China's authoritarian regime. Perhaps, many are now tempted to believe, a strong centralised state is exactly what is needed to get things done. In a controversial column in the *New York Times*, journalist Thomas Friedman did most to popularise this strengthening view for a Western audience. 'One-party autocracy certainly has its drawbacks,' he admits. 'But when it is led by a reasonably enlightened group of people, as China is today, it can also have great advantages. That one party can just impose the politically difficult but critically important policies needed to move a society forward in the 21st century.'[54] China's apparent top-down urbanism, its dictatorial planning and its ability to assert its will without compromise is being reassessed in light of the country's enormous success.

Others, however, maintain that as Shanghai's, indeed China's, showcase of urban development, Pudong perfectly illustrates all that is wrong with the authoritarianism of modern China. Like the high modernism epitomised by the totalitarian urges of Le Corbusier, who was willing—even eager—to bulldoze anything that stood in his way, the urbanism typified by Pudong is deeply inhumane. The district, according to these dissenting voices, is the product of an autocratic regime that pays little attention to the people under its power. It is the perfect emblem of a system that can magically build new cities, and miraculous bridges, tunnels, skyscrapers and subways, but only by forcing mass relocations, quickly securing massive faulty loans and stifling all dissent.

Even as it was being built, architects like Hong Kong's Tao Ho warned that Pudong's planners were making a big mistake in their embrace of the 'tall buildings and the car oriented mentality of the West'.[55] Indeed, planners in Pudong seem ludicrously blind to the needs of pedestrians, as anyone who tries walking around Lujiazui can attest. Disembark at Century Avenue station and at first the stroll seems, given Pudong's reputation, surprisingly smooth. The pavements are wide, there are benches for resting and the road is lined with pleasant parkettes. As you approach the towers, however, it all goes wrong. The path runs into a park, which turns into a maze from which there is no escape. Suddenly you are stuck. The only way out is to squeeze through bushes, balance on the kerb and then summon the courage to dash through mad traffic to get to the other side. Pedestrian overpasses were supposed to be the promised solution. Yet, when they emerged just in time for Expo 2010, they served to highlight many of the problems with Pudong.

Despite its many skyscrapers Pudong lacks density as its buildings are spaced far apart. The skyways are, thus, nowhere near as intense as similar structures in Hong Kong. They tend to ascend and descend in odd places and, lacking any commercial activity, often seem barren, just like the desolate paths on a very wide road.

Developer Vincent Lo and architect Ben Wood, famous for their work on the wildly successful preservationist-based project, Xintiandi, which is located at the heart of Puxi are devastating in their critique. Pudong, says Wood, is 'a regurgitation of everything wrong with 20th-century urban planning'.[56] 'I am always asked to replicate Xintiandi somewhere in the district,' echoes Lo, 'but I say, "Where? Where do I put it? The roads are just too wide." And it's so difficult for pedestrians. Pudong's planners are too car-oriented. They like wide roads because they look good on their models.'[57]

Pudong then, clamour its critics, is designed to look good from afar but get up close and the district has a Legoland feel—vast roads are devoid of street life, immaculate plazas are barren and desolate. 'Pudong is less a city', writes Daniel Brook, 'than an ad for a city.'[58] Without the usual hustle and bustle of the city (which the Chinese describe with the celebratory term *renao*), this zone of Shanghai seems dead. To quote Thomas Campanella:

Lujiazui indeed suffers from the same shortcomings that make so many American edge cities and office parks unpleasant places to be—an overemphasis on motor-vehicle infrastructure, huge parcel sizes, and large plazas and deep setbacks that create a poorly defined street wall and an almost suburban level of density. Exclusionary zoning makes matters worse still, banishing the kaleidoscopic array of uses that brings such vitality and life to the Chinese streetscape. The result is a pedestrian-unfriendly realm where those unfortunate enough to be on foot are buffeted by ricocheting winds and dwarfed by skyscrapers and sweeping vistas. Even the sidewalks in Lujiazui—148 feet wide in some places—seem to have been designed as parade routes rather than places to walk.[59]

In many ways Pudong appears to be a simple continuation of modernist planning; the latest manifestation of 'the future city' as it was imagined by the modernists of old. Yet, while Pudong does, at least at first glance, seem like a master-planner's fantasy, in fact, the forces that went into the making of Pudong are far more complex. Shanghai's showcase district emerged from quite singular and messy conditions. There was never a clear overarching plan that guided Pudong's development, and its growth has not been governed by the solitary vision of a single individual. Rather than the product of a plan administered from above, Pudong is the manifestation of state power just at the point that it began opening to a multiplicity of players.

Thus, though it may seem derivative, as if it is copying the ideas and practices of a modernity that has already been tried, Pudong, the showcase of Chinese urbanisation has actually emerged from a web of singular forces that have arisen through the particular forces of the contemporary East Asian entrepreneurial state, which is carving out the contours of its own singular modernity.

The dragon head

Despite appearances to the contrary, Pudong was not constructed through the top-down dictates of a centralised state. There was no master-builder of the Haussman-Moses type. Instead, the district was designed by committee, through a hodgepodge mixture of compromise and experiment that emerged precisely at the moment Shanghai opened its door to the outside world. While it may seem as if Pudong conforms to the rigours of a plan, in fact, it, more than anywhere else in the city, was built at the cusp of China's transition away from the planned economy. 'Compared with the traditional way of managing area development in China—closed, top down, opaque, bureaucratic and government controlled—the development of Pudong,' argues Yawei Chen, 'showed an evolutionary trend, more open and interactive, governed by a hybrid form of control.'[60]

The project of Pudong was always more concerned with what the district could do than how it should look. Most crucially, ambitions for the area were tied to a widespread and growing interest in globalisation. Rather than a rigid implementation of an idea conceived from on high, then, Pudong was built by harnessing global economic flows. Huang Fuxiang, who was leading the team at the Shanghai Urban Planning and Design Institute (SUPDI) at the time, sought to use Pudong to capture the winds of the global economy that were already sweeping in from elsewhere. According to Chen, he saw two possible trends that were exerting a powerful influence on the fate of Shanghai:

the first was a shift in the centre of activity from the West (the Atlantic area) to the East (the Pacific area), with the western rim of the Pacific Ocean as the possible centre of the boom. The second trend, associated with the further opening up of China and its integration into the world economy, involved a shift in economic development from south China, with its pioneering cities like Shenzhen, Zhuhai and Xiamen, to the north and east, and subsequently from the east to central and western China. Shanghai enjoyed a strategic location between these two movements. The researchers believed that without proper preparation, Shanghai would be unable to handle the approaching economic boom.[61]

Pudong, then, was viewed as a site through which Shanghai could take advantage of its strategic location. As the regional 'dragon head,'[62] it was to guide the future development of the entire Yangzi River region and thus operate as a portal through which China could integrate with the world.

Deng Xiaoping urged officials to view the development of Pudong as an opportunity to 'liberate thought' and not to be 'straitjacketed by predetermined ideas'.[63] Shanghai's eastern shore was thus positioned at the cutting edge of China's market orientation to planning. To fulfil these ambitions, Huang Fuxiang and the team at SUPDI began exploring ideas about how to best encourage China's new market system, examining what other cities did to attract investment,[64] since at the time, as Huang admits, Shanghai officials, 'were more familiar with Russian concepts of urban planning'.[65] In addition to looking outside the country, officials drew on experience in the Special Economic Zones (SEZ); testing grounds that were already proving so fundamental to growth. In China, as Chen explains, the SEZ's have functioned:

as laboratories for developing various methods aimed at overcoming the drawbacks associated with the central planning system. Fresh concepts and methods originating in market economies outside China can first be introduced into, absorbed by, and tested out in the SEZ. Those measures that prove to be effective and successful in the SEZs can then, wherever feasible, be extended to the rest of the country.[66]

Huang, in particular became interested in the idea of central business districts (CBD), paying special attention to how they functioned in the cities in America. 'After my visit to the World Trade Center,' he is quoted as saying, 'I begun to understand the role played by the CBD in the American urban economy.'[67] With an eye to Manhattan, Lujiazui was designated a CBD and in 1990 Pudong was earmarked one of the biggest SEZs in the country.

Pudong, then, is better thought of as an economic strategy than as an urban design. It was intended as a mechanism through which the city could transition from a rigidly top-down bureaucratic system to the more flexible and open networks of the global market. Only this explains, as Chen argues, why foreign capital so eagerly invested in Pudong, risking billions of dollars, especially in the early years when the district's development was little more than fantasy. 'The strong hand of an authoritarian state alone,' she writes, 'is insufficient to explain why so many investors and multinational corporations flocked to the area.'[68]

As the 'Wall Street of Asia,' explicitly established to rival Hong Kong, Pudong took the lead in carrying out a series of economic reforms, especially in the areas of finance and trade.[69] Pudong's growth demanded institutional reform, forcing the public sector to reinvent itself. Pragmatic innovations were especially geared at luring foreign direct investment (FDI). Ye Longfei, vice chairman of the Shanghai Investment Commission, advocated for a myriad of creative policies aimed at attracting money. 'We should not only try the Shenzhen method of "building nests to attract birds" (that is, building the infrastructure that will lure investors from overseas),' he commented colourfully, 'but also the Hainan method of "alluring birds to build nests" (getting foreigners to invest in the development of the land) and also Xiamen's model of "having birds come and bring their nests with them" (inviting foreign businesses to invest and bring with them their own investment partners).'[70] These adaptive strategies have proven immensely successful. Today Pudong, (now the site of Shanghai's newest 'free trade zone') is China's testing ground for any tactic aimed at liberalising finance.

Pudong's most vital zone of experimentation, however, lay in pioneering the practice of land leasing, the lynchpin of China's urban growth. Drawing on examples from both Hong Kong and Singapore, Pudong officials concocted a land leasing system which could separate land ownership from land use. This distinction, which was codified in the 1988 Regulation of Land Use Rights, created a mechanism through which land could became a commodity without challenging the Communist Party's public ownership. Though there is still no private property in China, the land leasing system established a private market where land can be bought and sold. The introduction of this trade in real estate has generated an immense amount of wealth. In about ten years Pudong alone earned more than 100bn yuan ($12.08bn) from the leasing of land.[71] Moreover, and arguably ultimately of greater consequence, the land leasing system had the unintended effect of wrenching power away from the central state, since in China the municipal or even district governments have ultimate control over land. Creating a market for land has therefore acted as an enormously powerful force of decentralisation. 'Although in China local governments and their officials form part of the administrative apparatus, part of the "state," writes Yawei Chen, 'they are also distinct entities, separate from central government and the rest of society, with their own agendas, and increasingly with their own resources.'[72] This dispersion of power has been crucial in the rapid rise of China's cities. It is thus an oversimplification to refer to China's urban development as a top-down state project ruled hierarchically from above. 'In developing countries, a major player in configuring the urban environment is the state,' writes scholar Aihwa Ong. Nevertheless, she goes on to argue that entrepreneurial governments throughout Asia have reconfigured the relation between the controlling tendencies of the nation and the complex and messy micro-politics that are embedded differently in each locale. 'Through the renovation of cities,' she writes, 'new political maps are drawn.'[73]

In Shanghai, centralised power was further ruptured through the establishment of companies tasked with the development of Pudong. In order to construct the new district, the Shanghai municipality, borrowing a model from the UK, created a number of public companies to act as commercial enterprises. At first these new entities were large state-owned enterprises (SOEs) closely tied to the city government. With no capital of their own and no means of raising funds through the private sphere, they had to rely on the Shanghai Municipal Government (SMG) to give them money so they would be able to purchase the available land. Companies bought land from the government simply by handing back cheques they were given for this purpose. At the beginning, then, the government acted as a major shareholder in these newly formed companies and had a large degree of control. It was soon recognised, however, that the variety and complexity of tasks involved in building Pudong—planning, relocating, developing infrastructure, finding a real estate developer—would become faster and more efficient if it was done through the creation of subsidiaries that could specialise in just one of these tasks.[74] As the process continued, ever smaller, ever more specialised companies began peeling away, increasing their autonomy by distancing themselves from their parent organisation. The Lujiazui Group, for example, one of five development companies set up by the SMG to develop Lujiazui has since diversified into a whole plethora of subsidiaries, holding shares in at least fifty-four other companies.[75] Through this splitting apart, development companies operating in Pudong quickly became, according to Chen, 'the pre-eminent representatives of the front line of entrepreneurial Chinese local government. These companies worked bottom-up, city wide and at district level, simultaneously involved in many different building projects involving private investors and investors from all around the world.'[76] Among the most crucial players in this economic flattening out were financiers from Hong Kong and other overseas Chinese whose 'sleeper networks' were stirred by the opportunities presented in Pudong. Operating through the tight webs of *guanxi* (connections), overseas Chinese have infused Chinese capitalism with a flexible, risk-taking diasporic culture that is notoriously adept at operating outside state control.[77]

Pudong's development thus occurred through an intricate mix of diverse entities. It arose through the complex interaction between traditional state bureaucracies and a multiplicity of agents including SOEs (controlled by the central government), enterprises run by the People's Liberation Army

(PLA), enterprises run by local government, diasporic capitalists and the mainland's new capitalist class, who are often old party members. These in turn 'follow the contours of provincial and local alliances and the business networks to which they connect.'[78] 'This bifurcation and complex set of relations,' argues Chen 'is shifting the foundations of future urban development in Shanghai further outside the reach of central government.'[79] Pudong, then, arises just at the point where centralised power meets the forces of decentralisation, and where planners become entangled with the unplanned. 'It is important to remind ourselves,' argues Seng Kuan,' that Lujiazui was and is, for the most part, a private development' and 'embodies much more meaning than the one-dimensional portrayals of Shanghai's economic vitality or its sometimes banal modern architecture.'[80] Pudong recalls the modernist projects of Hausmman's Paris and Moses' New York. Yet, despite these apparent similarities it did not emerge as the vision of a single authoritarian planner, but rather as an intricate negotiation at the cusp of a changing China as it opened to the world.

The streets of Pudong?

The best way to see Pudong is to ascend one of its super tall towers. Choose a skyscraper and take an elevator to the top. Turn your gaze away from the alien city-scape growing on the other side of the river and look down on the land below. The high-rise towers are all clustered around the river's edge and along Century Avenue, the district's central axis. Off these main strips are rows and rows of five- to six-storey white box apartment buildings, all with red or blue roofs, a Sim City labyrinth that stretches on for miles. The only way to explore these zones is at street level. Back down on the ground, turn off the main boulevards and walk a block or even less. The landscape is still dominated by the towers, but here, hidden from sight, an altogether different urban fabric comes into focus. Though still in the heart of Lujiazui, the glamour and gloss seem far, far away. Just a five minute stroll from the city's most momentous spectacle are the small neighbourhoods and communities that exist not for show, but just for the people who live there. The apartment blocks are all housing communities built twenty, thirty, even sixty years ago. Residents who have been living here for decades sit outside on folding chairs drinking tea, reading the paper and shelling peas. They tell of being moved by their *danwei* (work unit) many years ago. Most came reluctantly from their homes on the other side of the river. They were given apartments when they married or when their old neighbourhoods were torn down during slum clearing campaigns. At the time the Communist government sought to deal with massive housing shortages in Puxi by building blocks of living quarters in what was then the remote district of Pudong. At first there was only a ferry to take them across to the city, and their new neighbourhoods seemed like the end of the world. But over time the district has grown increasingly desirable. There are now convenient places to shop, an ever-growing subway line provides transport and the proximity to the towers provides a spectacular view. The value of the apartments has risen exponentially and, though their homes are run down, only a few are willing to go elsewhere. One old man proves the exception. He stands with a few friends near the front gate of his compound. He wears a grey suit, has a big belly and a hearty laugh. Soon his son will get married and he will have no choice but to give up his apartment since his son cannot afford to buy anywhere else. When that time comes the old man will relocate again, to a place miles away, where Pudong is still countryside and the growing city has not yet reached. Pudong, then, is still very much unsettled. Paris and New York have already had a monumental influence on our ideas of modernity. The impact of Shanghai, however, is still uncertain. We still do not know what Pudong is or what it might become. The 'worlding' city in Asia, as Aihwa Ong writes, 'is a milieu in constant formation.'[81]

Even in Lujiazui, the core financial zone, whole blocks are still under construction and overpasses remain incomplete. There are jarring juxtapositions that seem impossible to sustain. Rows of cheaply made public housing stand right next to the city's most expensive skyscrapers. Walk around and you sense a zone in flux. Turn off the main roads with their fancy towers and the small streets lined with micro businesses still exist. Narrow lanes stuffed with small restaurants sell *xiaolongbao* (Shanghai's famous special dumplings), noodles and breakfast bings. Inside a warehouse at the back of an alley is the wet market with fresh fruit and vegetables that are biked in from the farms just out of town. Colourful stands of fresh produce sit alongside the buckets of slithering snakes and sacks of somnolent toads. Most visitors, taken in by the façade, do not bother to come here. These side streets are kept backstage. They are not part of the show. Yet, sometimes due to their tight proximity, road and street bleed together. Back on broad Century Avenue an electronic sound-scape fills the air. The source is a migrant vendor that has rigged up his bike with a makeshift sound system. He is using his ad-hoc mobile stereo to advertise his wares, a suitcase stuffed with pirated CDs.

Today, the architects and developers working in the spectacular core of the district are becoming increasingly aware that an urban design meant for cars and not people lacks the vitality crucial for city life. Workers in the towers of Lujiazui complain that there is nowhere for them to eat and discussions on Pudong's development speak of humanising the scale, finding ways to recreate the street life that has been lost. Gensler's plans to open the sky gardens of the Shanghai Tower is meant to address these concerns by encouraging a neighbourhood feel. Mori is said to be working with the government on a plan to build a retail courtyard at the base of the SWFC as well as a pedestrian deck connecting the towers, complete with restaurants, shops, parks and even a monorail. Chris Choa, an architect at EDAW points to the 'exquisite irony' inherent in Mori's position. 'He was drawn to Pudong out of the frustration that he experienced trying to assemble large parcels in Tokyo. Now he finds that to make this project work, he must recreate the delicate tissue of community that makes urban life desirable.'[82] In the end, roads are not enough. The future city needs the dense and twisted tangle of the streets.

3

THE POWER OF SPECTACLE

That which lets now the dark, now the light appear is tao.

Laozi

Shanghai is a city obsessed with its own image. This was especially apparent in the lead up to Expo, when giant billboards and video screens unabashedly declared Shanghai's ambitions for growth. The self-reflexive PR, however, hardly needed the excuse of this mega-event. Here, hype forms an integral part of the landscape. Shanghai is often identified with its most stylish female inhabitants (Shanghai's femininity versus Beijing's masculinity is one of the key components of the long and ongoing *haipai* versus *jingpai* debate).[1] Living here one gets the sense that the city itself takes great delight in gazing in the mirror, preening. Shops selling luxury brands are multiplying everywhere, despite the fact that few Shanghainese can afford them. The malls that house them are so empty that locals call them ghost malls, but the fact that their clientele is only virtual doesn't seem to be a problem.[2] As China's image of growth, Shanghai is pure window display.

The city's fascination with façade is frequently condemned. To critics, Shanghai's embrace of urban spectacle is tied to a harmful neglect of the needs and desires of the real, living city. There is no doubt that this destructive construction of spectacle is increasingly at work in Shanghai. Aligned with the all too common conception that the modern is necessarily Western, it manifests itself in intermittent campaigns to clean up the streets. At their worst, these clean-up crusades accentuate a damaging lack of confidence, and seek to erase all signs of a local 'backward' and 'uncivilised' culture. Street food, hanging laundry and people in pyjamas[3] are all forcefully replaced with a tired, depressing view of Shanghai as a 'Global City' that is filled with Gucci stores and KFCs.[4]

There is, however, another much more positive notion of spectacle that is also at play in the metropolis today. In this alternative vision, spectacle is not equated with the falsity of illusion and the darkness of deceit, as it is in the Western philosophical tradition. Instead it is rooted in Chinese culture and thought, which has its own understanding of shadow and light, and operates with a decidedly different attitude to what is revealed on the surface and what is concealed beneath. Under this more indigenous conception, spectacle is itself productive, both because of what it can attract and also—even more vitally—because it allows for another realm to operate freely in the shadows. In this positive understanding, the power of spectacle can help create a twenty-first century metropolis in which a dazzling science fiction skyline can comfortably coexist with the rich, vibrant and chaotic urbanism of the street.

In his book *Postcards From Tomorrow Square*, which reports on his impressions from China, journalist James Fallows comments on the seemingly incomprehensible disjunction found throughout Shanghai, 'I have not before been anyplace that seemed simultaneously so controlled and so out of control,' he writes. 'The control is from on high … What's out of control is everything else.'[5] Inside China, a popular saying captures this critical dichotomy: *shangyou zhengce, xiayou duice* (policies above, counter-strategies below). Shanghai's singular futurism depends on the unfolding of this unprecedented, unpredictable mix of the planned urban spectacle on the one hand and, on the other, the city's unplanned culture that takes place in the darkness, hidden from view.

The showcase

Pudong has always been infused with spectacle. Dreams of Shanghai's re-imagined eastern shore date back to the beginnings of the twentieth century. In 1921 Sun Yat-sen proposed a plan for the 'Great Port of Pudong', deeming it essential to the project of national reconstruction. The imposing vision included redirecting the Huangpu, drowning out the colonial buildings of the Bund, and creating a new modern port.[6]

For decades, Pudong, as a site for extravagant fantasy, was buried by China's tumultuous history of revolution and war. But, in the early 1980s, as soon as Deng Xiaoping's strategy of opening and reform began taking root elsewhere, the seeds of the district's resurrection were planted. A decade later, in 1990, premier Li Peng officially sanctioned the development of the Pudong New Area.[7] Large-scale urban planning, however, did not occur until after Deng Xiaoping's 1992 tour of the south when, in an oft quoted statement, Deng expressed regret over his policy with respect to Shanghai. 'Looking back [I realise that] one of my main mistakes was not including Shanghai when I designated the four Special Economic Zones,'[8] he told his welcoming crowd. In Shanghai, Deng's words were interpreted as a green light for the spectacular ambitions for Pudong, which would be rebuilt as the sign of the nation's re-emergence—a symbolic commercial centre that would overshadow the colonial legacy of the Bund.

Zhu Rongji, mayor of Shanghai from 1988–1991, and the person most often credited with the development of the district, saw Pudong as a way of ending Shanghai's isolation; a test case for the new open door policies, which sought economic efficiency, an increasing role for markets and rapid economic growth. As boosters publicly stated at the time, Pudong 'demonstrates the determination of the nation to open a wider door to the outside world'.[9] To achieve this goal, Pudong's central business district was conceived, as research by Kris Olds reveals,[10] as a giant PR exercise. Planners impressed with the urban monumentality they had seen in the cities of Europe (Pudong owes much to Paris' La Defense) envisioned the gleaming skyscrapers and striking skylines as icons to the 'successes of China's open door policy.'[11] From the start, Shanghai's new CBD, said Huang Fuxiang, was to be a 'symbol and image of the results of reform'.[12] 'The tall buildings in Lujiazui were not built to satisfy the need for vertical expansion due to the lack of horizontal space,' argues academic Non Arkaraprasertkul, 'but for the purpose of generating monumental symbolic value'.[13] In overshadowing the Bund, an icon to a previous age, Pudong was thus designed as the emblem of a new Chinese modernity.

True to Pudong's spirit of openness, Zhu, who was dissatisfied with the level of urban expertise on the mainland, sought help from the outside. In 1993, in consultation with the L'Institut d'aménagement et d'urbanisme de la région Île-de-France in Paris, Zhu announced an international competition for the development of Lujiazui and invited a host of top architectural firms to compete. Four teams—Richard Rogers, Toyo Ito, Massimiliano Fuksas and Dominique Perrault—submitted detailed planning proposals for the heart of Pudong. Officials carefully considered all these plans and then, in a move that would later be frequently repeated, dismissed them all. In the end, the project was awarded to SUPDI, a local company that understood the environment, was familiar with the site and its politics, and could be trusted to work with the required speed. In creating their final blueprint the institute incorporated elements from many of the foreign proposals but gave them Chinese characteristics, adapting them to local needs. The final design had certain fixed elements, the wide central axis and the cluster of three super tall towers for example, but it also ensured a large amount of flexibility for future construction.

The importance of the international architectural competition, then, was not so much for the particular blueprints it offered but rather for its contribution to the district's early PR. The competition, writes Olds, 'was viewed by the Shanghai Municipal Government as a mediatised publicity show, a discursive event which would raise the international profile of Lujiazui and Pudong'.[14] The fact that, in the end, the foreign input had only a minimal impact mattered little since, as Olds explains, their role was largely promotional. Once the competition was complete, the images, diagrams and models created by the famous firms could be replicated in brochures and websites and used to lure in attention and investment. Pudong, even in its planning phase, was understood as a branding exercise, a method of attracting foreign investment and solidifying domestic support.

This strategy of constructing a spectacle in Pudong is still in explicit use today. The 1999–2020 comprehensive plan promises to 'further the image construction of Pudong New Area'. Pudong, then, is still conceived as a showcase. Its glistening, majestic super tall skyscrapers are the ultimate photogenic objects. They exist both to be to be gazed at and gazed through. Like all of Shanghai, they are best viewed at night, when the whole city is awash with lights and projection, and entire buildings are transformed into screens, further accentuating the flat surface of things.

Spectacle and deception

In a work called 'Santa's Little Helpers' local artist Chen Hangfeng cleverly captured this propensity of the city to present only its glittery façade. The piece consists of video recordings taken in the nearby villages of Zhejiang province where family-run back-room factories produce—painstakingly, by hand—the majority of the world's Christmas decorations. At the show, the videos were placed inside large boxes wrapped in paper and decorated with bows. To see them, viewers had to stoop over and peer through a peephole that was deliberately placed in an uncomfortable position. In Shanghai to look past the surface takes work.

Critics scorn this superficiality with derisive disdain. They berate the city for presenting a dazzling exterior that blinds people to the truth buried below the surface sheen. In Shanghai when old buildings fall into disrepair bricks are not repaired, they are simply painted over. In the mass urban clean-up that took place for the World Expo, doorways, gates and fences were made to sparkle and shine while everything that could not be easily seen was left in a state of ragged disrepair.

The most savage of this type of criticism is saved for Pudong. Here the fixation on face, it is argued, has produced an urban district that seems to lack all the conveniences and vibrancy that are so crucial to the creation of a successful metropolitan core. Urbanist Thomas Campanella's bitter attack on Lujiazui is one that is widely shared:

What appears so definitely urban from afar—as a skyline—is on foot not only dull but spatially unpleasant and even intimidating. In the end, Lujiazui is little more than a preening clutch of monuments lunging for the sky. This is the urbanism of naked ambition, if it is urbanism at all. Here was an opportunity to build a model city, and what has come instead is photogenic monumentality—a stage-set city intended to impress from a distance, from the Bund, from the air, from the pages of a glossy magazine. Lujiazui is indeed a good place for architectural photography; its austere vistas are most of the time unencumbered by messy pedestrians, bicyclists or street vendors with their stacks of steaming buns.[15]

Even before construction began, Pudong was being dismissed as a spectacle. In 1988 free-market economist Milton Friedman came to Shanghai for a conference organised by the Cato Institute on China and Economic Reform. During his visit, he was proudly shown early plans for the district. Yet the dazzling ambition did not impress. Pudong, Friedman quipped, is 'not a manifestation of the market economy, but a statist monument for a dead pharaoh on the level of the pyramids.' Over a decade later, when Pudong's astonishing transformation was well underway, *The Shanghai Star*, a local English-language weekly, echoed the libertarian sentiment. Quoting a Hong Kong newspaper, the magazine editorialised: 'Through sheer chutzpah and public relations guile Shanghai's super-smooth politicians somehow dissuade foreign investors, leaders and even journalists from looking too closely at their fair city's facade… Shanghai is arguably a Potemkin village on a massive scale.'[16]

Contemporary Shanghai's most searing critic, MIT economist Yasheng Huang, shares this vision of a city that is cloaked in a deceptive layer of glamour and gloss. 'Much of the admiration of Shanghai,' writes Huang with an angry frustration, 'is based on visual evidence.'[17] Mocking the veneration of 'foreign observers' who are too easily duped, Huang accuses Shanghai of being 'the world's most successful Potemkin metropolis'.[18] Huang's book *Capitalism with Chinese Characteristics*, dedicates an entire chapter to dissecting the truth behind Shanghai's shallow façade. The chapter, entitled 'What is wrong with Shanghai?' argues that the 'dizzying rise of skyscrapers from the rice paddies of Pudong' are 'both the sign and the culprit of what is structurally ailing the Chinese economy.' Rather than the mark of success, they are 'a glaring warning sign' of the fragility of a system that might one day collapse.[19]

The substance of Huang's critique is an attack on what he calls the 'Shanghai model of growth', which came to the fore in the 1990s. According to Huang, the Shanghai model is based on a high-speed urbanism that favours massive state-owned enterprise and giant multinational corporations. Its primary aim is the attraction of foreign direct investment (FDI) and its success is measured solely by rising GDP. He contrasts this economic model with a vibrant bottom-up sector of small, private entrepreneurs from the countryside, which dominated China's initial wave of economic reform that took place throughout the 1980s. This more organic, rural entrepreneurship creates wealth for individuals, not just for the state. It is these small private businesses, Huang argues, rather than the state-led crony capitalists responsible for the spectacular rise of Shanghai, that are the real force behind China's economic miracle. Reviewing Huang's book, *The Economist* magazine sums up the argument as follows: Huang 'has discovered two Chinas: one, from not so long ago, vibrant, entrepreneurial and rural; the other, today's China, urban and controlled by the state.'[20]

Huang is a careful researcher and provides plenty of data to back up his claims. Yet, perhaps the separation between these 'two Chinas' is not as neat as he suggests. China, after all, is currently in the grip of a mass wave of urbanisation, the biggest the world has ever seen. The rural entrepreneurs that once revolutionised village life are now seeking their fortunes on the city streets. Shanghai's dynamic rise rests not only on the spectacular projects of a state-led urbanism, but also on the vibrancy of the life and culture of these migrant workers. Outside the hyper-modern gloss of new roads and skyscrapers, there is a thriving micro-commercial culture—made up primarily of migrants from the countryside—which constitutes a flourishing informal economy that infiltrates the urban core. Moreover, as the 'dragon-head' of the Yangtze River Delta, Shanghai is intimately connected with the entrepreneurship of the region of the country Huang celebrates most. What, after all, is the urban gloss of Shanghai, if not a shop window for the back-alley factories of Zhejiang?

The notion of a Potemkin village stems from Russian minister Grigory Potemkin, who is said to have constructed elaborate fake villages in order to fool Catherine the Great on her tours of Crimea in the eighteenth century. In modern times, the idea has come to imply a stage set, a show that is designed to mislead. Those clever enough to see past the pretence will discover a pitiful reality that must be shamefully disguised. In Shanghai, however, the glittering artifice is not just a fraud but rather a show, a global attraction that—at least when conceived in this manner—need not interfere with the messy, vibrant entrepreneurial culture that continues to power the everyday life of the street.

The hidden layer

It is possible, then, to understand Huang's divide between 'two China's' not in terms of time (the 1980s versus the 1990s),[21] nor in terms of space (cities versus the countryside), but rather as an abstract distinction between two different economic orders that operate simultaneously in the city. This formulation is derived from the historian Fernand Braudel,[22] most famous for his monumental three-volume history of capitalism. The fundamental conclusion of this epic work is that there is, to use Braudel's words, a 'dialectic, still very much alive, between capitalism on one hand, and its antithesis, the "non-capitalism" of the lower level on the other. Capitalism as distinct from the market economy, is for me,' he writes, 'the essential message of this long quest.'[23]

Throughout his historical analysis, Braudel shows that these two economic realms—a higher-level capitalist order, consisting of monopolies and large corporations, and a substratum of market activity—have both been at work since as far back as the thirteenth century. Braudel identifies the mega-institutions of the higher level by their 'high-intensity capitalist endeavour; the privileges they are granted by the state; and their appropriation of whole sectors of overseas trade'.[24] Yet, while this more centralised and organised economic order has always been more visible, its secret is the strength it draws from the markets, which continually exist underneath and alongside it. Braudel repeatedly draws attention to 'the enormous creative powers of the market, of the lower storey of exchange…':

[This] lowest level, not being paralysed by the size of its plant or organisation, is the one readiest to adapt; it is the seed bed of inspiration, improvisation and even innovation, although its most brilliant discoveries sooner or later fall into the hands of the holders of capital. It was not the capitalists who brought about the first cotton revolution; all the new ideas came from enterprising small businesses.[25]

Walk through Shanghai's streets and alleys exploring the plethora of street vendors with their mobile carts, selling everything from stockings and fresh vegetables to houseplants and pirated DVDs, and it soon becomes clear that the city's spectacle exists only on the surface. The attention to glossy façade, massive state-owned corporations, concentration on FDI and support of monumental urbanism co-exists everywhere—just as Braudel suggests—with a lower level, bottom-up, thriving market activity that constitutes life in Shanghai's streets and alleyways.

The ongoing interaction between these two layers—or economic orders—is of fundamental importance to Shanghai's future. How is their relationship to be conceived? Are they poised on the brink of battle? At times it appears so. On one side, a monumental urbanism attempts to crush the micro-entrepreneurs that are helping to power China's growth. Deemed messy, unsightly and uncivilised, this organic street culture is continuously subject to the attempts to stamp it out and sweep it away. On the other side, the country's 'ongoing bottom-up transformation'—to borrow a term from theorist Kate Zhou[26]—bubbles up, gathering strength, waiting to overthrow the top-down planners responsible for the 'Shanghai model of growth'. Yet, in the rhythms of everyday life in the city, it is possible to catch a glimpse of another more murky type of interrelationship that, were it allowed to flourish, could help define a Shanghai futurism in which the gloss of urban spectacle could coexist with an emergent, micro-commercial and out-of-control culture that thrives in the shadows.

On the streets of Shanghai, this tension between freedom and control manifests itself in daily clashes that occur between the *chengguan* (the city inspectors) and street vendors. Though the *chengguan* are not official government employees, they are tasked with keeping the streets clean and have the right to chase off vendors and seize their money and goods. At times this unofficial policing becomes horribly violent—the *chengguan* are generally made up of unemployed state-owned workers and have a reputation for thuggery. Charged with maintaining the Shanghai spectacle, *chengguan* have beaten—even to the point of brain damage—migrant entrepreneurs. Outrage over their brutality has resulted in more than one urban riot.[27]

Nevertheless, there are zones of the city where a workable compromise between city inspectors and street vendors seems to have been reached. In these places the vendors have been working the same spot for many years and have developed relationships with the area's *chengguan*. When the inspectors are on duty (their daily schedule is no secret), the vendors disappear—or at least move off to one side. Their 'face' preserved and their duty done, the inspectors happily go off to eat or rest. As soon as they leave, the vendors return to their spots. This type of give-and-take relationship is a vital component of the contemporary Chinese city and anyone familiar with Shanghai will immediately recognise this kind of compromise. In China, goes another saying, 'green light means go, yellow light means speed up and red light means find another way around'. In these kinds of 'arrangements with Chinese characteristics,' the concept of spectacle is key.

The seen and the unseen

China loves a good show. It famously invented gunpowder, but rather than use it for deadly ammunition it created grandiose firework displays. This deep respect for pageantry is apparent in the Forbidden City, headquarters of China's imperial power, whose intricate layering ensures that every visitor participates in an elaborate theatrical performance. The Chinese skill at staging such performances was revealed to the world in the astonishing opening ceremony of the 2008 Olympics. A year later the 2009 celebrations for the sixty-year anniversary of the Communist Party occurred under a sunny blue sky. This did not happen naturally. The party manipulated the weather for the event. In China it is no secret that these spectacles are choreographed. That the Olympic fireworks were 'Photoshopped' for TV, that pretty smiling girls were brought in for the opening, or that the clouds were seeded for the Party's grand parade should come as no surprise. Here illusion has long functioned as a crucial currency of power. You only have to visit the Great Wall to realise that China's greatest monument was built more as a symbol than for any functional purpose. This profound attention to exteriority and façade attains an intensely personal expression in the Chinese concept of 'face'. To lose face, in this shame-based culture, is itself a devastating failure and thus functions, for both children and adults, as an enormously powerful mechanism for behavioural control. In China, people recognise that spectacle works.

In the case of Shanghai, and especially Pudong, this is blatantly obvious. Shanghai may be built on hype, but the hype has produced some very real results. The power of PR, Kris Olds tells us, was evident as soon as Pudong planners launched the international competition for the development of Lujiazui. 'The identity of the district was transformed immediately from a former industrial and residential zone, into a high-tech city set to rise out of Shanghai's shadow.'[28] 'Before the start of the Pudong development,' concurs researcher Yawei Chen, 'Shanghai was an unattractive place to invest, notorious for its rigidity, bureaucracy and red tape. Within 15 years all that changed.'[29]

Whilst intentionally directed to the flows of global capitalism, Shanghai's embrace of spectacle was also a very intentional expression of local power. Aihwa Ong, in her discussion of hyperbuilding as an illustration of the Asian 'art of being global', critiques the conceptualisation of spectacle as the expression of 'a global capitalist hegemon' (as theorised, for example, by Guy Debord or Jameson). 'Urban dwellers in Asia's big cities do not read spectacles as a generalised effect of capitalism, but rather as symbols of their metropolis that invite inevitable comparison with rival cities. Shanghai sees itself as the international gateway to China and is therefore a critical site of China's urban representations as well as symbolic encapsulation of the world and the potential of globality.'[30]

The Western philosophical tradition has a deep-rooted animosity to spectacle. This ancient and foundational hostility is captured by Plato's famous image of the cave, which tragically likens our existence to prisoners who are forced to spend their lives gazing at shadows that are projected on the wall. The prisoners, forgetting what they once knew of the outside world, are fooled into mistaking the illusion for reality. In Plato's parable one prisoner manages to escape and makes his way out of the cave. Slowly—after his eyes painfully adjust to the light—he sees the truth of the world illuminated by the brightness of the sun. With the truth revealed he returns to his friends, the prisoners, who reject his story of escape as a lie. The philosopher king— our hero—presses on. The shadows must be eliminated. The spectacle must be penetrated. All that is true and good must be brought to the light.

China has an altogether different outlook on the spectacular. It does not condemn illusion in the same way. One of most famous Taoist fables from the *Zhuangzi* tells of a man who dreams of a butterfly. When he suddenly wakes he finds himself again a man. In the end, the story teaches, we do not know whether it is the man dreaming the butterfly or the butterfly dreaming the man. Western thought encounters the idea that the world may have the character of a dream as the terror of epistemological uncertainty.[31] René Descartes, faced with a similar thought, recoiled in horror. His subsequent quest for certainty eventually formed the foundation for modern Western thought. The *Zhuangzi* is far more comfortable with the coexistence of the dreamer and the dreamed. To the Taoist both are equally real, equally authentic, equally valid. 'There must be some distinction between Zhou and a butterfly!' says the *Zhuangzi*, 'This is called the transformation of things'.

This acceptance of spectacle is rooted in a philosophical tradition that, unlike the West, does not associate brightness with truth and darkness with the falsity of illusion. One of China's oldest classical texts—and one of the few books to have survived the Qin Emperor's great book-burning in the third century BC—is the *Yijing*. At the heart of the *Yijing* is a divinatory system made up of sixty-four hexagrams that are composed of multiple variations of broken and unbroken lines. The lines represent the yin/yang dualism that is at the foundation of Chinese thought. Originally and literally, yin and yang denote the shady and sunny side of a mountain. Over time these principles accrued deeper significance. 'The *Yijing*, writes scholar Wonsuk Chang, 'depicts contrasting forces through a variety of terms relevant to different situations':

rest (*jing*) and movement (*dong*), softness (*rou*) and firmness (*gang*), within form (*qi*) and above form (*dao*), receptivity (*kun*) and creativity (*qian*), completion (*zheng*) and beginning (*shi*), simplicity (*jian*) and easiness (*yi*), progression (*jin*) and regression (*tui*), darkness (*yu*) and brightness (*ming*), ghosts or dissemination (*gui*) and spirits or stretching (*shen*), wisdom (*zhi*) and benevolence (*ren*), cold (*han*) and hot (*shu*), hidden (*cang*) and disclosing (*xian*), and enlarging life (*dasheng*) and broadening life (*guangsheng*).[32]

According to Chinese philosophy, yin and yang emerge together out of primordial emptiness. They are interconnected and give rise to each other. The world is produced through their constant rotation of shadow and light. Time itself, the *Yijing* teaches, is governed by this constant shifting change.

What's behind the curtain?

The fundamental dualism of shadow and light manifests itself in contemporary Chinese society in a multiplicity of ways. One of its most profound expressions is in the thin line that separates the Chinese government from the Communist Party. This dualism is essential to the structure of the state. In China today the government and other state organs perform on the front stage, creating an outward spectacle. Behind the scenes, the Party rules. In China, every segment of the public realm—the military, state-owned companies, each and every layer of government—is intricately shadowed by the Party which stealthily remains out of sight. 'It is backstage, in the party forums,' writes journalist Richard McGregor 'where the real stuff of politics is transacted.'[33] This concealment of the Party is the key insight of McGregor's well-known book. The theme is introduced in the preface. 'The problem in writing about the Party,' McGregor confesses, 'is that, as much as the Party might be staring you in the face, you can't easily gaze back... Sometimes, you can't see the Party at all.'[34] Throughout the book this idea of the Party dominating the country from the shadows forms an ongoing motif. 'The Party is the grand puppeteer.'[35] McGregor quotes one business-man working in the state-owned sector as saying. It is 'like a phantom', echoes a lawyer from Beijing.[36] The best analogy, though, comes from a professor in Beijing who writes 'the party is like God. He is everywhere. You just can't see him.'[37]

Left in the shadows

Liberals in China attack this lack of transparency as the dark side of China's recent reforms.[38] When a secret sub-sector of society has hidden access both to great power and to great wealth the inevitable result is corruption. The concealment of the party, they contend, has created a mafia state run off crony capitalism.[39] Hope for the future rests on the forces of openness—glo-balisation and cyberspace—that will eventually force light on this hidden realm. To these critics, there is something inherently dishonest, and morally suspect, in a city that so delights in pure show. It is no doubt true that the dualism of luminosity and shade that exists in Shanghai allows for nefarious dealings, and the growth of a power that is corrupt and unchecked. Yet, there is also a certain liberty in the acceptance that there is life in the shadows that does not need to be brought to light. The darkness provides space and free-dom (if not power) not only for those at the top of society, but also for those at the bottom. The Shanghai spectacle, with its concentration on the surface, can, at least sometimes, produce a toleration for the messy markets that thrive alongside and underneath the spectacular skyline.

In the lead up to Expo, a widely publicised anti-piracy campaign led to a frenzy of reconstruction inside the city's DVD stores. Proprietors well versed in the customs of face, converted the front of their stores into legiti-mate businesses—some sold sweaters and bags, others stocked their shelves with the few legitimate DVDs that are available inside the country (mostly Chinese films and films from Hollywood's classical age). Behind this front they all installed fake doors. Customers looking for illicit goods were ush-ered into the back where the real goods were being sold. Though some of these stores were busted,[40] the deception was hardly a secret. Instead, it was a clever arrangement serving a multiplicity of interests. Officials didn't have to lose face from the flagrant piracy in the city, businesses didn't have to shut down and customers could continue watching films. The day Expo ended all the DVD stores in the city closed for renovation. The fake walls and doors were taken down and business as usual resumed.

These types of arrangements—so strange to Western eyes—are what allow Shanghai's spectacle to co-exist with its street life. When spectacle is contained, relegated to its place, the Potemkin village ceases to be a shameful disguise. Instead, it enables a potentially productive dualism that can awe and attract while still allowing for the flourishing existence of a hidden realm. 'Urban development,' writes Ananya Roy, 'unfolds in differential and "unmapped" geographies of informality and illegality, and such city-making pivots on the flexible practices of powerful state.'[41] The grey or shadow economy—so vital to Shanghai's rise—is thus supported by the blindness that comes from all the urban gloss. It cannot function if all is brought to light. Critics should remember that to insist on penetrating the surface, to hope for face-to-face confrontation, runs the danger of destroying all that needs the darkness to survive.

PART 2

4

GOTHIC FUTURISM

> *The numbering of the past is flowing with the current.*
> *The knowledge of the future is countercurrent*
> *This causes the Yi to count backwards.*

> Yijing

> *Dare you state categorically that demons don't exist in modern Shanghai?*

> Shi Zhecun

Modern time

In 1899, at the dawn of the twentieth century, two events occurred in China that transformed the nature of time. The first was when Liang Qichao, the famous reformer of the late Qing, published diaries of his trip to North America that were marked with Gregorian dates. Liang, along with his teacher and mentor Kang Youwei, occupied a liminal position on the cusp of two worlds. Though trained in the classical Confucian tradition, they were, like all thinkers of the time, swept up by the forces of globalisation and modernisation that were spiralling through China in the last decade of the nineteenth century. Both Liang and Kang are most commonly remembered for their role in the 'hundred days reform', a short-lived movement based on a series of edicts implemented by Emperor Guangxu, which sought to bring about rapid and dramatic change. Sweeping plans included building a modern postal and banking system, laying down a railway network, promoting research centres dedicated to industrial innovation, transforming the educational system and the civil service examination, embracing capitalist democracy and creating a new China based on constitutional monarchy. The revolutionary moment lasted only for a brief flash before ending in failure, when conservative forces led by Empress Dowager Cixi staged a *coup d'etat* that ousted Guangxu and called for the reformer's arrest. In 1898, facing certain execution, Liang fled to Japan. A year later he made his first trip to North America to meet with Sun Yat-sen.

Liang's politics were tied to the culture of the modern city. He was heavily immersed in the emerging world of journals and newspapers made possible by the spirited combination of printing press technology and a new urban readership. Liang was a strong believer in the power of the press and worked throughout his life as a writer and editor. Lin Yutang called him, 'the greatest personality in the history of Chinese journalism'.

Liang's was not the first publication to use the Western calendar in China. Over twenty years earlier, in 1872, *Shenbao*, a Western-owned newspaper, started printing the Chinese and Western calendar dates side by side on its front page. Liang's diary, however, made a much greater impact. 'It was not until Liang Qichao proclaimed his own use of the Western calendar,' argues the great theorist of Chinese modernity, Leo Lee, 'that a paradigmatic change in time-consciousness was effected.'[1]

Liang was adamant that social transformation involved a shift in time-keeping practices and argued passionately for calendric reform. 'Till now, half of the nations of the world use the Gregorian calendar,' he wrote in 1902, 'unless it is in an extremely barbaric place, people are not using the imperial era way of counting years.'[2] A decade later, in 1912, the Chinese republic officially adopted the Gregorian calendar. Soon after, the calendar poster, which featured Western dates and modern girls, became a fixture in urban daily life. The posters, still found in the curio markets around town, are one of the quintessential creations of *haipai*—Shanghai's singular style.

Liang's early adoption of the Gregorian calendar was symptomatic of a much broader shift in the understanding of time that was seeping its way through urban China, reaching an apex in the culture of the May Fourth Movement.[3] This new temporality, which was already well established throughout industrial Europe, rested on synthesising the twin poles of modern time, the Gregorian calendar and the mechanical clock, thereby melding empty abstraction (the ubiquitous ticking of the clock) with a calendric, directional pull. Chinese modernity, it was widely held, rested on an embrace of this particular construction of time, which moves along a straight line, propelled by evolutionary progress. 'I believe,' writes Leo Lee 'that time—

and the system of calendric dating—is the foundation on which modernity is constructed.'[4] Shu-mei Shih, author of *The Lure of the Modern* concurs. 'Time,' he writes, 'was the crucial category in the radical rethinking of Chinese culture and literature during the May Fourth era (1917–1927).[5]

The primary impulse of a progressive linear temporality—that the old must give way to the new—requires that time be recoded in both directions at once. Developmental time needs both the construction of a past that lies behind and is available to be discarded as old and outdated, as well as a brightly lit future up ahead. The doctrine of progress thus demanded that China's indigenous, traditional time cultures and time practices be rejected and replaced.[6] Chinese modernists, under the powerful influence of social Darwinism, which Liang himself helped introduce, rejected the 'cyclical dynastic mode of traditional time.'[7] Instead, time, which had previously been governed by a rhythm of qualitative change, was re-conceived as a purely quantitative force that moved 'in a continuous stream' or 'tide' from 'past to present'. 'The evolution of human civilisation is replacing old with the new,' declared May Fourth writer Chen Duxiu, 'like a river flowing on, an arrow flying away, constantly continuing and constantly changing'.[8] Liang concurred with the typical confidence of the age: 'By examining the past and revealing the future I will show the path of progress to the people of the nation.'

In the May Fourth Movement, therefore, the two temporal coordinates, 'present (*jin*) and past (*gu*)' became, as Lee explains, 'polarised as contrasting values'.[9] In 'May Fourth parlance, to be modern means above all to be "new" (*xin*), to be consciously opposed to the old (*jiu*).'[10] Among the popular formulations of this embrace of newness were new policies (*xinzheng*), new schools (*xinxue*), new people (*xinmin*), new culture (*xin wenhua*), new literature (*xin wenxue*) and new time or epoch (*xin shidai*).

The construction of modernity embedded in May Fourth, then, celebrated the arrival of a discontinuous break; a clear split from what was perceived as the repetitiveness and stagnation of traditional Chinese time. The leaders of the new 'Chinese Renaissance', wrote its great spokesman Hu Shih, 'want to install in people a new outlook on life which shall free them from the shackles of tradition and make them feel at home in the new world and its new civilization.'[11] The present was therefore conceived as a pivotal moment—a new 'epoch' that was 'not only unprecedented and qualitatively different from previous eras but better'.[12] It marked 'a rupture with the past and formed a progressive continuum toward a glorious future'.[13] 'The light that died is born anew,' wrote Guo Moruo in his famous poem, 'The cosmos that died is born anew.'[14]

Deep past

In the same year that Liang published his diary marked with Gregorian dates, the scholar and antiquarian Wang Yirong stumbled upon one of China's greatest archaeological treasures: turtle shells marked with an ancient script that told the fortunes of those that had died long ago. Legend goes that Wang made the discovery through the chance purchase of a medicinal mixture used to treat malaria. For many years farmers near the modern city of Anyang had been digging up shells and bones for trade in the nearby medicine markets. The shells were ground up and sold as 'dragon bones', a potent ingredient in traditional Chinese remedies. Most often farmers scraped off any markings before bringing the shells and bones to market. In 1899, however, one that was still preserved fell into the hands of Wang whose familiarity with ancient bronzes allowed him to recognise the cryptic signs as an early example of Chinese script. Excited by his discovery, Wang spent the next year collecting as many bones as he could find.

His obsessive gathering was brought to an abrupt end in the summer of 1900 when Wang, who worked as an official for the Qing government, was called to Beijing to lead a battle against the Boxers, which ended in defeat.[15] Wang, despairing for the future, swallowed poison and jumped into a well. After his death, Wang's personal discovery of about 1,000 artefacts passed to his friend Liu E, who published a book on the collection in 1903. The modern study of oracle bones had begun. In the two decades that followed, locals and foreigners alike dug frantically for turtle shells and other relics. The anarchic search was brought to an end in 1928 when an official excavation was launched at Anyang. With this first dig, China entered the golden age of archaeology and joined the modern world in opening the chasms of deep time. Anyang turned out to be the former capital city of the Shang dynasty (c.1600–c.1100 BC), whose existence, until then, many believed to be only myth. At the dawn of the twentieth century, then, this most ancient culture emerged from the murkiness of legend, establishing itself with the certainty of historical fact.

The discovery of the oracle bones opened China to lines into the deep past. Yet, it also added a layer of complexity to the modern construction of time. Just as the revolutionary culture of May Fourth was gaining strength, with its evolutionary and progressive temporality, the archeological discoveries at Anyang were uncovering an indigenous futurism that refused to stay buried.

The shells and bones buried at Anyang were the main tool in Shang divination rituals. The conductors of these rituals—those skilled in consulting the oracle—would begin by recording the date, name and question. They would then proceed to drill small notches that could be prodded with a hot metal stick. The cracks produced were interpreted as the 'voice of the turtle', an entity with access to the fortunes that lie ahead.

> Tonight there will be no disasters,
> There may be someone bringing alarming news.
> The whole day he will not encounter great wind.[16]

The oracle bones thus enact a strange twist of time in which messages recorded from thousands of years ago tell us today about what tomorrow might bring. 'We often think of writing as history, and traditional culture is characterised by its tendency to idealise the past,' writes author Peter Hessler in his book *Oracle Bones*. 'But the irony of Chinese archaeology is that the earliest known writings tell of the future.'[17] In China, time is looped from the start.

Shadows and light

By the end of the nineteenth century, Shanghai had positioned itself as the indisputable centre of Chinese modernity. In this great modern metropolis the adoption of a 'Western', linear time had considerable sway. Clocks as symbols of modernity were prominently on display. The most notable example, as historian Jeff Wasserstrom points out, was the giant clock on the Customs House, which operated throughout the twentieth century as one of the most iconic symbols of the Bund and a critical sign that Shanghai was China's most modern metropolis.[18] Today, as Shanghai attempts to situate itself at the cutting edge of the twenty-first century, the legacy of May Fourth culture and its embrace of progressive time is apparent once again, most dramatically in Pudong, where, as we have seen, a clean-slate urbanism with its broad blocks of boulevards and gleaming glass towers deliberately recalls the raze-and-replace high modernism of the International Style. This clearing away of an older urban fabric to make way for a shining, luminescent futurism is found everywhere in the contemporary urban landscape. Viewed from this angle, 'neo-modern Shanghai' with its dazzling spectacle of glass and light follows a familiar template—destroy the old to make way for the new.

Yet, Shanghai's contemporary rise, as well as its future orientation, is also being influenced by the resurrection of another, darker, more shadowy modernity, rooted more in Puxi than in Pudong. In the looming Art Deco monuments behind the Bund, at the striking octagonal intersection at Jiangxi

Lu and Fuzhou Lu, in the dark brick intricacies of the Park Hotel, along with its contemporary echo—the Jinmao tower, a science-fiction pagoda that cuts across the blackness of the sky—Shanghai seems more like Gotham City than the luminescent imaginings of the City of Tomorrow. This more obscure manifestation of modernity is rooted in a gothic vision of the future city, which is tied to an alternative and more occulted notion of time. In this tangled temporality the future does not wait for us as a brightly lit beacon up ahead. It is not a point that can be easily located on the straight line of time and thus cannot ever be just a delayed borrowing from elsewhere. Rather this 'Gothic Futurism'—essentially unpredictable and unknown—lurks always in the shadows of the present and can, as the oracle bones show, be accessed by cities already buried as well as those that are still on the rise.

The gothic revival

The strongest counter current in Europe to modernity's embrace of light, linearity and evolutionary advance was the Gothic Revival. The movement began in England at the heart of the industrial age. Its emergence and subsequent spread posed a dramatic challenge to the ideology of reason and progress that seemed so married to the machine age. The Gothic expressed the dark side of reason, the anti-enlightenment, the unconscious of modernity. 'During its years of greatest influence,' writes Michael Lewis in his monograph on the style, 'it subjected every aspect of art, belief, society and labour to intense intellectual scrutiny, using the Middle Ages as a platform from which to judge the modern world … In the broadest view, [the Gothic Revival] is the story of Western civilisation's confrontation with modernity.'[19]

It was an Englishman named Horace Walpole (1717–97) who first reawakened the Gothic in modern times. In 1750, Walpole purchased a cottage in Twickenham outside London on a property now known as Strawberry Hill. Over the course of the next three decades he led a highly eccentric renovation, converting the simple cottage he had bought into an intricate, rambling Gothic mansion. This revival of Gothic's skeletal architecture summoned up an unconscious horror in Walpole. Asleep in his mansion one night, he dreamt of a ghostly hand dressed in armour that hovered above the castle staircase. Walpole immediately recorded the nightmare, publishing it under the title *The Castle of Otranto: A Gothic Story*. The tale is widely ridiculed. H. P. Lovecraft, one of the greatest horror writers of the twentieth century, calls it 'thoroughly unconvincing and mediocre'.[20] Nevertheless, as

Lovecraft notes, 'the hunger left by the sober rationality of the age' was such that Walpole's story was 'destined to exert an almost unparalleled influence on the literature of the weird.'[21] *The Castle of Otranto* is widely credited with founding the modern gothic novel. Crucially, the main character was the Gothic building itself, 'with its awesome antiquity, vast distances and ramblings, deserted or ruined wings, damp corridors, unwholesome hidden catacombs, and galaxy of ghosts and appalling legends'.[22] The Gothic castle writes Lovecraft, 'was a nucleus of suspense and demoniac fright'.[23] By building his mansion and publishing his story, Walpole fused together an intricate architecture with ghostly tales, which, from then on, became the twin faces of the Gothic in modern times.

Given its fascination with ruins and its conservative inclinations, the Gothic Revival is often understood as the product of a desire to return to a previous epoch. This regressive impulse is seen to have reached its apex during the Victorian age. Thus, by 1922 when Raymond Hood won the competition for the Tribune Tower in Chicago with an overtly neo-Gothic design, the decision was dismissed with outrage by the more avant-garde European modernists who saw the building as a triumph for traditionalism. Yet, while twentieth-century modernism saw fewer buildings being constructed in an explicitly Gothic style, the Gothic sensibility has retained its strength and allure. Contrary to common opinion, though, it has done so, not through its nostalgic recollection of the past but, like modernity itself, through its futurist orientation.

With its flying buttresses and vaulted arches, Gothic architecture, was, above all, an architecture designed to respond to the challenge of height. The desire to build ever upwards compelled it to find ways to stretch material to its vertical limit. The modern skyscraper—as the Tribune Tower, the Woolworth Building, the Chrysler Building and many other high-rises make clear—has been the direct inheritor of this Gothic obsession with buildings that reach up to the sky. In the Gothic Revival, however, the spirituality of this vertical architecture was combined with a looming sense of a world governed by shadowy forces. Through this strange synthesis (what after all does skeletal architecture have to do with literary horror?) Gothic futurism creates its own particular vision of the 'metropolis of tomorrow'. It imagines an urban landscape of vast elevations and dark caverns, most alive at night, which operates as a radical alternative to the radiant future promised by a modernity governed by the straight line of time.

This Gothic vision of the future city manifested itself most intensely in New York in the early decades of the twentieth century. In a series of lectures designed to accompany the show *New York Modern* put on by the Skyscraper Museum, curator Carol Willis shows how New York in the twenties and thirties embodied a realm far different from textbook notions of urban modernity. In the dark brick designs of Raymond Hood, who used the 'vehicle of the Gothic to express towering height',[24] or in Hugh Ferris' 'quasi nocturnal images' whose charcoal sketches envision, as Rem Koolhaas writes, a city 'of artificial night',[25] New York futurism produced an alternate modernity, rooted in urban life, that was only later eclipsed by the imposed dominance of the International Style.

Just as the Walpole's mansion motivated the first Gothic novel, so the architecture of New York in the early decades of the twentieth century inspired the two early masterpieces of Gothic futurism: *Batman*'s Gotham City and Fritz Lang's *Metropolis*. In Batman mythology, the 'Gotham style' was the invention of a young architect named Cyrus Pinkney, who was himself a participant in the Gothic Revival. Pinkney's urban 'creations', however, are clearly based on exaggerated versions of the buildings of New York City. Gotham City, says Dennis O'Neil, Batman's writer and editor, 'is Manhattan, below 14th street at 11 past midnight on the coldest night in November'.

The sight of New York at night is also said to be the muse for Lang's greatest film *Metropolis*. 'The view of New York' he is quoted as saying, 'is a beacon of beauty strong enough to be the centerpiece of a film ...At night the city did not give the impression of being alive; it lived as illusions lived.'[26] In *Metropolis*, Lang famously used the shadows and angles of expressionism to create, through only a few montages, the dark vista of an urban landscape made up of impossible heights and monstrous subterranean canyons. *Metropolis*' shadowy image of the future city is reanimated for today's audience through the popular genres of cyberpunk and manga. In stories and films like *Neuromancer*, *Ghost in the Shell* and *Blade Runner*, spectral entities unleashed by the modern machine haunt dark cities teeming with nocturnal life. The future they evoke is obscure and unknown, totally unlike the well-illuminated destinies guaranteed by the predictable march of progress.

The gothic style

Most interpret the darkness of the Gothic negatively. The very term originated as a pejorative description of something that was rude and barbaric. This perceived savagery in the style provoked intense hostility from its

critics. 'For three centuries,' writes Michael Lewis, the gothic style of architecture was the 'apex of barbarianism and the irrational.'[27] Kenneth Clark,
in the introduction to his celebrated essay on the Gothic Revival, calls it a
'style we cannot swallow'. Its buildings are 'monsters', 'ugly shapes', the
'unsightly wrecks stranded on the mud flats of Victorian taste'.[28] Gothic
Futurism is considered equally distasteful, a disturbing dystopia, a nightmare vision of foreboding cities filled with crime, degeneracy, illicit activity
and urban decay.

In his wondrous book *Form in Gothic*, the great philosopher of aesthetics
Wilhelm Worringer challenges this widespread view. The book, first published in English in 1927, aims to understand the Gothic on its own terms.
It begins, writes Worringer, with the 'hypothetical construction' that there is
a 'gothic will to form' that is as 'strongly and unmistakably expressed in the
smallest crinkle of Gothic drapery as in the great Gothic cathedrals'.[29]

To access this 'will to form', Worringer contrasts the Gothic with the
Classical style, which, he argues, we have elevated to the pre-eminent aesthetic. He defines the Classical regime through its 'highest ideal', the realistic representation of the human figure. Reflecting a world with man at its
centre, the Classical style, 'whose prejudices we have inherited',[30] is rooted
in the comforting sense of a well-ordered cosmos that can be mastered
through knowledge and rationally controlled. The Classical-European aesthetic is secure in its comprehension of the universe and thus delights in the
truthful reproduction of natural models, especially the human form. It awak-
ens, writes Worringer, the 'feeling for the beauty in living things…for the
joy inspiring rhythm of the organic world'.[31] This intrinsic organicism is
particularly evident in the honour that the Classical style gives to stone
sculpture, which privileges the 'literal, plastic representation of beautiful
human beings'.[32] The greatest aspiration of the classical artist, writes
Worringer, was to 'animate the lifeless nature of stone', by carving it into 'a
wonderfully expressive organism'.[33] For Worringer even Classical buildings
were based on this admiration of the human. The rounded column, the ultimate expression of Classical architecture speaks, he argues, of this intense
organic vitality.

Ultimately, however, the impact of this profound celebration of life was
to strip the cosmos of its mystery. Classical Aesthetics succeeded, to use the
language of Max Weber, in producing a world disenchanted of its gods and
demons. 'A well-ordered cosmos,' says Worringer, 'leaves no room for a
belief in wild, spectral doings.'[34] With the Classical regime, there is an 'easing of instinctive fear' as the universe becomes knowable, controllable, and

no longer 'strange, inaccessible and mystically great'.[35] In the human-centred Classical Age, 'life becomes more beautiful, more joyful, but it loses in depth, in grandeur and in force. For, in the increasing security of his knowledge, man has made himself the measure of all things, has assimilated the world to his finite humanity.'[36]

The Gothic, by contrast, does not find joy and beauty in the human body. Instead of the organic representation of nature, the gothic 'will to form' exalts in the expression of abstraction. This abstract tendency began with ornamentation and reached its apex in the complex brickwork of Gothic architecture. Whereas the Classical Age revered sculpture, the gothic venerated buildings. 'We need only utter the word Gothic,' writes Worringer, 'to awaken in us immediately the powerfully associated idea of Gothic architecture. The stylistic epoch of the Gothic was completely dominated by architecture.'[37]

The underlying impulse of Gothic structures was, as we have seen, the desire to soar upwards. The Gothic 'sought to lift stone, free it from its heaviness'. Through the pointed arch, ribbed vaulting and flying buttresses, the Gothic unleashed a 'strong upward movement of energies in opposition to the natural downward weight of the stone'. It became the bearer of 'an uncontrolled upward motion',[38] unleashing what Worringer describes in a dramatic crescendo as a 'vertical whirlwind', an 'upward soaring of energy', a 'vertical movement from which every law of gravity seems to be eliminated'.[39]

One explanation for the difference between the Gothic and Classical style is that the Gothic has a Northern nomadic heritage while the Classical Age has sedentary roots. The Northern, or nomadic world, which lacked comfort in an organic nature, did not treat the cosmos as something that could be known, mastered or contained by the limited realm of human beings. On the contrary, it perceived a universe filled with 'gods and ghosts, spectres and spooks', in which 'everything becomes weird and fantastic'.[40] The Gothic, writes Worringer, was 'distressed by actuality, debarred from naturalness'.[41] This drew it to the transcendental possibilities of the abstract line. It is through the expression of this transcendental abstraction that the Gothic ties together the intricacies of its architecture with the terror of its tales.

For Worringer, then, the Gothic 'will to form' is not simply negative—it is other. The Gothic form sought to put the play of light at the centre of its cathedrals, but with this light came shadows. Its affinity with night and darkness arises from the inherent exteriority of its sensibility. The Gothic counters the dominant forms of modernity not through a direct or straightforward critique but rather through a sensibility that is intrinsically alien.

The 'nomadic line invested with abstraction'—to use the name given to it by philosophers Deleuze and Guattari—is both unnatural and non-organic but nevertheless expressive of an intense vitality. The Gothic line is inorganic but alive. Or, to borrow Deleuze and Guattari's phrase it is 'all the more alive for being inorganic…This streaming, spiraling, zigzagging, snaking, feverish line of variation liberates a power of life.'[42]

This exteriority of Gothic Futurism, which is capable of connecting the deep past with the far future, belongs equally to the twelfth, eighteenth and twenty-first centuries. It is impossible to date and can never be dated. Cyberpunk theorists Bruce Sterling and William Gibson call it 'atemporal', since the modern countercurrent it summons is not of a past era but of another type of time. For the Gothic Futurist, then, it is not only the straight line of evolutionary history that produces the City of Tomorrow. An alternate temporality is also at work, forming the modern metropolis.

Shanghai noir

The modern culture of the May Fourth Movement sought to banish traditional belief in ghosts and other supernatural entities. In the wake of the May Fourth Movement, writes David Wang in his book *The Monster That is History*, 'authentic modern literature was expected to highlight themes such as enlightenment and revolution'.[43] The guideline was 'art for the sake of life'. In the grand exorcism, modelled after nineteenth-century European canons of realism, ghosts 'were associated with obsolete superstition, feudal practices, or merely decadent imagination, and were thus impediments to modern epistemological and ideological advancement'.[44] Both Wang and Tsi-an Hsia, author of *Gate of Darkness*, an illuminating study of the period, take Hu Shih, champion of the 'Chinese Renaissance', who boasted of his ability to 'chain the demons and subdue the ghosts', to be the key representative of this cult of reason. Hu Shih's commitment to progress 'appeared to be unequivocal and consistent', writes Hsia; 'over his life shone the steady, serene light of optimism. Ghosts, indeed, became powerless in his world of enlightenment.'[45] Wang echoes this emphasis on disenchantment quoting one of Hu Shih's poems: 'let us summon like minded friends … flogging and expelling the whole carriage of ghosts, and welcome the arrival of a new era'.[46]

Yet prominent theorists of Chinese modern literature—Tsi-an Hsia, Leo Lee, David Wang and Shu-mei Shih—all agree that despite the pull of an 'enlightened' modernity, there was a strong gothic undercurrent to

Shanghai's urban culture in the early decades of the twentieth century. The writing and architecture of the city's golden age combined to create a 'Shanghai Noir' aesthetic that was picked up by Hollywood depictions of the city as the 'Paris of the East'. Shanghai's own neo-Gothic productions can be glimpsed in the sorcerous writings of Shi Zhecun; the reinvention of tradition of Lu Xun; the Brick Expressionism of Hungarian architect László Hudec that linked modern Shanghai to the dark futurism of Fritz Lang; and in the delirious borrowings of Art Deco, which, inspired by a golden age of archaeology, sought to create a modern language through reanimating mysterious patterns that were being uncovered from the ancient world.

The tales

There is something I dislike in heaven; I do not want to go there.
There is something I dislike in hell; I do not want to go there.
There is something I dislike in your future golden world; I do not want to go there.[47]

Lu Xun

In the realm of literature, modernity's counterculture was most actively embraced by a group of Shanghai-based writers known as the 'new sensationists', or 'new perceptionists' (*xin ganjuepai*). This movement comprised writers like Mu Shiying, Liu Na'ou and Shi Zhecun, who sought to 'immerse themselves in the sights, sounds, and feel of the new urban experience'.[48] These experimental writers embraced the winds of a global transformation and welcomed modernity as their own. 'I think modernism in the 1930s was not local or national but international,' says Shi Zhecun in an interview conducted by Shu-mei Shih in 1990. 'Modernism in the West was influenced by Eastern culture ... To say that I "Easternised" modernism is wrong. It is Western modernism that is Easternised and my modernism Westernised.'[49]

New sensationist writers went 'against the grain of realism' propagated by May Fourth modernism. They were deeply influenced by Freudian ideas and by modern art's great engagement with the unconscious—surrealism. Shi Zhecun, in particular, also tapped into a widespread interest in occult dabblings and admired the gothic fiction of writers like Edgar Allan Poe. His story *The Devil's Road*, is told through the unconscious paranoid ramblings of the narrator, a technique Shi uses in many of his tales. The plot centres on a trip to the outskirts of Shanghai and is riddled with witches, mummys and opium-crazed hallucinations. Shi, writes Leo Lee:

had developed a penchant for the bizarre and the supernatural—not only about dreams and hallucinations, but also about sado-masochism, dandyism, fetishism, sorcery, witchcraft, necromancy, black magic and Celtic myths. This medley of strange materials was put to good use in a dozen 'fantastic' stories set in present Shanghai. He would have developed a subgenre, a kind of urban Gothic romance of repressed and not so repressed eroticism if he had not been so hard pressed by his leftist colleagues to give up this 'bewitched journey' of literary experimentation.[50]

A decade later, Eileen Chang, who David Wang calls 'the priestess of Shanghai's decadent cult in the 1940s',[51] inherited something of this same style. 'Her tales, though couched in realistic rhetoric, constantly suggest a chilling gothic world.'[52] 'A strange feeling emerges toward surrounding reality,' Wang quotes Chang as writing; 'a suspicion that this is an absurd, ancient world, dark and shadowy, and yet bright and clear.'[53]

China's formulation of a Gothic Futurism, however, was articulated most profoundly in the writings of Lu Xun, the country's greatest modern writer. In his most famous stories and even more stridently in his prose poetry, particularly those recorded in the astonishing collection *Wild Grass*, Lu Xun evokes a realm that haunts the celebration of reason. Lu Xun, 'was committed to progress, to science and to denial of the backward, superstitious, cruel and shameful old China', explains Hsia in his gripping study of the author. Yet, 'his beliefs in the enlightenment did not really dispel the darkness'.[54] Hsia's *Gate of Darkness* is worth quoting at length:

Lu Hsun was not a true representative of the May Fourth Movement insofar as that term is understood to mean a popular movement with positive aims to discard the old and adapt the new. He embodied rather the conflict between the old and the new and some deeper conflicts, too, that transcend history ... his militant advocacy of progress, of science and enlightenment, is well known. But this does not make up the whole of his personality, nor does it account for his genius unless we take into consideration his curiosity, his secret longing and love for what he hated... Few authors are able to discuss the macabre with so much zest ... [Lu Hsun] tried to find a reason that we should all love these ghosts. With his vivid imagination he called them back to life, as it were, and affectionately showed them around to his readers ... To take Lu Hsun as merely an angel who sounded the trumpet for daybreak is to overlook one of the more profound souls of modern Chinese history, and a morbid soul too. Some trumpet he did sound; but the music he made was sombre and sardonic, expressive of despair as well as hope, a mingling of heavenly and infernal notes.[55]

Lu Xun's most engaging works, then, deal not with his reasoning about China's fate', agrees David Wang, 'but with the dark side of reason':

When the representational order of the world he establishes for himself breaks loose, demons, superstitions, and macabre fantasies haunt him in the form of a spectral carnival. In other words, beneath his project of edification and enlightenment, something ghastly always looms. And strangely, before these dark forces can be exorcised, he is first hopelessly deceived or even charmed by them.[56]

A fascination with modernity's shadows can be found in all of Lu Xun's best work: in the cannibalism of *A Madman's Diary*, the lunacy of *The True Story of Ah Q* and the occulted poetry of *Wild Grass*. Despite his commitment to modern revolutionary change, Lu Xun was too great an artist to do away with tradition entirely. His writing thus occupied a position between darkness and light. What compelled him, argues Hsia, was the 'interesting variety of shades of grey. The twilight hours hold ghostly shapes, shadowy whispers and other wonders, and phantasmagoria, which are apt to be dismissed in the impatient waiting for the dawn.'[57]

The urban landscape

There was, then, a gothic impulse at the very heart of Shanghai's modern culture. As with the neo-Gothic everywhere, its presence emerged not only in literature but also in architecture. One of its starkest manifestations was in the work of László Hudec, particularly those of his buildings which, following the architectural historian Luca Poncellini, we can recognise as built in a 'Brick Expressionist' style.

Hudec was born in a town, now in Slovakia, that was then part of the Austro-Hungarian Empire. During the First World War he was taken from the battlefield and imprisoned in a Siberian labour camp. In 1917 he managed, during a moment of political chaos, to flee the frozen rivers and escape into China's northern town of Harbin. Hudec had trained as an architect in Budapest, however, and was thus drawn southward to the cosmopolitan city of Shanghai, where he lived for thirty years. In this period, between 1918 and 1947, Hudec designed well over sixty buildings including hotels, apartment blocks, personal villas, a hospital and churches, as well as other large-scale projects, many of which still count among the city's finest buildings. To tour Hudec's work in Shanghai is to witness the birth of modernism in the city. His enormously influential legacy includes the Park Hotel, the Grand Theatre and the Moore Memorial Church in People's Square, the Ambrosia restaurant, Arts and Crafts Museum and Normandie apartments in the former French Concession, Wu's House on Tongren Lu and the Union Building (now known as Pier One) beside Suzhou Creek.

Hudec's buildings are notoriously lacking in a singular style. He artfully embraced a wide range of approaches (including Beaux-Arts, Georgian Revival, Streamline Moderne and Art Deco). His own house on Panyu Lu is a Tudor-style cottage that seems more at home in a British village than on the streets of Shanghai. Detractors argue that this lack of uniqueness diminishes his imprint on the city. Fans counter the criticism by claiming that Hudec's profound eclecticism was true to the 'haipai culture' of the time.

According to researcher Luca Poncellini, however, the key to understanding Hudec is to consider his clients. Hudec's practice mutated dramatically depending on whom he was working for. When building for Westerners, he tended to function more as an engineer than an architect and happily followed the decisions of his clients. He was, claims Poncellini, like a tailor, designing buildings specifically to meet his customer's tastes and need. A prime example of Hudec's method is Columbia Circle (Lane 329 Xinhua Lu), a residential complex built for Asia Reality Company in the 1920s that offered a variety of standard homes deliberately designed in different styles (English Tudor, Spanish Villa, Hollywood Style). His work for Chinese clients, on the other hand, was totally different. These local patrons were members of a flourishing new social class. Part of an economic and cultural elite—many of who were educated abroad—they were intent on helping to construct a new, modern China. Their preferences in architectural style were neither strict nor settled. All they required from their creations was something that looked modern and unique. According to Poncellini, this demand—simply to be modern—allowed Hudec the freedom to experiment and enabled him to discover his own personal style.

The style Hudec embraced—and ultimately helped create—was that of 'Brick Expressionism', (an offshoot of German expressionism) that was developed by architects such as Fritz Schumacher and Fritz Höger. This design approach was characterised, Poncellini explains, by using dark brickwork on the façade in order to explore the 'expressionist power of details'. The style was based on 'the reinterpretation in the modern taste of the gothic tradition', and was 'far away from the avant-garde tendencies of the time (Le Courbusier, Bauhaus etc)'.[58] Hudec, Poncellini maintains, was not just copying an architectural trend from Germany, but was instead completely contemporary, participating in the invention of the style. He was thus able to transfer—and even anticipate—the modes of German expressionism directly, and without any delay to China.

Hudec's choice of this dark and moody style forged a link between Shanghai's twentieth century modernity and the futurism of Fritz Lang's *Metropolis*. Hudec's expressionist aesthetic is most evident in the twin buildings on Huqiu Lu (the China Baptist Publication Society and Christian Literature Society Building) and, even more prominently, in the Park Hotel, which is widely considered the pinnacle of Hudec's achievement. The Park Hotel was Asia's first skyscraper and was the highest building on the continent until the 1980s. For decades it marked the geographical zero point of the city. The design arose out of Hudec's trip to America, where he went to study the most recent development of high-rises. In Manhattan the neo-Gothic buildings of Raymond Hood mesmerised him with their 'emphatic verticality'.[59] The Park Hotel is clearly based on Hudec's sketches of Hood's American Radiator building at Bryant Park, a modern expressionist construction in central Manhattan that, as Carol Willis tells us, was deeply influenced by the Gothic architecture of Brussels.

In the 1930s, however, Hudec moved away from expressionism towards Art Deco, and in the end it was Deco, 'the twentieth century's other modernism',[60] that would come to establish itself as Shanghai's most signature style. At its height in the 1930s architects such as Fan Wenzhao (Robert Fan), Li Jinpei (Poy G. Lee), Guan Songsheng, Yang Tingbao and Zhuan Jun, as well as foreign firms such as Palmer and Turner, built a plethora of homes, apartments and monuments in the Deco style. These structures, which include the Peace Hotel, Grosvenor House, the Metropole, the Paramount, the Capitol and Grand Theatre, made Shanghai one of the great Art Deco centres of the world.[61]

Art Deco began, according to its own retro-chronic history, with the 1925 Paris Exposition: The International Exposition of Modern Industrial and Decorative Arts. The Exposition took place on an enormous site, occupying both sides of the Seine, on twenty-two hectares in the centre of Paris. Electric lights lit up the Eiffel tower, presenting Paris itself as a great urban spectacle. The exhibit drew sixteen million visitors, awarded thousands of prizes and established—in retrospect—the Art Deco style. The fact that Deco formed itself only in hindsight is, as Nick Land notes, revealing of its nature:

Art Deco is a (retrospective) label patched crudely over mystery, it never had a manifesto, or a master plan, and—due to its inarticulate self-organization—it has eluded historical comprehension. This is the sense, at least in part, of Art Deco's pact with night and darkness. Beneath and beyond all ideologies and centralized schemes, the spontaneous culture of high-modernism that climaxed in the interbellum period remains deeply encrypted.[62]

Art Deco, despite its refusal of an overarching unity, had a global reach. It 'spread like wildfire all over the world, dominating the skylines of cities from New York to Shanghai and sheathing offices and factories from London to Rio', writes Ghislaine Wood, curator of *Art Deco 1910–1939*, a wonderfully extensive exhibit held at the Victoria and Albert Museum in 2003.[63] Deco was profoundly eclectic, drawing life from many sources.

Particularly influential were the materials, techniques and geometric forms and motifs of East Asian decorative art.[64] In addition to this virulent global intermixing, Art Deco fed off the avant-garde. Cubism, Futurism and Constructivism all had a deep effect on the designers of the style. Arguably the most important impact, however, was the revolutionary change in consciousness brought on by the golden age of archaeology. Archaeological findings—especially the astonishing discovery by Howard Carter in November 1922 of the tomb of Tutankhamun—fuelled a fascination with long-lost ancient cultures. The unexpected riches that were buried with the boy-pharaoh in an undisturbed tomb near Luxor in the Valley of the Kings far exceeded all previous digs. The excavation gripped the global imagination, sparking a major cultural phenomenon virtually overnight. '"Tutamania", as it was known, pervaded all areas of design and culture, from jazz music to fashion and its accessories, furniture, bookbinding, everyday objects, interior design and architecture.'[65]

Feeding off these new discoveries, Art Deco—with its zigzag lines, golden geometrical designs and mummy wraps—incorporated motifs from the deep past into an expression that was absolutely modern. In linking these ancient patterns with the imagery of the machine age, it generated a highly abstract mode of expression that seemed to unlock a futurism from long ago. Art Deco creates the uncanny suggestion that the cultures of antiquity were already in contact with a far distant time. With 'the deeply encrypted "language of Art Deco"', writes Land 'prophetic traditions inter-mesh with commemorative innovations, automatically hunting the point of fusion in which they become interchangeable, closing the circuit of time. The past was something other than it once seemed, as the present demonstrates, and the present is something other than it might seem, as the past attests.'[66] Art Deco visualises this temporal spiral in a return to tradition that simultaneously celebrates the mechanised, modern world. It thus helps construct a modernity 'at home in the *Yin* World, comfortable with secrets, and with night'.[67] The Gothic Futurism of the Deco metropolis is not a brightly lit destination waiting for us on the road up ahead, but a virtual presence that haunts the world of yesterday as well as that of tomorrow.

5

CREATED IN CHINA

> *The revolution will not be televised.*
>
> Gil Scott-Heron

In September 2011 an old industrial complex near Suzhou Creek opened with an exhibit entitled *Rebirth*. The show was a branding ritual designed to launch the space before it had been occupied. In this moment, between renovation and re-use, *Rebirth* sought to celebrate the rejuvenation of urban spaces that were abandoned long ago. The opening took place before the building was complete. Outside, bulldozers were still running. The construction workers—migrants who lived in the makeshift encampment across the street—gathered in clusters, smoking on the sidelines, amidst piles of rubble that had yet to be removed. Newly empowered security guards enthusiastically shuffled them off the red carpet and away from the elaborate entrance display.

Inside, a collection of Shanghai's avant-garde artists produced a high-tech display showcasing the city's creative potential. Videos and installations by artists Qiu Anxiong and Sun Xun occupied huge rooms throughout the complex. Near the entrance Hu Jieming built what looked like bits of an old submarine with flotsam projected in the windows. In another room massive light-boxes showcased the ingenious collage of Yang Yongliang. Meanwhile, in the courtyard, Chen Hangfeng carved a landscaped mountain of ice cream for the cosmopolitan gathering to enjoy. Guests wandered throughout the vast and still unfinished network of buildings holding their glasses of imported wine. The complex, now renamed '800 Show' was originally constructed over the span of two decades, between the 1920s and 1940s. Its architectural mix perfectly illustrates Shanghai's history of urban eclecticism. Though it appears today as a single compound, the site consists of fifteen buildings of various ages and diverse styles, including the factory and workshop of the Xinan Electrical Machine Plant as well as a Modernist Style garden villa built by an entrepreneurial family from Northern China who established their home in Shanghai, with undue optimism, in 1942. Today '800 Show' comprises part of a hugely ambitious project by the district government who plan a 'megacluster of creativity', which will fashion 'a new face for Jingan'.

Shanghai is riddled with developments like '800 Show', many of which stand vacant and unused. Scattered throughout the metropolis are the shell-like containers of newly revamped creative clusters. Often—as was the case in *Rebirth*—the spaces come alive for a moment, to host an exhibition or a launch, and then, when the event is over, they retreat into a near oblivion, incapable of sustaining momentum. In its ardent quest for creativity, one wonders just how many of these 'creative' spaces the city can absorb.

The German firm 'Logon' was hired to oversee the restoration of '800 Show'. Wang Fang and Frank Kruger, who were part of the team, recorded in the catalogue for *Rebirth* their impressions of the ghostly population that haunted the space when they first arrived:

Two years ago when we first visited 800 Changde Road for the first time, the area looked like a typical disused and abandoned factory: the buildings were dirty, windows were broken, moisture soaked the walls, rubble and trash lay around and weeds grew everywhere. Sometimes we came across traces of people who worked or lived here before: cast-away playing cards, clothes, shoes and work gloves. A broken basketball lay on the ground of the old foundry.

Despite being refashioned and rebranded, much of Shanghai's industrial heritage still contains the traces of a virtual population. Today, however, the ghosts are from the future, not the past. Shanghai's old factories and warehouses—now revamped as creative clusters—architecturally express the latent potentiality of the city. They are the holders of a destiny that lies in wait, occupying a time that has yet to arrive.

Cities and their golden ages

In *Cities in Civilization*, urbanist Peter Hall explores the discontinuous nature of historical time. Civilisation, as it unfolds in his book, does not evolve in a straight, continuous line, but is generated, instead, through the ruptures and starts produced by great bursts of human creativity. These momentary innovations, which 'flower for a few years', and then 'disappear as suddenly as they come'[1] operate as a historical engine by engendering revolutionary change on a global scale.

In his book, Hall attempts to dissect how and why these creative instants occur. His first and most important insight is that the great creative flowerings always happen in cities: Athens in the fifth century, Florence in the four-teenth, Paris at the end of the nineteenth, New York in the early twentieth, Hollywood with films, Memphis with the Blues. 'Every golden age,' writes Hall 'is also an urban age.'[2] In these instances of intense inventiveness, the city becomes more a time than a place. The metropolis becomes an epoch.

'What is it,' Hall asks, 'that makes a particular city, at a particular time, suddenly become immensely creative, exceptionally innovative?' His answers are tentative but illuminating. First, he concludes, it helps to be big. Despite the many criticisms of megacities, large urban centres tend to help foster moments of exceptional innovation. 'The biggest of cities,' writes Hall, 'for all their evident disadvantages and obvious problems, have throughout history been the places that ignited the sacred flame of human intelligence and human creativity.'[3] Second, the most conducive hosts are places in the midst of rapid, economic and social change. Creativity most often arises in urban centres that are growing at an enormous speed and are in 'transition forward to new and unexplored modes of organization.'[4] Also crucial is a steady stream of outsiders. Exceptional moments of urban cre-ativity are almost always the product of people that are both of the society but also, somehow, exterior to it; people that both belong and do not belong. 'A creative city will be a place where outsiders can enter and feel the state of ambiguity: they must neither be excluded from opportunity, nor must they be so warmly embraced that the creative drive is lost.'[5] Cosmopolitanism therefore, is essential. 'Probably no city has ever been creative,' writes Hall 'without continued renewal of the creative bloodstream.'[6] Cities in their golden ages are 'magnets for the immigration of talent, as well as generators of the wealth that could help employ that talent'.[7]

Reading Hall's book in Shanghai, the question invariably arises. Where will the next great outburst of innovation be situated? Is Shanghai, a vast metropolis in the midst of high-speed change, filled with migrants from both China and abroad, capable of such a period of inventiveness? Does the city's 'golden age' already lie behind it, or has it just been interrupted; a suspended epoch waiting for the right moment to return?

The story of Suzhou Creek

In Shanghai's ambitious blueprint, the city is cut in two by the Huangpu, with a finance capital in the east (Pudong), and a cultural capital in the west (Puxi). Yet, while so much of Shanghai's futurist imaginings are based on the banks of the Huangpu, it is arguably the city's other less glamorous waterway that has, ultimately, a more vital part to play in Shanghai's development.

The 125 km-long Suzhou Creek flows out at the Taihu Lake in Suzhou (from where it derives its name) to meet the Huangpu river at the northern section of the Bund, snaking its way along an east-west axis through the heart of Shanghai. 'In the early decades of the twentieth century, the drama of urban modernity—its industries, battles, and glamorous rise—played out along the river's edge.'[8] As a vital shipping route, with a rich network of tributaries and waterways, it allowed for the convenient transit of goods and materials into the interior of China. The country's most famous industrialists established factories, warehouses, cotton and flourmills, gasworks, breweries and a power station along the banks of the creek. Suzhou Creek thus became a key site of modern industry and a hotbed of finance, industry and logistics. By 1949, there were more than 10,000 factories in the city, many of them located on the banks of Suzhou Creek.

In the early 1990s, however, when Shanghai was finally able to participate in the policies of opening and reform, the city embarked on a vast project of industrial relocation. A campaign to promote the transition 'from Secondary to Tertiary Industry' entailed the 'closure, suspension, merger and conversion of pollution-emitting industrial enterprises in the central urban area'.[9] An enormous amount of industry (which, by this time, was all state-owned), was thus moved from downtown zones into new factory towns in the suburbs. 'Between 1995–2005 there was a 67 % decrease in the industrial activity in the urban core.'[10] Scores of industrial buildings and warehouses were left empty and the buildings along the once vital creek were left increasingly abandoned.

The spark of revitalisation occurred in 1997 when the Taiwanese architect Deng Kunyen leased a 2,000m[2] warehouse overlooking the Creek to use as his studio.[11] The story goes that Deng discovered the 1930s edifice while riding his bike by the river. The warehouse—by then decrepit—had been used for grain storage, and was also rumoured to be the private storehouse of notorious Green Gang boss Du Yuesheng. By the time Deng found it, it was totally dilapidated, infused with the stench of the severely polluted waterway and was serving as an informal dormitory for industrial workers:

When I first moved in, around 150 migrant workers used to reside inside, in separate and semi-separated areas that almost blocked up the whole warehouse: there were a minimum of 10 open and semi-open kitchens spread all over, imbued with smoke and soot at mealtimes. There was no bath, the only toilet was on the roof...[12]

Deng used a minimalist strategy of subtraction, removing at least 100 truckloads of scrap. He gutted the interior, and increased the light by widening windows and adding a skylight. Instead of paint, traditional limewater was used to preserve the brickwork. Deng thus conserved the building's original form, while creating an open, meditative and ultramodern space. 'Suzhou Creek Warehouse' was based on an industrial chic aesthetic, which, Deng hoped, would spread the idea of urban rejuvenation through preservation:

I understand that destruction is sometimes irresistible and even necessary for the city's development. But it's nevertheless a pity to see the valuable historical fabric destroyed. I wanted to show the government and decision makers that there could be other ways of development, that there isn't always just conflict between the old and the new. As you know damage to historical buildings is irreversible—what's gone is gone … So I wanted to quickly choose a place that would act as an example of a different type. In 1998, I started working on the Suzhou Creek warehouse and then, in 2004, on an area on Yangshupu Road. I hope that these would serve as successful examples for a new concept of 'development' and push forward the protection of our urban industrial architecture.[13]

In 2004 Deng's pioneering architecture was acknowledged by the UNESCO Asia Pacific heritage awards, which cited Suzhou Warehouse as a 'catalyst in the conservation of the city's industrial history'. The award noted the 'large-scale impact' of the project and praised Deng's 'innovative adaptation', which demonstrated how 'heritage structures could be rehabilitating for modern use'.[14] Today, Suzhou Creek Warehouse is widely recognised as triggering an artistic revival along the banks of Suzhou Creek.

Liu Jidong, a local designer who had been working in America was among the first architects to follow Deng. In 1999 Liu secured a lease on 'Sihang Warehouse', a 5,000m² property located only a few doors down from Deng's reconverted space. The four-storey concrete building was built in 1931 to house four banks, but the warehouse had acquired historical significance by playing an important role in the Battle of Shanghai. From 26 October to 1 November 1937, 800 Kuomintang soldiers took advantage of the structure's thick walls to resist the encroaching Japanese. Their mission was to hold out against the complete loss of control of Zhabei district, help martial international support and buy time for Chinese troops to regroup elsewhere. Though many soldiers were killed, and the remainder eventually forced to retreat, the active resistance at 'Sihang Warehouse' did, for a time, receive international attention and was an important morale booster for the Chinese. The edifice, therefore, had already been pinpointed as an important heritage site, though the municipal government had no idea what to do with it. When Liu Jidong gained control of the building, he redesigned the entire structure, using part to house his own office. He billed the complex as 'Shanghai's first creative industry facility' and attracted a number of local and overseas design firms to set up offices inside.

Soon, an organic, bottom-up process of urban rejuvenation was spreading throughout the area. Artists, in search of low rent and large spaces, began converting the factories and warehouses into galleries and personal studio spaces. Activity was especially concentrated at the northern bend of the creek a little west of where Deng Kunyen and Liu Jidong had set up shop. Artists clustered in the Chunming Textile Mill Compound, an old industrial enclave located at 50 Moganshan Lu. Within a couple of years many of Shanghai's most prominent artists including Xue Song, Ding Yi, Zhou Tiehai and Xu Zhen had studios in the complex. A number of foreigners, as well as locals who had had exposure to the outside world, supported the burgeoning art scene by opening galleries in the neighbourhood.[15]

In this same period, the Shanghai government, along with the assistance of a number of international firms, embarked on a determined effort to clean up the waterway. 'The Suzhou Creek Rehabilitation Project', which was launched in 1998, was an ambitious twelve-year-programme. When the project got started industrial waste and domestic sewage had left the river heavily polluted:

In the 1970s and 80s, Suzhou Creek was China's dirtiest river. All aquatic life was obliterated, the water was black and the odor so great that locals referred to it simply as 'the smelly river'. Silt accumulated on the creek bed putting an end to water traffic and closing it to transport. According to urban legend, during this period Suzhou Creek was so dirty that it would, on occasion, spontaneously burst into flame.[16]

'The Suzhou Creek Rehabilitation Project', which must be counted as one of the most impressive examples of urban environmentalism anywhere, worked to improve water quality, mitigate flood impact, introduce wastewater and water resource management, reconstruct the river banks and engage in extensive urban revitalisation by constructing commercial, entertainment and residential complexes as well as ninety-five beltway parks.

In the beginning, the government-led project clashed with the bottom-up, artist-led growth at Moganshan Lu. Under pressure to raise money to complete the task of river cleaning the Shanghai Municipal Government sought to sell the land along the Creek. In 2003 a demolition order came for the newly established artist community. In an important example of Chinese civil society, artists and urbanists responded with an orchestrated campaign to save the now reanimated Chunming Mill. They joined together to rally the public and gain media attention (both at the local and international level), arguing that the industrial buildings on Moganshan Lu formed part of the city's cultural heritage and should thus be guaranteed protection. By this stage the Municipal Government was already quite image conscious and sensitive to media pressure. Moreover, the issue of conservation had been pushed onto the government agenda by the work of Deng Kunyen.[17] Nevertheless, the threat of destruction only subsided once it became clear that the studios and galleries of M50 were powering a dramatic boom in the visual arts. In 2005 the Chunming Art Industrial Park site (now rebranded as M50) was given official recognition. It was sanctioned with the designation 'Creative Industry Clustering Park' and upgraded with special signage and plaques specifying the historical significance of each building. Today M50, which is surrounded by encroaching high-rises, has more than sixty galleries and studios, cafes and stores, and is one of the city's premier art spaces (and one of the most successful creative clusters in Shanghai).

China and the creativity economy

The developments along Suzhou Creek fed on, and ultimately into, a world-wide discourse on the creative economy that became immensely popular at the end of the last millennium. Briefly stated, the concept of the creative economy rests on the idea that with the decline in heavy industry, post-Fordist modes of social organisation and the increasing influence of digital technology, there has come a transition to a 'new economy'. What matters most in this novel 'information' or 'knowledge' economy is no longer the physical production of stuff but rather, the creative realm of inventive ideas. 'Creativity,' writes John Hartley, a well-known academic in the field, 'will be the driver of social and economic change during the next century.'[18]

The notion of the creative economy was popularised by the celebrity-scholar Richard Florida, who gained an instant notoriety with his books on the 'creative class'. The world today, Florida argues dramatically, is under-going a process akin to the industrial revolution, and in this new age, the industrial proletariat are being succeeded as the key drivers of growth. 'Human creativity,' Florida writes with typical rhetorical fervour, 'has replaced raw materials, physical labor, and even flows of capital as the primary generator of economic value.'[19] The rise of the creative worker, he further contends, is potentially 'bigger and more powerful' than the transition from the agricultural to the industrial age. 'For the previous shift substituted one set of physical inputs (land and human labor) for another (raw materials and physical labor) while the current one is based fundamentally on human intelligence.'[20]

Together with the theorisation of a 'creative class' came the concept of 'creative industries'. The term first appeared in Australia in the early 1990s but later came to be associated with the UK and the New Labour government of Tony Blair. Under Blair's charge, the Department for Culture, Media and Sport (DCMS) established a 'Creative Industries Unit and Taskforce', whose job was to help rebrand the stuffy image of the UK (dominated by visions of double-decker buses and the changing of the guard at Buckingham Palace) into a younger, hipper, more 'creative' place. The punk attitude that permeates UK culture was not altogether conducive to this PR branding exercise, however, and there was a fair amount of resistance to a 'coolness' that was trumpeted by politicians. Nevertheless, while the 'Cool Britannia' campaign was something of a flop (the top-down mega-project of the Millennium Dome was especially ridiculed), the DCMS did manage to transform (or at least rebrand) arts-related practices—architecture, advertising, software and game design, fashion, music and film—away from what had previously been thought of as a non-economic 'cultural sphere' into high-growth industries, now widely considered to be 'good for the economy'.[21]

Crucially for its adaptation in China, much of the work on creative industries drew heavily on the theory of the industrial cluster, a concept formulated most succinctly in the work of Michael Porter. Porter's research focuses on a series of successful locales—Hollywood, Silicon Valley, Wall Street—in order to study the benefits of geographically based innovation, or what he calls 'the competitive advantage of location'.[22] Particular fields tend to gather together in clusters, Porter maintains, because concentration allows the sharing of common pools of knowledge, skills and infrastructure. These networks create new capabilities, new companies and new industries and are, therefore, themselves the drivers of economic development. 'Competitive advantage lies *outside* companies ... and even outside their industries,' Porter concludes, 'residing instead in the locations at which their businesses are located.'[23]

For the proponents of the creative economy, the positive attention given to industrial clustering helped reinforce the growing emphasis on the importance of cities. Countering the widespread contention that digital technology had rendered place irrelevant and that people could now create from anywhere, researchers noted that the freelancers and micro-businesses that power creative industries most often cluster in certain urban areas as part of highly localised scenes. 'The world is not flat but spiky,' Florida opines.[24] Due to the clustering that lies at the heart of invention, cities now matter more than ever. Economic growth, as Jane Jacobs so persuasively illustrates, depends on urban cores that can support the network effects associated with innovation.[25] In the new globalised economy, cities, not states, are the fundamental nodes. 'Place,' writes Florida, 'has become the key social and economic organizing unit of the creative age, replacing the industrial corporation as the main vehicle for matching people to jobs. My emphasis is more on place than on culture or subculture; thus my focus on urban and regional questions and quintessentially urban and regional thinkers.'[26]

The idea that cities needed to breed creativity in order to grow gained traction. The 'creative class' was understood to be highly mobile and extremely finicky about where they worked and lived. The right type of place, it was increasingly argued, could attract these key drivers of economic growth. Thus the 'art of city making' or 'culture-led urban regeneration' started to proliferate everywhere and consultants (Florida key among them) flew around the planet advising city governments and business leaders on how to nurture the creative industries by promoting quality of life, an open tolerant culture and the types of places in which creativity could thrive. Particular attention, notes the scholar Justin O'Connor, was paid to 'cultural venues and quarters, street markets, alternative retail, new forms of public art and signage, urban landscaping, architectural and larger scale regeneration projects, and campaigns such as the "24 hour city"'.[27] Throughout, the emphasis was on that indefinable 'atmosphere', the buzz, the scene, the genius loci, which make up a 'creative milieu'. Build the right kind of place, went the argument, and the talent, business and money would arrive.

China's embrace of creativity

In the mid-2000s the theory of the creative economy came to China with full force. Previously, the country had focused almost exclusively on the manufacturing sector, which had been so successful at powering such incredible rates of growth. Yet, after more than twenty years of opening and reform, there was a growing sense that more attention should be paid to the knowledge economy and the ultimately more valuable service sectors. It was not enough just to make things. China needed to create.

In December 2004 China held its first forum on creative industries. The concept was zealously cheered from the start. In a plethora of research meetings, conferences, industry forums and government policy papers, officials, scholars, practitioners, entrepreneurs and developers celebrated the introduction of the new buzzword. Enthusiasm was especially intense in Shanghai, which was influenced in part by its close ties to Hong Kong.[28] By welcoming the idea of creative industries these most sophisticated urban centres hoped 'to construct an alternative vision of an emerging China'.[29] Officials were seduced by the creative industries' promise of a new model of growth. Creativity quickly became the 'industry of the future', the key to a necessary and inevitable transition that would shift the country away from low-cost labour and the production of cheap consumer goods and allow it to move up the value chain. Addressing a 2005 forum on creative industries, Wu Qidi, former vice minister of education, expressed this growing sentiment: 'Creative industries play a key role in enhancing China's core competitiveness and raise the added value of products and services. The development of creative industries is an important opportunity in the process of China's modernisation and development.'[30] The aspiration was captured in a clever slogan: 'From made in China to created in China'.

In addition to the hoped-for economic benefit, there were a number of other factors that played into the adoption of creative industries in China. First was the fact that the country is enormously attracted to, and has had huge success in, experimenting with urban clusters. Science and technology parks were already pervasive and the clustering effects produced by the Special Economic Zones were well known. Also enticing was the fact that the creative industries offered a model of urban regeneration that could address the problem of a barren inner city landscape left by the ongoing reform of the State Owned Enterprises (SOEs).

In the West, 'creative clusters' have grown organically over an extended period of time. The process—widely analysed and discussed—typically begins with artists, designers and other members of the 'creative class' looking for large cheap spaces to use. They rent, and sometimes buy, rooms in disused industrial zones, which they then convert into studios and shops. Other individuals and developers are attracted to the area and, in time, the by now familiar process of gentrification sets in.

In China, however, the situation is complicatedly different. Shanghai's industrial zones are built on state-allocated land and the buildings themselves—even after the policies of urban de-industrialisation have left them empty and abandoned—are typically still owned by the SOEs. The Shanghai

Municipal Government has protected this right of ownership by decreeing that in the conversion of factories and warehouses for commercial use the 'land use rights and the underlying ownership of the subject properties remain unchanged'.[31] As property owners of closed factories and warehouses, SOEs are free to rent leases of twenty years to private developers. The state-owned manufacturing company is thus able to reap huge benefits from the booming property market and exploit the most profitable sector of Shanghai's economic boom. Occasionally, SOE management gets into the business of creative industries themselves. M50, for example, is owned and operated by the former state-owned textile mill and the old factory manager is still in charge. District governments enter the mix by negotiating rent between the private development company (who usually has close ties with officials) and the SOE. Tax policies, too, play a critical role as enterprises setting up business and renting properties in designated 'creative zones' get preferential tax breaks. Creative clusters are thus produced through an intricate web of district governments, SOEs, private developers, and the companies and workers of the creative class. In this unique form of economic activity, not exactly private, not exactly public, the tangled networks of relations frequently fold back in on themselves. Some creative clusters, for example, are said to have formed 'creative companies', as researcher Xin Gu has argued, simply in order to take advantages of tax incentives that are available in other, nearby, clusters. Tax loopholes and property speculation have thus joined forces to help generate the boom in creative clusters in Shanghai. The explosive growth in these complexes is such that today, 'the dominant symbol of creativity in China' has, as Michael Keane argues, 'become the "creative cluster" itself'.[32]

The clusters: Bridge 8, Redtown, 1933

The first group of eighteen clusters was granted official licence by the Shanghai Economic Commission in April 2005. Included in this early wave was a complex known as Bridge 8, a 20,000m^2 factory that once belonged to the state-owned Shanghai Automotive Brake Company and is located at the corner of Jianguo Lu and Ruijin Lu, near the edges of the former French Concession. Bridge 8 was the first cluster given over to a professional developer. In 2003 the Luwan district government, which had control of the property, sought strategies to redevelop this abandoned lot, situated on prime downtown land. They turned to Tony Wong, former general manager of Xintiandi, whose idea was to convert it into a creative cluster. Bridge 8 was to function as both incubator and testing ground. With government support, Wong's company, Lifestyle Ltd, acquired a twenty-year lease from the state-owned factory, with a promise to return the property in a better state. The renovation, which was done under the guidance of Japanese architect Kenji Mantani, whose company HMA was the first client at Bridge 8, deliberately retains the rawness of the industrial past. Shells of old buildings remain and steel staircases and piping are left exposed. Grey bricks taken from the demolition site provide the basic visual elements and texture of the place while light, ultramodern additions and subtractions—skylights, glass walls, open courtyards and networks of balconies—are meant to convert the cluster into a singular whole.

Bridge 8 is among Shanghai's most successful creative zones. Walk the corridor and it seems that all of urban China is being designed from within these walls. The converted factory complex hosts the offices of fashion and product designers, brand consultancies, animation and post production studios, and some of the most influential architectural firms in the world. Tony Wong is explicitly calculating in the role Bridge 8 has in developing the creative industries in China. 'Though China is emerging as the world's manufacturing powerhouse, it is not yet known for originality and creativity, which are cornerstones for the sustainable development of an economy,' he says. 'Around the world, cities that are known for creativity attract creative people. They flock together to trigger mutual inspiration.'[33] In pioneering the development of creative zones in Shanghai, Wong and his colleagues have closely analysed models from other cities in Europe, Japan and America. What they want, however, is to adapt these gradual processes to the high-speed intensity of China time. 'We looked to developments in the West, West Chelsea is a good example,' Wong reflects. 'There development took fifty years. What we are trying to do is shorten the period, to try to compress it into a decade.'[34]

Another relatively successful example of an industrial heritage site refashioned as a creative cluster is Red Town, a 55,000m^2 complex located at the corner of Huaihai Lu and Hongqiao Lu. The buildings were constructed in 1956 as No. 10 Steel Factory, but when the SOE was relocated in 1989 the plant was left abandoned. It was remodelled as a creative cluster when the Urban Cultural Bureau's Sculptural Development Department chose the space as a home. The government hired a private developer who commissioned a number of architects to renovate the old industrial zone. Today the 'Shanghai Sculpture Space' has emerged from the hulk of the former steel factory and refill has converted the central courtyard into a reclaimed green space where families come to play. Surrounding buildings within the complex house offices, some retail and a small art school. The complex had a lacklustre feel until 2010 when the Minsheng Art Museum, a privately run museum initially curated by the renowned local artist Zhou Tiehai, opened adjacent to the Sculpture Space.

The most spectacular of Shanghai's creative clusters, however, is a complex known as 1933, an adaptive reuse of the old slaughterhouse of the Shanghai Municipal Council, one of the city's most astounding architectural relics. The site consists of a number of buildings including a long narrow barracks, known as the Doghouse, that once served as workers dormitories as well as a four-storey Art Deco power plant complete with a brown brick chimney, as well as a massive warehouse that is now covered in glass. Most stunning of all, however, is the abattoir itself. The façade is covered in an elaborate geometrical design. Inside, ergonomic engineering gone mad has produced a concrete labyrinth of interlocking ramps, bridges and elevated walkways with hidden staircases, cavernous corners, columned halls and light open galleries. Clearly designed by a rogue architect who, when tasked with directing flows of animals, humans and meat, created an Escher-like, form-follows-function, singularly intricate maze. 1933 was built in a global collaboration illustrative of Shanghai modernity. It was commissioned by Zhejiang businessmen, designed by British architects and constructed by a Chinese firm who used concrete cement imported from the UK. The first drawings date from the 1920s but the building didn't open until 1933. Once complete, it was one of the three grandest abattoirs in the world. During the Cultural Revolution, the abattoir was converted into a medicine factory, which was in operation until 2002. In 2005 the buildings, which were by then abandoned, altered and in a state of disrepair, were recognised as an important part of Shanghai's industrial heritage and put under state protection. The government-run Shanghai Creative Industries Corporation began restoration under the leadership of architect Zhou Chong Xin, who, through a now familiar process of subtraction, returned the slaughterhouse to its original look and feel while adding some modern amenities. Considered as architecture alone, 1933 embodies the future nostalgia that permeates Shanghai. It perfectly articulates the city's temporal twist, which encases its industrial heritage—putting a past modernity on show—precisely so as to anticipate its future creative potential.

The failure of the clusters

Though it is an astonishing place to visit, as a project, 1933 has failed. The initial grandiose plans, which included innovative restaurants, world-class exhibitions, unique boutiques, educational facilities and artist studios, have never been realised. Instead, much of the building remains empty, while those spaces that have been filled host only high-end chain restaurants and a few VIP clubs. For a brief moment in 2009 the abattoir's warehouse—converted into a raw concrete frame wrapped in glass—hosted a micro-culture with interesting potential. Backed by a UK branding firm, 'The Factory', as it was called, contained a restaurant, sound studio and design laboratory. Its mission was to gather Shanghai's young creative talent for collaborative projects worldwide. Sitting on the plush couch of a private room, latte in hand, the manager expounded on the vision. 'Shanghai,' he said with the confidence of a seasoned salesman, 'is the world's fourth great city.' With great exaltation he expanded on his analysis:

In London there's culture—you dig deep and you keep on going; in New York there is this tremendous engine of tripping up, making mistakes, and reinvention, mixed with an incredible optimism—blow the place up and it rebuilds itself very quickly; Tokyo has richness and integrity, with this incredible sense of detail; Shanghai is not there yet. There is huge expectation that Shanghai is this very creative place but once you scratch beneath the surface, beneath the bling there's not a lot there. But in 15 years it will be, it will buy its way there, it's got a huge volume of people and there are people like me that will put stuff there because of greed and opportunity, it will get there, it's a self-fulfilling prophecy … that's why it deserves to be called the fourth great city … but its really just a designate.[35]

'The Factory', he declared at the time, was based on a long-term bet, an intentional willingness to invest in creative talent in the early years for a pay-off that would come three, five, ten years down the line. Yet, only a year after it opened, the place had already closed down. What was once a thriving office filled with purposeful workers gazing intently at their big screen Macs had been completely stripped clean. Not a single chair had been left behind. In the Shanghai rumour mills, which are steeped in superstition, 1933's blatant lack of success—the enormous discrepancy between the singularly astounding space and the uninspiring reality of what goes on inside—is due to the fact that it's haunted. It is not only animals, go the whispered tales, who were killed within these walls.

Be that as it may, as a failed creative cluster, 1933 is hardly alone. All throughout Shanghai newly renovated industrial zones lie empty and unused. Some, like the former 'Creek Art', which was housed in the famous Rong family's flour-mill, have now closed their doors entirely. Others like 'Tong Le Fang' have abandoned all pretence at urban creativity and now host little but seedy bars. Still others like 'Pier One' keep desperately trying to reinvent themselves with new renovations and businesses models that seem to change every year. In conjunction with a massive expansion (there are now said to be close to 200 creative clusters in Shanghai) is a city littered with 'creative developments' that lie deserted or grossly underused.

One of the main culprits is a glaring disjunction between the imagined 'creative class' dreamt up by developers and the actual inhabitants of Shanghai. The PR material put out by the creative zones is filled with stock images of beautiful people (few of whom are Chinese). The illusory nature of the imagined population is revealed by the fact that they most often shown in profile (or, as was the case in the hyper-designed brochures for '800 Show', illustrated only as shadows). Caught up in fantasies of *Bobos in Paradise*,[36] the developers of Shanghai's clusters tend to view the local population as an obstacle that must be relocated so that the creative class can move in. In doing so, they sometimes fail to see the potential that lies right outside their doors. This was particularly apparent in the case of 'Creek Art', which billed itself as a high-end gallery, and hosted weekly champagne brunches. Patrons who looked down into the alleyways below could catch a glimpse of a fascinating instance of Shanghai's genuine street culture as a community of peddlers, scrapers and metal recyclers went about their business, without being seen or engaged.

This fissure between a culture that is real and an imagined creative class was illustrated with preposterous precision in the case of 'Weihei 696', an art cluster located in the heart of the Jingan district. The property contains a richly layered historical structure that served as a villa, army barracks and electrical factory. Artists found the dilapidated structure in the mid-2000s and—especially as prices at M50 started to skyrocket—transformed the rambling edifice into a warren of artists' studios. In 2011, however, the Jingan district decided that 'Weihei 696' should be turned into a creative cluster. Their first act was to kick out all the artists.

Developers of the creative clusters are after high rent. Spaces tend to be large, and as is the case with so much of Shanghai, they often cater to luxury shops, upscale boutiques and fancy restaurants. Yet their mandate to help foster urban creativity requires precisely the type of heterogeneous intermixing that their prices won't allow. Jonah Lehrer, in an interview for his book *Imagine: How Creativity Works*, worries about this sterile version of urban innovation. 'Cities induce creativity by allowing mixing,'[37] he writes. Without the random encounters and radical variation that invention requires all that is left is a 'kind of city in a bottle':

I think we need to ensure that we don't surrender too much of our cities to the loveliness of upscale boutiques, fancy espresso bars and high-end restaurants. Money in a metropolis typically buys isolation—we get a little peace of mind and our very own parking space—but the creativity of a city depends on our constantly mixing and mingling.[38]

Places conducive to innovation need flexible 'Low-Road spaces', Lehrer argues, where 'creative tinkerers' can do what they want.

Shanghai's determination to position itself at the forefront of the twenty-first century is intimately bound to its ambition to transform itself into a 'creative' hub. At the heart of this fervent aspiration is the conversion of Shanghai's old industrial heritage into creative clusters, many of which are still blank canvasses anticipating a creativity that has yet to come. In constructing these spaces, the state-backed developers often assume that creativity is something that can be planned for, programmed and projected. The arrival of a creative metropolis, however, does not emerge gradually in a step-by-step process that can be tightly controlled. Rather, true creativity is necessarily unprecedented. It arrives suddenly, as a total surprise, an unpredictable eruption from outside that inevitably disrupts the linear unfolding of time.

Creative deficit

Today the viral-like spread of renovated industrial zones refashioned as creative clusters has reached almost comic proportions. Many in the city now scoff at the mere mention of these developments and research has shown that most of the actual cultural activity in Shanghai (concerts, exhibitions, design studios etc.) actually occurs outside the designated creative zones.[39] The problem, however, lies deeper than the clusters themselves. Shanghai envisions itself as the next great global cultural hub, a key site of China's 'soft power'. The city now teems with infrastructure. Along with the plethora of creative clusters, over the past decade Shanghai has built a whole host of new theatres, concert halls and galleries. In 2012 two vast buildings used for the 2010 World Expo were converted into major museums, part of a major boom in museum building that is occurring throughout the country.[40] Yet, despite these ambitions, and even with the burgeoning art scene, rock bands, nightclubs, coffee shops, trendy boutiques and an ever growing hipster community, there is a widespread sense that the city's creative content does not match its future-oriented designs. Shanghai, goes the common cliché, has the hardware but not the software. 'Ours is a city of the mediocre and the mild,' writes Shanghai scholar Xu Jilin. 'In the Republican era, Shanghai enjoyed a bifurcated pluralism: there was the bourgeois tradition of the middle class, as well as the bohemianism of the cultural leftwing.

They both contributed to the invaluable tensions that generated a unique Shanghai culture. But the edge of Shanghai was long ago worn down. All that remains is a bourgeois culture that is as comfortable and reassuring as a warm bath.'[41] This paucity of true cultural inventiveness, Xu maintains, ultimately stands in the way of Shanghai's aspiration to become a 'global city'. 'As China's largest city and a global centre of commerce,' he concludes, 'Shanghai will continue to be castigated if it fails to become a major cultural centre like New York.'[42]

The most commonly cited obstacle to a truly innovative culture taking root in Shanghai is the censorship imposed by the authoritarian regime. Even party officials admit that the flourishing in art and literature that happened in Shanghai in the early decades of the twentieth century could not be replicated today because of the stifling stranglehold on free expression. 'The thorniest question triggered by the paradigm of creative industries is that of "creativity"—the least problematic in the western context,' writes scholar Jing Wang in an essay entitled 'The Global Reach of a New Discourse: How Far Can "Creative Industries" Travel?' 'How do we begin to envision a parallel discussion in a country where creative imagination is subjugated to active state surveillance?' she asks.[43] Indeed, China is caught in a potentially explosive paradox as its active pursuit of a creative economy clashes so profoundly with the tendency to suppress the most creative among its population. 'The government talks about how to make national culture strong and creative,' writes China's most famous dissident artist Ai Weiwei:

Of course, if a person has never had the right to choose their information, freely associate with any kind of ideology, and develop an individual character with some passion and imagination—how can they become creative? It is against human nature. If you are against every essential value of individualism and independent thinking, and the willingness to take risks and bear consequences, and have a sense of responsibility—what kind of creativity do you expect?[44]

The immensely popular blogger and cultural critic Han Han echoes this point in a quieter manner. 'The restriction on cultural activities makes it impossible for China to influence literature and cinema on a global basis,' he writes, 'or for us culturati to raise our heads up proud.'[45]

Government censorship, however, is far from the only difficulty. The emergence of a creative epoch in Shanghai is profoundly hindered by the violence of modern history and widespread amnesia, with its coinciding loss of traditions and skills; the rampant piracy and total disregard for intellectual property; the stifling education based solely on rote learning and memorisation, and a culture that does not pay enough heed to passion and play. While

Westerners tend to emphasise the lack of freedom and democracy in discussing this creative deficit, locals tend to be more concerned about this paucity of spirit. It is this shortfall in human sensibility, for example, which leads angel investor Xu Xiaoping to conclude that it will be '20 years before China can produce a Steve Jobs.'[46] Artist Ai Weiwei concurs: 'You can't create generations just to labour at Foxconn. Everyone wants an iPhone, but it would be impossible to design an iPhone in China because it's not a product; it's an understanding of human nature.'[47]

These obstacles to innovation, however, are often double-edged. It is undoubtedly correct, for example, that the lack of respect for intellectual property rights in China hinders the country's creative potential. Yet, piracy has not only been an impediment to creative culture, it has also served as a catalyst. In a place where barriers restrict the flow of information, piracy has long served as a corridor to traffic with the outside. Sitting on a worn-out couch in the top floor of a rundown warehouse he refashioned as 'The Lab', hip-hop DJ Gary Wang reminisces about the black market in music where he bought his first cassettes. The country was totally locked down and officially almost nothing was available. Wang remembers buying a Madonna tape in a licensed store that cost twenty RMB, almost half a month's salary. By the mid-1980s the pirates had arrived and everything started to change. 'They set up a weekend market at the corner of Maoming Lu and Yanan Lu where bootlegged cassettes tapes were sold in black and white packages,' remembers Wang.[48] In an instant, the lost decades of music history flooded in. Today the same impulse to connect with the exterior leads millions to use proxy servers, which allow those caught inside the great firewall to climb over and see what's on the other side. Some theorists go so far as to maintain that China's relatively cavalier attitude to piracy, which is rooted in a culture that accepts—even values—the skills learned by copying, is more attuned to the open, distributed systems and the 'Rip, Mix, and Burn' ethos of contemporary technology. Today's creativity, writes Taiwanese researcher Han-Teng Liao, 'thrives on distribution, derivation and appropriation of others' work'.[49] Rather than simply capitulating to the imposition of a regime of individual property rights, with its deep emphasis on proprietary notions of culture and copyright, Chinese cyberculture, thinkers like Han-Teng argue, should embrace its own traditions of sharing, transmission and collaborative production. 'In an age of downloading, sampling, remixing and re-versioning, [Confucian] statements such as "I transmit rather than create" may take on new significance.'[50]

A similar ambiguity exists with respect to the authoritarian regime. Revolutionary creativity, as Peter Hall has shown, rarely emerges in times and places where all tensions have already been smoothed over. Sinophiles Kaiser Kuo and Jeremy Goldkorn point to the example of Leonardo da Vinci in order to argue that there are 'any number of authoritarian states in human history, where nonetheless there has been inarguable innovation'.[51] Rather than places and times that are absolutely free it is more often societies in the process of transition that inspire sudden bursts of inventive imagination. Hall writes:

As a massive generalization, but one that stands up surprisingly well 'urban golden ages' tend to occur in places that were in a state of uneasy and unstable tension between a set of conservative forces and values—aristocratic, hierarchical, religious, conformist—and a set of radical values which were the exact opposite: bourgeois, open, rational and skeptical. These were societies troubled about themselves, societies that were in the course of losing the old certainties but were deeply concerned about what was happening to them.[52]

The most conducive 'creative urban milieu', is not, then, necessarily, or at least entirely, open and free. Creative cities, writes Hall, 'are places of great social and intellectual turbulence, not comfortable places at all'. The most potent periods of cultural reinvention, he argues, occur in cities that are in the midst of what he terms *kicking over the traces*. 'Kicking over the traces: that means that there must be traces to kick over. Conservative, stable societies will not prove creative, but neither will societies in which all order, all points of reference have disappeared.'[53] Ai Weiwei, with all his anger and defiance, appears at least sometimes to agree that there is something stimulating in the current environment. 'Without censorship, I think it would be much less interesting,' he has said. 'Trying to find possibilities through the difficulties can make life more interesting. I often see my cats put their toys in an area littered with obstacles, and their play becomes interesting and dramatic.'[54] In an article for the *New York Times* commemorating the events of Tiananmen Square, author Yu Hua expresses the same, troubling thought. The article entitled 'The Spirit of May 35th', discusses how in adapting and circumventing the regime of control, young Chinese have created a new linguistic art form. In this ultramodern 'Netspeak', *Ai Weilai* (love the future) stands for Ai Weiwei, May 35th stands for June 4th (the date of Tiananmen) and the term *hexie* (harmonise), a Confucian concept at the core of Hu Jintao's political agenda, has been hijacked by the public such that in contemporary urban China to 'harmonise' now means 'to censor':

To evade censorship when expressing their opinions on the internet, Chinese people give full rein to the rhetorical functions of language, elevating to a sublime level both innuendo and metaphor, parody and hyperbole, conveying sarcasm and scorn through veiled gibes and wily indirection … Surely our language has never been as rich and vital as it is today. Sometimes I can't help but wonder, if one day the June 4th kind of freedom were to arrive, would we still be so creative, so ingenious?[55]

Dancing with Shackles On, a short film on Chinese cyberspace, further explores this disturbingly complex theme. The film ends by quoting an old Chinese saying 'the misery of the state, brings the emergence of the poets'.[56] In the good times, explains one of the bloggers, there is no need for poetry. This is not to say that the buttoned-up situation in China's cultural sphere is good for creative culture, patently it is not. There is no doubt that the creative sphere in China would have a better chance of flourishing if the censors would loosen their grip. It seems doubtful that China's great cities can foster a creative epoch when the country's best writers and artist can so easily be jailed. Nevertheless, there is an inventiveness that comes from being forced to push against the edges. And there is nothing that crystallises the fascinating contradictions in contemporary Shanghai more than the tension between the ambitions of a creative metropolis and the fervent desire to maintain control.

Inviting the unexpected

In a prime location near the subway hub at Wujiaochang in the Yangpu district, Vincent Lo of Shui On Group—the developer behind the 'real' Xintiandi—has embarked on a massive project. Knowledge, Innovation, Community (or KIC) occupies a space of more than one million square metres. It seeks to take advantage of the more than fourteen universities in the area including Tongji, with its enormously influential departments of architecture and urban planning, and Fudan, which is widely considered to be Shanghai's top university. Lo has the support of the district government, which views KIC as part of its core strategy to 'Revitalize the City with Science and Technology and develop the Yangpu Knowledge and Innovation Zone.' The development consists of four distinct parts, and includes housing, sports facilities and a high-tech park. It was inspired, says the brochure, 'by the technological innovation and entrepreneurial spirit of Silicon Valley in the United States and the cultural ambience found in the Left Bank of Paris'. The dream is to build a 'factory of innovation', incubate entrepreneurship and 'construct a space where art and science meet'. PR billboards announce 'a huge technology spider', whose web of interconnection breed collaborations between R&D divisions of multinational corporations and research institutes, venture capitalists and universities, and technology companies. Lo himself is increasingly focused on creating a good environment for venture capital and is intent on attracting local and international venture capital firms. KIC has its own seed stage investment company whose aim is to find and incubate start-ups as well as educate and guide entrepreneurs. KIC, then, aspires to invent an ecosystem capable of breeding creativity. It is a grand example of the typical Shanghai strategy—*build it and they will come*. On the tree-lined University Avenue that connects Fudan University to KIC plaza all the SOHO housing was sold out before it was even built. Yet, two years later, the street still had the feel of a deserted film set. Despite a gradual increase in traffic in the area and the fact that KIC has hosted some genuinely innovative events (the 2013 Shanghai Maker Faire, for instance), few would maintain that this zone of the Yangpu district has either the culture of Paris or the vitality of Silicon Valley that drove the developer's initial designs.

The problem for Lo and for the city more generally is that no matter how meticulously programmed, a government-backed development company cannot hope to recreate the dynamism, culture and enterprise that results from bottom-up growth. True innovation is not something that can be so calculatedly engineered. Creativity, when it does arrive, is always inevitably unplanned, an invader from outside. Planners, of course, refuse to concede this incapacity to imagine what has not yet been. The PR agent at '800 Show' smilingly introduces the third phase of the project which will incorporate the surrounding *shikumen*. Relocation has already begun. In an excited tone she describes the tired vision. The retail zone will be 'like Xintiandi,' the restored *shikumen* will be 'like Tianzifang.' Yet, enthusiasm cannot veil the incoherence of a creative vision based purely on mimicry and stolen ideas.

The creativity that powers the future is by definition, as the economic philosopher Nicholas Taleb has written, impossible to predict or project. Its 'black swan' nature must necessarily catch you by surprise. Jane Jacobs, who recognised the essential uncertainty of the creative process, advocates that cities follow an 'esthetics of drift'. 'Successful economic development', she wrote, 'is open ended rather than goal oriented'.[57] It occurs through 'drifting in an empirical or practical fashion', and is driven not of necessity but by an 'esthetic curiosity', which follows no clear goals and in such a way that no one knows what will happen next. 'Targets', 'long-range planning', 'resolute purpose' and 'determined will' are, according to Jacobs, part of a 'military mindset' that does not lead to urban innovation or economic growth.[58] Instead, innovation emerges accidentally, through positive feedback circuits, between unforeseeable problems and the improvisation of unplanned open drift.

In seeking to anticipate the unanticipated, all that Shanghai—or indeed any metropolis—can do is prepare, cargo-cult style, for that which has yet to arrive. Looked at from the perspective of the city itself, rather than from the viewpoint of any particular developer, the best of the creative clusters succeed in doing just that. In renovating and restoring the empty shells of a bygone era into offices, galleries, studios and boutiques, the clusters operate as an invitation or landing pad. The significance of these cutting-edge refurbishments of the city's long-abandoned industrial core is not their content—which many so desperately lack—but their form. By deliberately encasing and exhibiting the modern past, the clusters architecturally express a revival or reanimation of Shanghai's modernity. They act at once as homage to the city's industrialisation and as recognition that industrialisation as it once was, is no more. In their attempt to unlock the latent potentiality of the metropolis they serve both to root Shanghai in its own history while, simultaneously, making it anew. The creative clusters are thus themselves an integral expression of Shanghai's neo-modernism, in which looking back and looking forward have become indistinguishable and the nostalgia for the past plugs directly into the desire to occupy the future. This process of adaptive reuse is, of course, not unique to Shanghai. Cities throughout the world have refashioned old industrial zones as spaces that might nurture the promise of creative industry. Nevertheless, the scale of this activity in Shanghai, and more importantly its flatness with the time-consciousness of the city in which the most future-oriented zones are deliberately designed to reawaken a lost past, speaks to the special affinity the creative clusters have with the particular temporality of Shanghai's own restoration.

As architectural sites, the finest of clusters contribute to the fundamental mutation of creativity that Shanghai's new modernity entails. At their best, the clusters serve to reanimate the craftsmanship and sensibility of tradition while, simultaneously, generating something new. Deng Kunyen, whose work lies at the crossroads of heritage and development, preservation and innovation is one of the most striking practitioners in this quest. Saddened to see Shanghai's historical fabric destroyed, Deng helped launch the movement to save the city's industrial heritage and in so doing helped spark an artistic renewal. Work on the Suzhou Creek Warehouse was completed in the late 1990s. Deng then embarked on another project at the former General Electric site in the Yangpu district. Working with colleagues and associates linked to an organisation called 'mAAN' (modern Asian, Architecture

Network), Deng brought together more than sixty students for a fourteen-day symposium titled 'The Great Shanghai Industrial Heritage Revitalization Workshop'. The result is one of Shanghai's most remarkable architectural achievements—the metamorphosis of a disused factory into an urban oasis. Inside the gates at 2200 Yangshupu Lu an extraordinary transformation of industrial detritus and pillaged recycled materials has taken place: floors are made of old roof tiles, walls are constructed from pottery moulds, gutted buildings reveal the raw beauty of exposed brick and wooden beams. Throughout, a garden grows. Giant vines climb through rusted metal frames, lotuses bloom in ponds made from moulded concrete, masses of wild flowers mushroom through the tiles. Light touches of design—glass structures, an angled mirror, an oversized door, a curving wall, an innovative staircase—transform this wreckage of the past, now overgrown, into a showcase complex of design studios, galleries and shops.

Deng is deeply influenced by both Taoism and Buddhism. The spaces he creates are meant as models of architectural restoration but also, more fundamentally, as manifestations of a modern Chinese aesthetic entrenched in ancient traditions. 'I hope that these would serve as successful examples for a new concept of "development" and push forward the protection of our urban industrial architecture,' Deng says speaking of his projects in Shanghai. 'At a deeper level I wanted to take the chance to promote traditional Chinese culture and philosophy—Confucianism, Taoism, Buddhism. If China wants to build its own brands and make them internationally successful, local artists, designers and architects have to seek inspiration from our own culture, which is the most abundant source of creativity.'[59] At 2200 Yangshupu Lu, a classical Chinese garden grows out of a modern factory generating architecture that is unequivocally avant-garde. Asked about this fusion of nature and industry, and how it produces a layering of culture and time, Deng responds from the philosophy within which he is steeped. 'When you create something, you have to go back to the original form to see the "Nothing", so you know there is no difference between new and old, good and bad, the alive and the dead.'[60]

For a number of years Deng was based at the Yangshupu site waiting for the city's frenzied redevelopment process to reach him. In the front of the redesigned building he opened a Buddhist bookshop and in the back a stunningly ingenious 'coffee shop' that served traditional medicinal drinks with glass walls and tables that showcased the herbs that were served. The place, however, far out and without easy transport, was almost always empty, and eventually the doors were locked and visitors were no longer free to roam.

By climbing the stairs of the abandoned building next door and peering over the fence, however, it's possible to catch a glimpse of the remarkable site. Thankfully the buildings are standing and the garden still grows. Hopefully, one day, probably only once the creative clusters lose their designated purpose and break free from the preprogrammed plans, the place will be revived once again and help host the singular creative awakening that the city so hungrily awaits.

6

NEO-HAIPAI

A thoroughly renovated Shanghainese culture, or xin haipai, is inextricably entan-
gled with the city's historical discontinuity, or interruption, and with a broader
Chinese national (or even civilizational) modernization that was anticipated by the
'Old Shanghai' and revives today as a futuristic memory.

Nick Land

Shanghai's built environment was skyscraper and shikumen both—a mirror of the
Janus face of Shanghai Style, with the up-to-date on one side, the immemorial on the
other.

Lynn Pan

Xintiandi

In the late 1990s, when the Shanghai boom was well underway and cranes
peppered the city, the main symbol of the new metropolis was the towers
rising on the eastern shore. Yet, despite the frenzied construction, something
substantial was missing from the urban landscape that was growing out of
the barren flatlands of Pudong. Shanghai was becoming a generically futuristic city, one that could be relocated anywhere. The new Shanghai, to use
postmodern parlance, had 'no there there'.

At the same moment, however, on a patch of land in downtown Puxi,
Shanghai embarked on an altogether different pattern of growth as Hong
Kong developer Vincent Lo partnered with American architect Ben Wood
on a project that came to be known as Xinitiandi. The downtown property

111

consists of a series of low-rise structures, which today host restaurants, bars, boutiques and two small museums (one of which was the birthplace of the Communist Party). Yet, it is neither the historic nor the mundane content that makes this one of the most important urban developments in the country. Rather, by introducing the concept of adaptive reuse into China and showing, in a single stroke, that there was more money to be made in preserving old buildings than in tearing them down, Xintiandi sold Shanghai to the Shanghainese. It thereby generated the promise of a future city with a singular sense of place.

The project began in 1998 when Lo invited Wood to come to Shanghai as one of five architects to bid on his downtown development. Wood, who had never been to China and knew little of its culture, spent his days exploring the rapidly changing metropolis. He wandered through the confusion of streets and alleyways, encountering the exciting, inspiring transition between old and new. When he returned he wrote Lo a letter imploring him not to destroy the richness of that which was already there. 'I have just returned from Tuscany with my family,' he wrote; 'if you owned an Italian village would you tear it down?'[1] Lo, it happened, had also recently come back from a trip to the European countryside. 'When I saw what you wrote about Tuscany,' he later told Wood, 'I knew exactly what you meant.'[2]

Wood was the only architect to bid on the project to tell Lo to save the buildings. After being awarded the job, his first step was to change the master plan, which, as was typical for Shanghai in the 1990s, called for a wholesale destruction of the area. Then, guided by his mentor Benjamin Thompson, he set out to create the 'one space that was missing in the Shanghai of 1998'—a 'place of romance', a 'beautiful place' where 'people came to feel beautiful'.[3]

Lo's board of directors, who were feeling the sting of the Asian Financial crises, refused to fund the project. The idea of saving these buildings—with their hyper dense population and lack of indoor plumbing—seemed crazy. 'These,' Wood recalls, 'were the slums.'[4] Lo was determined to continue, however, and bankrolled the project himself using 150 million dollars of his own money. 'I am paying you out of my own pocket,' he confided to Wood in the midst of construction.[5]

Today's preservationists are often critical of Xintiandi, but the project never had a purist's intent. 'I am not a preservationist, so it was easy for me to alter buildings.' Wood says in an interview with Shanghai based researchers Moving Cities, 'Had I been a preservationist this project would have turned into a museum.'[6] Many buildings were eliminated in order to clear an open space for pedestrians, patio seating and public events. A further 70 per cent of the structures were demolished and then rebuilt on the same spot with the addition of more modern amenities. New architecture was added using a contemporary style. 'I wanted to leave a trace that we had been there,' Wood explains, justifying his decisions, 'otherwise, it does not feel honest.'[7]

Today, Xintiandi has become one of the main landmarks of Shanghai and 50,000 people pass through on any given day. With 170 million visitors every year, it attracts more people than Disneyworld. In China, 'to Xintiandi' has become a verb. Municipalities all over the country, including Hangzhou, Wuhan and Chongqing, have lined up to Xintiandi their city. Wood is proud of the achievement and its influence on Shanghai. 'When I first came to Shanghai, in 1998, nobody cared about the area, not even the government; the stone door houses were considered to be expendable.'[8] 'Demolition goes on,' he says, 'but Shanghai has done the most of any city in China to preserve its heritage.'[9] This attention to preservation stems from the temporal loop inherent in Shanghai futurism, which is well understood by scholars of the city. It is essential to look backwards, argues Wasserstrom, to engage with Shanghai's process of 'reglobalization'[10] Shanghai's urban development, echoes Bergère, is 'a remake.'[11]

Shanghai's hidden alleyways

The architecture of Xintiandi is the *lilong*, a singular form of lane-way housing that constitutes the archetypal element of Shanghai's built form. *Lilongs* were constructed in clusters in and around the foreign concessions for a period of approximately one hundred years, dating from the mid-1800s to the mid-1900s. By the time the Communists took power they had became the major type of housing in the city and the quintessential architecture of Shanghai.

Lilongs consist of narrow alleyways that branch off between blocks, often hidden from view. They are bounded by rows of steep multi-storey houses known as *shikumen*. The name is derived from their outer stone framed door (*shi* means stone and *men* means door). In each individual home these outer doors open onto an inner courtyard or 'sky-well', usually used as a small garden space. Behind this is an inner door beyond which the residents live. The lanes themselves are protected by a guarded entranceway and are often given auspicious or uplifting names.

Lilongs open up areas in between the streets, producing a type of inner block that is separated from the chaotic noise of the urban traffic outside.

They thus offer areas of safety and tranquility amidst a dense and bustling metropolitan core. Life inside the lanes has the feel of an urban village with neighbourly gatherings (and disputes) as well as all kinds of residential activities. Shanghai's everyday life, as historian Hanchao Lu reminds us, has traditionally unfolded away from the fashionable boulevards in the back alleys where 'the majority of the people of Shanghai lived'.[12]

Visitors can wander through the city for days without even realising the *lilongs* are there. These alleys give Puxi (Shanghai's western core) an inherently obscure nature that is dramatically opposed to the translucency of Pudong and the intrinsic transparency encoded in the dominant forms of modernism that it represents. In reviving the *lilong*, Xintiandi served as a reminder that Shanghai's futurism, whenever it emerges, comes from the *shikumen* just as much as from the skyscraper. In Shanghai, then, the brightly-lit outward facing spectacle has always been twinned with an intimate, more shadowy life in the lanes that takes place hidden from view.

Haipai or Shanghai style

Only people that don't like cities think all urban landscapes look the same. Great cities are like sophisticated biological organisms. Each has a distinct personality. One knows a city like one knows a friend. The Londoner, New Yorker, Delhiite or *Beijingren* embodies the urban fabric s/he is from, and becomes, through their views and tastes, gestures and tones, an expression—however unconscious—of the municipality itself. Open your door in any neighbourhood of a great city and you immediately know that you are in that city and not any other.

Urbanatomy, a comprehensive guidebook to Shanghai,[13] starts with the assumption that cities are 'developing bodies of singular complexity':

Part alien, sedentary animal, part cybernetic fungus, with crystalline, vegetable and mechanical aspects, they heap themselves upwards and outwards like termite mounds, spreading like mould, feeding, excreting, respiring and cephalizing, building a new life ... The city is a body of countless precisely interlocking parts, supporting an emerging intelligence and a maturing personality ... When Shanghainese burn incense for the city God, they honor this vast metabolizing, maternally nurturing beast.[14]

Shanghai, then, is best thought of as an entity with a unique personality, culture and style. The name given to this individuation is *haipai*, a term that was coined in the 1920s. It arose initially, according to historian Lynn Pan, who has written a detailed account of the Shanghai Style, to describe alterations in the local staging of Beijing opera. In Shanghai, where tradition is modernity, operatic forms were reinvented in a variety of ways. In an attempt to modernise Chinese opera and give it more box office appeal, the city embellished it with 'lighting, sets, props like real swords or even animals, arias sung in the vernacular, or snatches of local folksong'.[15] From the start, then, Shanghai's singular style has defined itself in contrast to a more conservative and traditional form of Chinese culture headquartered in Beijing. The two, Beijing and Shanghai, writes Pan, 'came to exemplify the two sides of that familiar question':

> whether to cleave to tradition, or to modernise. Through any area—writing no less than art and design—this problem ran as a leitmotif, manifesting itself as a conflict between old and new, nostalgia and progress, self absorption and openness, country and city, indigenous and foreign, disdain for the marketplace and eagerness for profit. The Jingpai versus Haipai controversy is but another face of this conflict.[16]

Haipai eventually came to encompass all the arts, from literature and opera to fashion and design. Shanghai Style, writes Pan, was 'constituted as much by an attitude, a context, a way of living and behaving as by an aesthetic or a set of definable formal features'.[17] *Haipai* became the 'style of the metropolis'.[18] 'The key to the singulariy of Shanghai lay in the rise of the haipai', agrees Marie-Claire Bergère in *China's Gateway to Modernity*, '*Haipai* or "the Shanghai Style" was the very expression of the commercial and cosmopolitan culture of modern China.'[19]

Cosmopolitanism

Haipai is sometimes translated as 'ocean culture' (*hai* literally means the 'sea'). Shanghai's watery nature (its very name means 'on the sea'), stems from the importance of its port, but also, more profoundly, from the intense intermixing that takes place on and through its urban waterways.

> The culture of Shanghai was, in short, "of the ocean" [*hai*]' Xu Jilin explains. 'The ocean is boundless and expansive, taking into it the flows of a myriad of rivers. But after the ocean subsumes those estuarine waters, they become part of a larger whole, a cultural vastness. After reaching Shanghai local Chinese and foreign cultural material was decoupled from its place origins to become part of what was known as the "Shanghai Style" [*Haipai*]. And what developed therefrom was: *Haipai* Western food, *Haipai*-Western-style dress, *Haipai*-English (pidgin or *yangjingbang Yingwen*). There is even *Haipai*-Sichuan cuisine and *Haipai*-Beijing Opera![20]

Shanghai, like New York, is a city of migrants. It is, and has always been, constituted by cultural crossings and openness to the outside. 'Being mixed up,' writes Pan, 'was a Shanghai condition.'[21] 'Foreignness is integral to *haipai*, and it is because the city was given its character by people from a dozen countries, planners and architects included, that the style evolved.'[22]

Lilongs, the architectural embodiment of *haipai*, were initially built in response to a great wave of immigration that began impacting Shanghai at the start of the 1850s. People seeking refuge from the savagery of the Taiping Rebellion that was sweeping across the mainland poured into the city in vast numbers. These new inhabitants were fleeing the chaos, violence and banditry of the civil war, and sought the security and social stability that the foreign settlements could provide. By the early 1860s well over 100,000 refugees had flowed into the concession areas and 8,740 houses had been constructed in the British Concession alone to cater to these new inhabitants.

Chinese refugees arrived from everywhere, but two populations had a particularly critical impact. First were the migrants from the surrounding areas of Zhejiang and Jiangsu who—taken as a group—were remarkably prosperous. Along with their money, these early settlers brought their families, their dialects, their culinary tastes and their business skills. Many came from the sophisticated elite of *Jiangnan* society and thus ensured, from early on, that Shanghai gained a paramount place in the cultural landscape of China.

The Cantonese also played a crucial role. Due to the early British settlement in Guangzhou, a long history of European and American trade in the area, as well as the Portugese control of Macau, this population was already familiar with foreign culture and many found work as compradors in Shanghai. Together they forged a go-between culture with its own hybrid language (pigeon English) and a fusion of customs, fashion and taste. The compradors thus facilitated an exchange that became intrinsically tied to the city's growth. At the same time, they established Shanghai's intimate links with Guangzhou and later Hong Kong, whose enormous influence continues to impact today.

From the start, internal migrants mixed with an influx of foreigners: Japanese traders, White Russians, Sephardic tycoons, French officials, American missionaries and, of course, British adventurers and businessmen who sought to make a profit from the richness of this recently pried-open place.[23] A great opportunity presented itself in the desperate Chinese migrants, many of whom had transplanted a great deal of wealth and had an enormous demand for housing above all.

At first, the conservative English elite had no interest in creating housing that would enable the Chinese to live in the concessions, which had originally been intended exclusively for foreign inhabitants. They complained that the cheap houses sheltering Chinese refugees had transformed the settlement into 'a native Alsatia, the southern portion being blocked with abominably overcrowded and filthy hovels, fraught with the danger of fire and pestilence, rife with brothels, opium shops, and gambling dens'.[24] Yet, the British merchants of Shanghai were in China for one purpose alone: to make money. One trader, in a much-quoted statement to then British Consul Rutherford Alcock, explained the situation with a disarming frankness:

You, as H. M.'s. Consul, are bound to look to national and permanent interests—that is your business. But it is my business to make a fortune with the least possible loss of time, by letting my land to Chinese, and building for them at thirty to forty per cent interest, if that is the best thing I can do with my money. In two or three years at farthest, I hope to realise a fortune and get away; what can it matter to me, if all Shanghai disappears afterwards, in fire or flood?[25]

Lilong architecture is both the result and embodiment of this pragmatic cosmopolitanism. Developers, working within the constraints of space, time and cost, devised an architectural solution that was influenced by Western thinking while, simultaneously, catering to Chinese residential traditions and expectations. The general pattern of the *lilong* recalls British row housing, which was designed for the efficient mass-housing of urban workers. With the *shikumen* structure, this was conjoined with the traditional patterns of Chinese courtyard dwellings (the *san-he-yuan* or *si-he-yuan*). The *lilongs* were thus 'not only hybrid, but multi-hybrid; at once Western and Chinese, modern and traditional, urban and rural. Within the *lilong* structure, two enormously different—almost antithetical—architectural lineages were folded together into an elegant, functional whole.'[26] In becoming the exemplar of housing in Shanghai, the *lilong* produced an urban texture that was at once exotically Chinese yet familiarly European, and vice versa.

Commercialism

Hapai's cosmopolitanism is tied to its deep commercial tendencies. In the arts, the emergence of a Shanghai Style arose specifically to please the mutating taste of a new group of patrons, the merchants of Shanghai. Even from its earliest 'fishing village' days, Shanghai was a city of trade. The 'essence of being "Shanghainese"', to quote Hanchao Lu 'derived from commerce':[27]

Modern Shanghainese have been stereotyped as astute, resourceful, calculating, quick-witted, adaptive and flexible (always ready to compromise but not budging an inch unless absolutely necessary). All of these are characteristics associated with commerce. Shanghai was arguably the epitome of modern China's commercial culture, in which commerce served as the primary motor of society. It seems legitimate to name such a culture after the city, hence the term *Haipai* (the Shanghai school or Shanghai type), in contrast to the supposedly rigid, tradition bound, and orthodox *Jingpai* (the Beijing school or Beijing type). The Shanghai type even in its original meaning as a school of painting or drama, was part of a broadly defined commercial culture: as Lu Xun pointed out *Haipai* is just the helper of commerce, whereas *Jingpai* is the hack of officialdom.[28]

Shanghai's essential commercialism was made manifest in the *lilong*s, which is where China's market in modern real estate first emerged. Shanghai's population tripled in the first decades of the twentieth century, from around one million at the end of the nineteenth century to three million by 1930. The majority of these new residents chose to settle in the foreign concessions. The tremendous flow of incoming wealth had the power to transform 'the boggy ground on the outskirts of the Chinese city, which had been allocated to the British and French consuls and which their nationals had begun to occupy ... into a potential "gold mine"'. Faced with intensifying Chinese demand, Western landowners came up with a lucrative business model. Real estate speculation took hold very quickly as land was parceled up, divided into lots and large quantities of hastily built housing were rented out to the refugees. The implications, as Land notes, were revolutionary:

Neither commerce nor housing was new to China, of course, but their combination within a commercial real estate market, resourced by speculative capital, and mass-producing identical residential units, was entirely unprecedented in the country. The mixture of urgent, large-scale need, affluent customers, eagerly opportunistic developers, and minimal administrative restraints, lent an extraordinary zest to proceedings. Financial returns of 30–40% were not uncommon, and the urban landscape of the concession areas underwent dramatic metamorphosis. Alongside trade and finance, real estate development added a third pillar to the economic foundations of the rising metropolis.[29]

Contributing to the vitality of Shanghai's real estate market was a secondary trade in subletting. Subletting was technically forbidden by standard lease contracts but was always tolerated and eventually became a near-universal practice. In addition to the original or 'big' landlord (*da fangdong*), who owned the property, secondary landlords (*er fangdong*) proliferated throughout Shanghai's inner city lanes. 'By 1937, over two-thirds of tenants in the *lilong*s were subletting from a secondary landlord (this number would reach 85% by 1948).'[30] Prompted by the popular practice of subletting, people began carving up their homes. Houses were sliced into micro portions: living rooms were split into a front and back living room (*qian* and *hou* *ketang*); second floor bedrooms into a front and back bedroom (*qianfang* and *houfang*); vertical divisions cut off portions from the ceilings to create second and third lofts (*er* and *san ceng ge*) or false third floors (*jia san ceng*); courtyard space was absorbed and converted into extra rooms. Such modifications could increase the floor area of a *lilong* housing unit by up to 50 per cent and transform a small house designed to accommodate a single family into a home for dozens of people from several different families.

The most culturally significant of these divisions was the pavilion room (*tingzijian*), a virtual cubby-hole located just above the kitchen, between the first and second floor. *Tingzijian* typically faced north and were famous for being both too hot in the summer and too cold in the winter and because of this negative *feng shui*, *tingzijian* were the cheapest rooms available. Their low cost, however, as well as their relative privacy (the rooms have their own entrance off the second floor), attracted Shanghai's growing population of bohemian intellectuals. As a result, a huge amount of revolutionary writing of the May Fourth era was composed inside these spaces, so much so that the style has come to be known as '*tingzijian* literature'.

The commercialism of the *lilong*, which gave rise to Shanghai's remarkable urban density, extended far beyond the real estate market. Ultimately, more crucial were the myriad micro businesses that were housed within the lanes. The *li* houses, writes researcher Samuel Liang:

> were provisional lodgings centering on business activities. To pay high rents and sustain an expensive urban life, a house was used not only as a home, but as a space that facilitated the constant flow of capital. Merchant residences were used for many different purposes as the sojourners sought every means to maintain their lifestyle or strike a fortune. Thus, extremely diverse functions—residential and commercial, private and public—were found in the *li* compounds.[31]

Though they were intended as purely residential, in fact, the *lilongs* were thoroughly 'mixed use' from the start, as historian Hanchao Lu details. In and among the multiplicity were factories, schools, traditional Chinese banks, warehouses, bathhouses, fortune-tellers, restaurants, law offices, medical clinics, even government bureaus and Buddhist temples. Streets in residential neighbourhoods were crowded with small stores selling food, clothing and household goods, small 'proletarian' restaurants and the ever-popular *yanzhidian* tobacco and paper stores that marked the entrance to practically every lane. There were silk and tea wholesale stores, bookstores and publishing houses. Inside the alleyways, dozens of hawkers gave life its colour and rhythms. The most common and popular goods were Shanghai's famous *xiaochi* (snacks), which were advertised with a song and often served from portable kitchens, which street peddlers carried on a pole. Besides the food vendors, barbers and seamstresses were stationed in the alleys and small businessmen and women regularly frequented with their carts or stalls selling 'newspapers, flowers, fresh vegetables, rice, salt, needles, thread, socks, handkerchiefs, towels, soap, cigarettes, mats, bamboo poles (for hanging out clothes to dry) and many other things'.[32] *Shikumen*, generally, did not have indoor plumbing. Instead, every family used a 'night-stool' (or chamber pot) as a toilet. Every morning farmers/traders came to the door to collect the night-stools, which were used as fertiliser. In the commercial culture of Shanghai even human waste was bought and sold. By generating this 'extraordinary mixture of residence and commerce', the *lilongs* thus produced the space in which Shanghai's 'vibrant commercial culture was born'.[33] The 'dazzling life symbolised by the Bund and Nanking road' were, as Lu reminds us, 'only ever interesting asides to the real commercial life of the city … What mattered most in daily life was the petty but vigorous commerce and activities conducted in an area within walking distance from home.'[34]

The modernity of the street

Shanghai's cosmopolitan commercialism laid the foundations for its embrace of the modern. In the early decades of the twentieth century, the thriving metropolis witnessed revolutionary transformations in everything from art, to food, to dress. 'Shanghai accepted what the twentieth-century world had to offer more readily than other parts of China,' writes Pan 'be it new technology, ways of thought, cultural forms or artistic styles. Where but in Shanghai would a Chinese so quickly find such modern symbols as escalators, cinemas, dance halls, advertising billboards, popular magazines, gramophone records, motor cars and women's fashions?'[35] It was here, in Shanghai, that Chinese modernity was born.

Modern Shanghai was forged in the *lilong*, a mode of housing that was both the creator and the creation of a new social class. *Lilong* residents were typically deterritorialised urbanites that came to the city as sojourners and thus tended to treat their dwelling as intrinsically temporary, discarding the auspicious rootedness that Chinese typically give to the family hearth. Shanghai's population, always to some extent floating, was in the city to make money, and their new urban existence profoundly reinvented the concept of home. For many of these new urbanites, traditional ties to the extended family were disintegrating. The *lilong*s appealed because they were able to accommodate a whole range of family structures and living arrangements.

For the wealthy elite who had recently returned from studying abroad—in Europe, America or Japan—larger 'New-type *Lilongs*' and luxurious 'Garden *Lilongs*' were constructed. These ambitious travellers returned after the fall of the Emperor, and were determined to participate in the development of a new nation. Settled in their new lane-way homes, they mixed with entrepreneurs from all over China as well as the compradors who mediated between West and East. All of these novel groups preferred life in the foreign concessions, which enjoyed greater social amenities and better infrastructure than was available in the Chinese-run parts of the city, and also could reflect upon their new social status and way of life.

In his book *Mapping Modernity in Shanghai*, researcher Samuel Liang argues that the most vital contribution to Shanghai modernity, however, lay in the spatial transformation produced by Shanghai's sojourners and the particularities of the architecture within which they lived. With the *lilong*, argues Liang, came the street, an urban form that transformed China's typical spatial order making Shanghai into a modern metropolis.

Traditionally in China, residential and commercial spaces were strictly divided with barriers that split them apart. Urban geography was thus hierarchically constructed, with a physical, psychological and sociological gap forming a boundary between the more honoured, peaceful and protected 'house mansion-palace centred on the courtyard' and the more chaotic and crass 'shop along-the-street'. 'The courtyard and the street,' writes Liang, 'were antithetical spaces separated by walls: the one represented the elite order and the other the amorphous and vulgar; the one was the centre and the other always was marginalised in Confucian ideology.'[36]

The *lilong*s, Liang contends, reversed this spatial hierarchy. As the city grew, many *lilong*s built on the periphery came to occupy highly-valued downtown land. Economic necessity thus ensured that their outer façade be given over to commercial activity. The lane-housing of Shanghai was typically bounded by rows of shops, at the back of which was a wall enclosing the residential area. Rather than try to remove themselves from the busy streets their outer edges produced, the *shikumen* opened themselves to this intrinsic exteriority of the modern city. Instead of facing inward into the courtyard, the space of traditional domesticity, *shikumen* houses had upper-storey windows that looked out onto the street and alleyways. Shanghai's architecture thus turned the traditional courtyard house inside out. 'The street,' writes Liang explaining how the *lilong*s enacted this powerful urban reversal, 'became an infinitely extending space central to everyday life, while the house had to open itself in order to be a sustainable unit in the city.' In Shanghai, then, the walls that had long closed off the private space of the family weakened, and life inside the home became increasingly integrated with the surrounding streets and shops. 'The *li*,' writes Liang, 'erased the borderline between orderly walled spaces and promiscuous streets ... As Western colonial expansion battered down the walls of the Middle Kingdom, the social space of the *li* demonstrated an analogous transformation: the walls of self-contained residential space were similarly breached.'[37]

This geographical intermixing created zones where people who were traditionally kept apart would mingle and meet. In the busy street of the city 'visibility and openness replaced walls and containment'. Everyone was free to see and be seen. Absorbed by the city's new spatial order, where the public and private were conjoined, Shanghai's floating population—its sojourners—felt the dissolution of customary bonds and boundaries:

Enjoying this freedom from the self-contained household and rigid social hierarchy, the sojourners were increasingly submerged in the city's sprawling commercial fabric and uneven geography. In contrast to traditional homeowners residing in a set of courtyard spaces, they were mere passersby with uncertain identities and fortunes on the city's promiscuous streets, where the Confucian ideal of social order and hierarchy had always been compromised. This is the true image of the social space in the *li*, where the courtyard adjoined the street.[38]

At home, in the new spaces the *lilong* produced, the Shanghainese were liberated to create their own modern rituals of everyday life.

Preservation

The development of *lilong* housing began in the early 1840s and lasted for about a century. After the Sino-Japan War, Shanghai's real-estate development stagnated and the economy sunk into depression. As Shanghai fell under the control of the Japanese, the construction of *lilong*s come to a halt. The Communists deemed the *lilong*s inefficient and once they took control of the city, mass prefabricated apartments that could shelter a new working-class society were built in their place. *Haipai* culture began to recede. 'By 1949, the year of the communist victory,' mourns Lynn Pan, 'Shanghai Style had had its day. The passing of styles is a familiar story everywhere, but Shanghai Style was a chapter not so much ended as blotted out, excised by fiat from the collective memory along with an entire way of life.'[39]

For the first thirty years of Communist rule, the government neglected the *lilong*s, treating them only as a convenient form of low-cost housing. People were piled in to the *shikumen's* already overstuffed spaces. During the Cultural Revolution a home originally designed for one family would typically house five to seven groups of multigenerational relations. The problem of overcrowding, which had long been present in the city, became evermore acute. With no funds given over to maintenance, the overflowing buildings that once carved out the streets of Shanghai deteriorated into a state of squalor and disrepair.

It is thus hardly surprising that when Shanghai finally began participating in the era of openness and reform it was commonly held that the best strategy was to tear the ramshackle *lilong* housing down. The burgeoning preservation movement faced a host of serious challenges including, as scholar Zhang Song notes, the 'large number of heritage structures located throughout the city'; the 'serious maintenance problems associated with these buildings' and the 'complex network of ownership and right to use that is extremely difficult to untangle'.[40] 'The original city landscape faces unprecedented threat,' Wan-Lin Tsai wrote in a thesis on *The Redevelopment and Preservation of Historic Lilong Housing in Shanghai*, 'old and deteriorated *lilong* blocks are not qualified to display the progress brought by economic reform, and the land they occupy is usually in a good location of the inner city'.[41]

Nevertheless, the Shanghai government, hardly immune to the seductive nostalgia of the city's golden age, had a sense, early on, that there was something worth saving in the megacity's urban heritage. In the late 1980s government and academic groups began working together to survey the most important historic buildings of Shanghai and catalogue the work of prominent architects in the city. Various types of buildings were put on the list, including hotels, theatres, hospitals, banks and *lilongs*. By 1989, the city's most iconic architecture was guaranteed protection, and by the mid-1990s the strategy of adaptive reuse was put into practice, starting with the enormously influential project to redevelop the Bund. A decade later by the mid-2000s, and prompted in part by the enormous success of Xintiandi, Shanghai had adopted the strictest laws in China on the protection, adaptation and preservation of its historic architecture.

Tianzifang

Today, many of Shanghai's remaining *lilong*s are under protection and a number are being restored and revitalised. This architectural renovation is invariably connected to a reanimation of *haipai*. The old buildings are haunted by a culture that has lain dormant, but is not dead. Nowhere has the

123

revival of this link between *lilong*s and *haipai* been more consciously under-taken than in Tianzifang, the *lilong* development at 210 Taikang Lu.

The architecture of Tianzifang is layered by time. The residential *shikumen* were built in the 1920s. Then, during the 1940s in a pattern of growth that was typical of the times, some light industrial state-owned factories were added to the lane. When companies were relocated at the start of the reform era, these structures were left empty and, eventually, some small businesses, a barbers shop, a scissors shop, a noodle shop, a bath house, took over the abandoned workshops. In the late 1990s, however, the Luwan district gov-ernment decided to redevelop this central urban zone. They called in Wu Meisen, now the general manager of Tianzifang, and tasked him, initially, to devise a plan to make better use of the 4,500 sqms of old factory space. Wu had seen the transformation of urban industrial heritage in other parts of the world and was particularly inspired by Granville Island in Vancouver, Canada. 'I decided this place could be a "Granville Island" in Shanghai,' Wu later said, 'containing some of old Shanghai's unique flavour.'[42]

Wu's first step was inviting some American friends to take a tour of the lane. 'They helped me hold a big party with hundreds of artists from different countries as guests,' he recalls. 'At the end of the night the whole 4,500 sqms factory workshop was rented out.'[43] Among the first tenants were the famous local painter Chen Yifei and the well-known architectural photographer Deke Erh. Later, other members of the 'creative class' joined them and gradually opened up businesses throughout the *lilong*. In the beginning the pace was slow and the lane stayed quiet for a number of years. Then, in 2008, an imperceptible threshold was crossed and Tianzifang became, suddenly, wildly popular. Today, tightly packed crowds snake through the converted *lilong*, which is stuffed with designer boutiques, coffee shops, galleries, res-taurants and bars. Locals and foreigners alike are drawn to this zone of urban hybridity, which infuses the global (organic salads, Thai curries, a kung-fu studio and a Japanese coffee shop) within a quintessentially local space. Wu is quite explicit that his intent with Tianzifang was to spark a resurgence of Shanghai style. From the beginning, he played a strategic role in choosing new tenants, insisting candidly on renting only to three categories of people: 'foreigners, Chinese with overseas experience and beautiful women'.[44] This mix of cosmopolitan, stylish Shanghainese and foreigners is precisely what '*haipai* culture' refers to, he maintains, an amalgamation of characteristics of different cultures from both home and abroad.[45]

The time of authenticity

Urbanists frequently compare Tianzifang and Xintiandi, as a case study juxtaposition of top-down development and bottom-up growth. Wu Meisen, a Shanghai native who has been living in a *shikumen* for decades, delights in the debate. 'I really dislike the model of Xintiandi, which is purely commercial and fake. I consider it the biggest fake product in China,' he declares with satisfaction. 'Of course, maybe after a century, when it has 100 years of history behind it, it will become "true". But Taikang Lu has already had over 200 years of history. There is a culture and history inside and around these *shikumen* and *lilongs* that no one can copy.'[46]

The stated idea behind the renovations of Taikang Lu was to preserve as much as possible of the old historical buildings as well as the internal structure of the lanes. The key to this, Wu asserts, was to ensure that land developers did not get involved. Xintiandi, claims Wu, seems like an alien implant because it is the product of a single developer who has imposed his plans from outside. 'It is the imported vision of a Hong Kong-based real estate company who has no real knowledge of local culture and history,' he declares.[47] Tianzifang, on the other hand, has grown more organically, and therefore heterogeneously. Without a single developer in control of the entire space, Tianzifang spread in an ad hoc fashion, seeping into the surrounding homes. For years the government had been trying to relocate residents in the area. Yet, due to the high costs and difficult logistics involved they were not able to move forward with their plans, and the people living in the *lilong*s off Taikang Lu remained while the area was transformed around them. Eventually, the residents and business owners of Tianzifang made agreements among themselves. According to Wu a resident named Zhou Xinliang was the first tenant to rent his thirty-three square-metre room. This occurred at the end of 2004, and since then soaring rent, along with the growing noise of this increasingly dynamic hub, has convinced close to 300 personal landlords to rent out their homes. Tianzifang set an example for the city of successful bottom-up growth, pioneering a model of self-organising urban development in Shanghai.

With projects like Xintiandi, where the pre-existing local population is relocated and the developer is handed a clean slate, the switch from old to new occurs all at once. With Tianzifang, on the other hand, the area's metamorphosis took time. For a number of years the lane occupied a transitional zone in which the new restaurants and shops coexisted with people who had been living in the *shikumen* for decades. The result was a dislocating mix that had the aura of authenticity. Amidst a slew of trendy shops, photo studios, wine bars and pizza joints, one could find the signs of Shanghai's 'living history': laundry hanging from bamboo poles and exposed wires, men crowded around folding tables playing *mah jong* or cards, old women gossiping from their doorways.

Today, however, as a result of the area's enormous success, little of this mixture remains. Instead, the site is packed with tourists, restaurants are loud and photographers are everywhere. Moreover, the money one can make as a landlord offers a strong incentive for the original residents to settle elsewhere. Few now remain. To get a sense of the intense intermixture that Tianzifang once held, it is better to head to other *lilongs* that are undergoing an even more recent transition.

Jingan Beishu is one of the largest and best-preserved 'New Style *Lilongs*' in the city. It is located at 1025 Nanjing Lu, in one of the most prosperous parts of Shanghai and the lane, which is nestled amidst glitzy new shopping malls, has long held a privileged residential community. Like all *lilongs*, this one is mixed use and small businesses that serve the community—a vegetable seller, a tailor and a masseuse—have long-established shops inside the lane. At the end of 2009, however, in a process even more ground up than the one that refashioned Tianzifang, some small entrepreneurs began to convert the micro spaces and courtyards of the ground floor into cafes, tea houses, artisan studios and boutiques. At Jingan Beishu the *lilong* revival occurred informally, outside any official plan and without the involvement of a developer or government body. The off-the-books status of the businesses inside the lane has caused tensions, and stores and cafes have, periodically (and now perhaps permanently), been forced to shut their doors. When they are able to open, however, Jingan Beishu illustrates the delightful mélange of contemporary life in Shanghai's lanes with their radical mixture of culture and class (in which the vegetable stand, repair shops and an old Chinese acupuncturist stand side-by-side with the designer boutiques and stylish tea house). In this way the *lilong* reproduces the everyday rhythms of Shanghai life and *haipai* culture reconstitutes itself for the new millennium.

The contemporary rejuvenation of Shanghai's *lilongs* raise a host of questions—familiar to urbanists everywhere—about gentrification and the interrelationship between cultural history, development and change. In the Shanghai context, however, as the restoration of the *lilongs* make clear, much of the debate over authenticity (or the reanimation of *haipai*) is centred on the difference between a homogeneous environment that tends to arise from top-down developments (the Disneyfication effect) and the intrinsic heterogeneity of bottom-up processes that emerge from the street.

Authenticity's conceptual ties to history—the idea of 'staying true to the past'—is problematic everywhere, but the culturally specific notions of age and architecture make it particularly thorny here. In China, buildings were traditionally constructed from wood and were, therefore, easily destroyed. Edifices, even whole cities, were, and are, constantly being rebuilt. As a result, Chinese culture tends to consider a building old if it resembles something that once stood in its place, even if it itself was only erected yesterday. The 'real' past, and the 'copied' present are thus inherently entangled.

In Shanghai the temporality of authenticity is even more intricate. *Lilong* life and the *haipai* culture that they incarnate and inspire are themselves a mode of modernity that does not belong essentially to any particular moment in time. 'Instead of seeing the *li* as a transitional type in a linear historical process,' writes Samuel Liang, acknowledging this temporal complexity, 'we should consider it as a distinct space, embodying a Shanghai or Chinese modernity, one full of complexities and hybridities and in sharp contrast to the modern marked by purist designs and functionalist planning.'[48] Modern Shanghai, which emerged in the lanes, has never followed the requisites of linear time but rather involved, as Lynn Pan has written, 'a search for new ways of being new and new ways of being old'.[49] Upon seeing Wood's plans for the development of Xintiandi, Shui On's E.C. Liu, commented precisely in this vein: 'I really think the future of Shanghai lies in its past.' Xintiandi's marketing slogan, 'Where yesterday meets tomorrow in Shanghai today', captures this sentiment exactly. As they rediscover life in the urban alleyways, Shanghai's contemporary sojourners continue to reenact a time spiral that lies at the heart of the city's contemporary cultural revival.

PART 3

7

DREAMS FROM THE EDGES

Thames Town

The first thing you notice are the brides. Women in flowing white dresses sit on the lawn by the cathedral or stand by the closed door of the church. At first, it seems there are only a few, but gradually you take in the crowds. They arrive by the busloads with their elaborate attire and matching grooms. Traditional wedding gowns and tuxedos soon give way to a whole host of colourful costumes. Couples wearing outfits modelled on Ming dynasty China, a 1920s jazz bar or the palaces of the French Versailles stand only a few feet apart, infusing the surroundings with a postmodern cacophony of time and place. Their movements are directed by professional photographers who mould them into a standard series of poses—the playful moment, the romantic gaze, the amorous embrace. Once the set is complete, the pictures will be packaged and ceremoniously displayed. Producing them is among the most important rituals of a modern Chinese wedding. Couples have come to this spot—'Thames Town'—to take advantage of one of the most spectacular backdrops in the city, a faux English village on the edge of the metropolis which offers a slice of the British countryside in the suburbs of Shanghai.

Thames Town is located in the new town of Songjiang, about an hour from downtown. It was built by the Songjiang New City Construction and Development Company, a semi-private enterprise, linked to the local government. They, in turn, hired the British firm Atkins Consultancy as designers. Despite the surreal nature of the project, 'Thames Town' is stunningly large. Built to house 10,000 people, it consists of a village green, a waterside promenade, a main shopping district with terraced town houses and suburban style villas. In both scale and in the rigorous manner in which it sticks to its theme, Thames Town—perhaps more than anywhere in the giant megalopolis—gives the impression of an urban experiment gone mad.

Though they were constructed all at once with the typical urgency of China's high-speed construction, the buildings that make up the town are designed to replicate the different styles and periods of a typical English village. The aim was to manufacture something that gives the illusion of having grown up over time. Thames Town 'squeezes 500 years of British architectural development into a five-year construction project, [with] half-timbered Tudor-style buildings at its centre, a waterfront of Victorian red-brick warehouses, and an outlying area of gabled 20th century buildings bordered by hedges, verdant lawns and leafy roads'.[1]

A tour of Thames Town begins at the parking lot on the perimeter. From this approach it is the villas on the boundaries that are visible first. These vast homes, which are protected by gates and guards, are constructed in the style of manor homes with landscaped gardens that line the banks of a mean-dering stream. Through careful landscaping, the traditional canals of the Zhejiang basin have been transformed into an idyllic English river. The 'Ye Olde England' effect is augmented by some kitschy additions placed spo-radically on the grounds: castle 'ruins', British-style phone boxes and vari-ous statues of the UK's most famous figures—Florence Nightingale, Winston Churchill, and even Harry Potter.

A man-made lake borders the town and nearby is a large municipal square. Its emptiness is entirely predictable since no one could have ever presumed that Thames Town would have its own municipal government. Nevertheless, a bank and post office have somehow been persuaded to open branches here, and they share the square with some (not very convincing) signs of galleries 'opening soon'. The main attraction to this part of town is the Urban Planning Museum, which showcases the staggering development of the new town of Songjiang of which Thames Town is only a small part. In meticulous model replicas of the area, the museum showcases the pleth-ora of new university campuses that form the heart of Songjiang, as well as the planned but not yet built Central Business District, the surrounding industrial zone, the amusement park, the vast botanic garden, the golf course and the new underwater museums and old mine shaft transformed into a five star hotel. All this, it is hoped, will transform Songjiang into one of Shanghai's key tourist destinations.

Wandering up out of the square, the roads lead downtown into Thames Town's 'historic' core where the streets are narrower and the housing denser.

In the middle of the town is a pedestrianised zone with cobblestone lanes lined with shops. Though few are open, they have already been given signs, names and phone numbers. Most are just fronts, their emptiness contributing to the weird sense of mirage that Thames Town exudes. The high street consists of a record shop that never was, which advertises its fantasy stock in the window. Nearby is the remnant of The Cobb Fish and Chip Shop, which was the subject of a court case since the owners of the real Cobbs in Dorset weren't amused at being replicated in the Shanghai suburbs. They needn't have worried though. There is little evidence in 'Thames Town' that a single piece of fish has ever been sold. Though the sign on the pub and bed and breakfast reads 'open all day' you only have to peek inside to know that this was never meant to be taken literally. The stores that do exist have followed the most important rule of globalisation and localised. Most are make-up studios, photo shops and dress stores designed to cater to the brides. The longest standing coffee shop, Incomplete Café, is the perfect satiric comment on the state of the shopping district downtown.

Just beyond the shops a wide-open lawn is surrounded on three sides by a large covered market, empty of course. The 'village green' is dominated by the church, which according to Atkins is almost an exact replica of a church in Bristol, UK. Though it is highly unlikely that anyone ever imagined a Christian community living here, the church functions as a key element of Thames Town. For marketing reasons the developers insisted it be included from the start.

Thames Town, with its design that takes the Chinese penchant for copying to a delirious extreme, its attempts to synthetically reproduce organic time while simultaneously wiping out all traces of real history, and its plan to artificially implant the culture of suburbia where none had existed before, may seem utterly inauthentic. Yet, carving out a space on the periphery of the megacity for the implantation of a bucolic village, modelled after a foreign culture and style, is an entirely local endeavour. Everything about Thames Town—its scale, ambition, remarkable success and obvious failure—is quintessential Shanghai. Like the wedding photo industry for which it serves as a backdrop, Thames Town is rooted in the specificities of China's contemporary urbanisation and shows that what is happening on the edges— no less than the core—is, despite the most blatant forms of mimicry, not a copy from elsewhere but rather a singular experiment that is bound to its own particular history, socio-economic conditions, culture and dreams.

SHANGHAI FUTURE

Fantasy and experimentation of the urban periphery

Visions of the future city are frequently bound to the metropolitan core. Yet the most radical urban experiments often unfold on the periphery. The boundary where city meets countryside opens a space for utopian imaginings. In Shanghai the urban fringes have served as a fantastical frontier. Among the cutting-edge conceptions concocted for the city's edges, perhaps the most outlandish was the eco-city of Dongtan. Designed in 2001 for the island suburb of Chongming, Dongtan was meant as an experiment in leapfrog development. The plan was to catapult this poor rural hinterland to the forefront of the 'green movement'. The eco-city was to be a 'model for sustainability for all of China' and 'the first self-sustaining city environment on Earth'.[2]

The radical plans for Chongming were stopped before they got started. Due to a drop in the market and a massive corruption scandal that rocked the Shanghai government, causing a change of leadership, the Dongtan project came to a dramatic halt. Yet, while the island eco-city was shelved before it began, growth elsewhere in the suburbs has been guided by a blueprint that is equally grandiose. Shanghai is developing according to a poly-central vision, known in planning circles as 1–9–6–6, in which the central city is complemented by the construction of nine new cities, sixty new towns and six hundred central villages meant to house between 30,000 and 100,000 residents. The model, writes researcher Harry den Hartog, editor of *Shanghai New Towns: Searching for Community and Identity in a Sprawling Metropolis*, aims to 'reduce congestion in the central city through the rehousing of over a million people to the outlying areas and to coordinate development between the urban and rural zones, and protect as much agriculture land as possible from unstructured development (urban sprawl).'[3]

In order to counter the danger of a homogeneous undifferentiated spread, in which all these new projects bleed into each other, the 'One City, Nine Town' master plan calls for each satellite area to have its own special theme. These 'themes' were based on storybook visions of cultural identities, mostly drawn from Western Europe. Today, therefore, the district of Luodian has a Swedish Town, Pujiang; an Italian Town, Gaoqiao; a Dutch Town; and Songjiang, the 'English' community of Thames Town.[4] Huang Ju, then Shanghai Communist Party Secretary, conceived of the themed towns as a way to celebrate Shanghai's history as a global city, with the European-style suburban communities functioning as an outward extension of the organic eclecticism of the urban core.

The faux cosmopolitanism found in the Shanghai suburbs also flourishes on the outskirts of many of China's cities, often in the form of actual theme parks. Some speculate that this is due to the relative isolation of the population (international reproductions are the next best thing for Chinese citizens who don't have the chance to go elsewhere). Others maintain that the theme park reproductions are the result of an age-old sentiment that China (*Zhongguo*) or the 'Middle Kingdom', as the country at the centre of the world, contains everything within its borders. In any case, locals seem to have a great fondness for this pseudo-internationalism. Early visitors to Shenzhen who wanted to witness the spectacular rise of one of China's first SEZs (Special Economic Zones) remember having to engage in Houdini-like escapes from tour guides who insisted that the only thing to see in Shenzhen was its famous amusement park 'Window of the World'. Jia Zhangke, in his hypnotic film *The World*, captures the odd, haunted atmosphere of a similar theme park on the outskirts of Beijing. This Baudrillardian hyper-reality sprouting at the city limits meshes perfectly with China's penchant for copying. Surf the web and you find them—the fake Eiffel Tower, the imitation White House, the shopping mall that looks just like the Pentagon. In Songjiang New City the cross-cultural pastiche reaches a fever pitch at the new campus of the Shanghai International Studies University, where each building is modelled after the architecture of a different country. Departments are housed in elaborate constructions built in the styles of Florence, Greece or Turkey. Walk up the stairs of the central building of the sprawling grounds and the view out of the columned balcony is of a golden dome rising above an English garden.

Yet another curious fabrication of the Shanghai suburbs is Anting New Town in the district of Jiading, which is home to Volkswagen and Formula 1. The town was developed by the Shanghai International Automobile City Property Management Co Ltd who commissioned the son of Albert Speer, Hitler's main architect, to oversee the design. The initial idea for this German-based theme town was to construct a stereotypical Weimar village.[5] At first, reports den Hartog, 'the clients and authorities wanted a medieval German town with a clock tower, gabled roofs and half-timbered facades like the Black Forest. They even wanted Germans to run the shops!'[6] These wishes were only partially fulfilled. Anting, like Thames Town, has some overt signs of its 'themed' identity (the memorial sculptures to Goethe and Schiller for example). It also tries to encode a simulated history. 'The circular shape of the new core suggests it was fortified during the medieval era and grew organically over the years.'[7] Yet, for the most part, the final design veers way off script. 'Instead of faking old architectures,' den Hartog explains, 'Albert Speer & Partners opted to reinterpret the international Bauhaus style as well as the modern thinking of Walter Gropius and Mies van der Rohe.'[8] Their plans were influenced by the ideas of the New Urbanists, who stress public neighbourhood squares and pedestrian-friendly streets. They placed a high value on sustainability, hoping for high-quality buildings that conserved energy. The idea was to use Anting New Town to display the excellence of German engineering techniques. For the architects and urban planners, writes Dieter Hassenpflug in an illuminating article comparing Shanghai's suburban developments, 'Anting revives the possibility of modernism.' It was a city that Speer would have built in Germany, were it still possible to build like that there.[9]

Reality, unsurprisingly, diverged from these preconceived ideas, and the attempt to impose a town from elsewhere collided with local conditions. The inevitable result was a hodgepodge: 'Germany with Chinese Characteristics'. In part this was due to shoddy standards in material and workmanship. Cheap Chinese builders untrained in skilful German techniques had no hope of meeting the ideal for sustainable, energy-efficient architecture that the planners designed for. Instead, the buildings in Anting showed signs of decay almost as soon as they were complete. An even greater difficulty was that Anting was planned according to the European tradition of an open city, while the socio-cultural norms of China demand that each neighbourhood be closed off. A space intended to be free of barriers, therefore, has now been segmented into fragments, a patchwork of micro-communities each with their own gate and guard. In Anting New Town, writes, Dieter Hassenpflug:

the principle of the inclusive city was implanted naively into an exclusive cultural context. Thus, the inclusion staggers across the exclusion. There has been too little recognition of the fact that, in China, the residential unit belongs to the family and community, commerce and market however to the open city. Accepting this dual structure would be the precondition for a successful transposition of spatial competence from Germany to China.[10]

More seriously still, the foreign architects didn't understand the Chinese tradition of orienting all houses towards the sun. This principle is so vital to Chinese homeowners that the developers insisted on altering the layout of the city, which was originally intended to be built around a central market square. The planned east-west buildings were never constructed. Instead, Chinese architects changed the floor plans to ensure that the main rooms all had windows facing south.

The tendency for Chinese builders to pick and choose, selecting from blueprints as they see fit, is often frustrating for foreign architects and planners. But the problem lies just as much with the outsiders who are blind to the merits of localisation. 'Most Western firms consider sustainability a Western feature,' notes den Hartog. Yet while 'much criticism has been voiced concerning a lack of sustainability in China, in fact, the Western model is the least sustainable'.[11] In facing their homes to the south, Chinese take advantage of the sun's heat. They save on electricity by putting on a jacket rather than use heating, make frequent use of solar water heaters and hang their laundry out to dry. 'Having all homes face south,' argues den Hartog, 'is thus essentially a form of sustainable housing.'[12] To emphasise his argument on the merits of globalisation, Hartog quotes Wu Jiang, former vice director of the Urban Planning Administration Bureau of Shanghai:

China urbanises rapidly and needs help, also from abroad. But why do most foreign architects see China as a white paper? They give us punk that they don't even dare to present in their own countries… China is not a white paper! It has a 5,000-year-old culture! To be able to make a good design you must understand how people live here. You cannot make your ideal utopia.[13]

In some ways Thames Town—no less odd and artificial—has been far more successful (remember the busload of brides). Atkins, the British design firm, was better able to adapt to the client's desires and their plans were flexible enough to accommodate local preferences. The new town was intentionally designed with the Chinese use of open and closed spaces and is made up of distinct neighbourhoods with localised, south-facing, villas and apartments. 'Thames Town cannot be compared to Anting New Town,' Hassenpflug contends. 'Anting is a project brimming with idealism—in this respect, it is typically German. It wants to be authentic, make the world a better place, indicate solutions for problems—and, incidentally, demonstrate the German art of engineering, adored everywhere.'[14] Thames Town counters this German idealism with Anglo-Saxon pragmatism. Its 'Ye Olde Englishe' deliberately conforms to a dream held in the imagination of the Chinese. 'You want the image of an English city? Nothing easier than that! The client loves the charm of the baroque? Got it!'[15] Recently, even the church seems to have found a use. For many years the main doors of the cathedral were bolted shut. The walls gave off a hollow sound, which made one suspect that the cathedral was nothing but façade. In 2011, however, suddenly the building was opened. Inside were stained glass and pews. Women stood by a table near the entrance advertising weddings services that they promised were to be held soon.

As an exercise in speculative real estate, Anting is a success. All the villas are sold and the rising prices reflect buyer confidence. Though the stores, restaurants and cafes all have hopeful signs that read 'coming soon', the town is eerily empty. Street signs direct the virtual pedestrians to a school and a hotel, but though the signs are up, the buildings are not. In the vast town square the buildings—a church, a town hall, a cultural centre—stand waiting for occupants that few could have thought would have ever arrived. Who are the imagined churchgoers of the Shanghai suburbs? What form of government would ever occupy the town hall? Today the main residents are the ubiquitous security guards, who dutifully follow the tour groups as they stare at each other passing by, awed by the post-apocalyptic feel of one of China's many ghost towns.

Almost all of Shanghai's most ambitious suburban developments have suffered a similar fate. In Luodian, at the model Swedish town, a clock tower rings out on an empty square. In 2009 Thames Town's official web-page offered 'news', already three years old, promising a 'commercial area'; a school where 'the authentic English learning style is assiduously promoted and cultivated'; a supermarket that 'stocks goods and supplies of greater variety and appeal'; the 'personalised services of the clinic'; and a hotel that 'gives everyone a chance to experience for themselves the unique flavour of the English way of life'. Five years on and few of these show any signs of materialising. Instead, chipped bricks and decaying roofs are the symptoms of overhasty construction and of buildings that have remained vacant for too long. Throughout the theme towns the occasional line of hanging laundry suggest signs of squatting (probably from the guards and gardeners who work there during the day).

One of the most potent critiques of the foreign-themed satellite towns comes from the Qingpu district, the most successful of the nine new towns. Qingpu's themed ethnicity is Chinese. In addition to this somewhat twisted concession to localisation, the district benefited enormously from the enlightened leadership of Sun Jiwei, who took over as Qingpu vice chief in 2002. Since then Qingpu has become famous for innovative architecture that reflects—as well as modernises—the cultural heritage of the locale. Sun came to Qingpu from his job as chair of the construction committee for Shanghai's central Luwan district, where he had helped oversee Xintiandi. A graduate of Tongji University's architecture school, Sun already recognised the importance of good buildings. The enormous success of the downtown project, however, further reinforced his belief in the value of urban heritage. Under Sun, Qingpu pursued a policy of 'identity through preservation' luring foreign as well as Chinese practitioners to engage in architectural experimentation that could modernise traditional Chinese architecture. Ben Wood created Cambridge Water Town, a residential village just outside Qingpu's water town of Zhujiajiao. Celebrated architect Qingyun Ma of MADA s.p.a.m. designed a community, shopping plaza and central green space in Qingpu, Yichun Liu constructed the award-winning Xiayu Kindergarten and Liu Jiakun the prize-winning Exhibition Centre. Qingpu thus shows that even in the construction of suburban fantasies, modernising tradition works better than hijacking cultures from afar.

Garden cities

Urbanisation in modern times is marked by two competing tendencies—congestion and dispersion. In conjunction with the rise of the great metropolis came an ardent desire for its dissolution. The cities of the industrial age were dynamic but dismal places, filled with squalor, pollution, poverty and disease. Peter Hall follows the Victorian poet James Thompson in referring to urban centres of the nineteenth century as 'The City of Dreadful Night'.[16] Quoting extensively from clergyman Andrew Mearns, who wrote vividly of the London slums of the late 1800s, Hall repeats graphic descriptions of 'tens of thousands crowded together', 'courts reeking with poisonous and malodorous gases', 'rotten staircases and dark and filthy passages swarming with vermin'.[17] While millions were drawn to the opportunities, freedom and culture that only living in a city could offer, the attraction to the city coincided with a profound repulsion against urban life. Alongside the overcrowding of the urban core came the yearning to flee. 'The modern suburb,' writes Ted Fishman 'was a direct result of unprecedented urban growth.'[18] Even Howard Kunstler, suburbia's most searing critic, admits that 'the spread of slums, hypergrowth and the congestion of manufacturing cities, the noise and stench of the industrial process, debased urban life all over the Western world and led to a great yearning for escape'.[19]

The story of the suburbs often begins with Ebenezer Howard, even though those who know his work best insist that his vision is distinct—even opposed—to the typical manifestations of contemporary suburbia. Howard was, by all accounts a modest man. He worked for most of his life in England as a stenographer. Yet, from this humble clerk emerged a monograph of enormous influence. According to the famous urban theorist Lewis Mumford, Ebenezer Howard's *The Garden Cities of Tomorrow* has done more than any other single book to guide the modern town planning movement and alter its objectives.'[20]

Howard maintained that the industrial cities of the late nineteenth century were unlivable and that most people preferred the relative purity of country life. He fervently believed that, 'large cities had no place in the society of the future'.[21] 'These crowded cities have done their work,' he adamantly declared, 'human society and the beauty of nature are meant to be enjoyed together.'[22] Yet, Howard's vision did not entail a simple return to rural life. Unlike the anarchists who influenced him, Howard recognised the allure of the metropolis and was sensitive to the pleasures and opportunities it offered. He also understood the unappealing hardships of life in the country. His solution was to imagine a future world which fused urban activity with the 'health and sanity' of the rural village. 'Town and country must be married,' Howard declared, 'and out of the joyous union will spring a new hope, a new life, a new civilisation.'[23] Garden cities, then, were never intended as satellite towns or bedroom communities. They were not meant to supplement the cities but to replace them. In Howard's vision the 'great cities would shrink into insignificance as their people desert them for a new way of life'.[24]

Howard proposed his alternative civilisation with both text and diagrams. He imagined an ideal society composed of small communities of about 30,000 people, all participating in the dream of co-operative living. The garden cities were to be supported by small business and agriculture, surrounded by a perpetual green belt and filled with the volunteer life and culture of a small town. They were to be relatively dense and built around a downtown core. Howard was never himself an advocate of urban sprawl. 'I must utter a warning against those who mistake Howard's programme for one of breaking down the distinction of town and country and turning them into an amorphous suburban mass,' writes Lewis Mumford in his celebrated introduction to the 1965 reprinted edition of *The Garden Cities of Tomorrow*:

Howard had no such end in mind; indeed the whole project is an attempt to guard against its happening ... the Garden City, as conceived by Howard, is not a loose indefinite sprawl of individual houses with immense open spaces over the whole landscape: it is rather a compact, rigorously confined urban grouping ... The Garden City, is not a suburb but the antithesis of the suburb.[25]

Howard was greatly concerned with the practicality of his plans and worked hard to have his ideas realised. The first and most famous Garden City arose in the early years of the twentieth century, when the architects Parker and Unwin built the towns of Letchworth and Welwyn in England. Following these initial experiments, multiple new towns in Europe and America sought to establish an urban experience based on the Garden City model. Yet, despite the proliferation of these planned communities, the future has not unfolded as Howard envisioned. Far from threatening the great metropolis, Garden Cities most commonly act as satellite towns revolving around megacities that have grown increasingly dense. Nor have they succeeded in dominating the zones between town and country. Instead of compact towns—formed and limited—what has prevailed on the fringes of the metropolis is something else entirely: urban sprawl.

The car

The most potent force pushing people out of the city was not, as it turns out, the idealised dreams of the planner but, rather, the decentralising impetus of new technologies. H. G. Wells recognised and recorded this already in 1901 in his collection of prophetic essays entitled 'Anticipations'. Writing at the dawn of the new century, Wells predicted that revolutions in communication and transportation—the railway, motorised vehicle and telephone—would combine with the inherent desire for light and space, and unleash a potent centrifugal force whose power would disintegrate the city. In his essay 'The Probable Diffusion of Cities', Wells forecast that the 'whirlpool concentrations' of the great metropolis would soon be obliterated. 'These great cities are no permanent maelstroms,' he wrote; the 'present congestion' would not last. 'The limit of the pre-railway city was the limit of man and horse. But already that limit has been exceeded, and each day brings us nearer to the time when it will be thrust outward in every direction with an effect of enormous relief.'[26]

The idea that urban density is doomed by technology's dispersive potential continues to gain strength today. The new technologies of globalisation, it is frequently argued, especially the aeroplane and the internet, have revolutionised both transportation and communication, and made it possible to live and work anywhere. 'It is almost as easy to communicate with ties (both strong and weak) across the globe as across the street,' writes Diana Mok, who has pioneered a study of distance in the internet age.[27] Place, many now believe, has become increasing irrelevant. This apparent sociological trend—the 'death of distance'—is captured by the well-used slogan 'geography is history' that was meant to define the information age.

Yet, despite the predictions, railways (even in their current high-speed form), flights (regardless of how cheap), the ubiquity of cell-phones, even the immensely decentralising power of the internet has—so far at least—occurred in conjunction with a countervailing trend that pushes people together in an ever tightening mass. Notwithstanding the convenience and ubiquity of Skype, Facebook and instant messaging, many people, whether executives, families or friends, find that online communication doesn't come close to matching, never mind replacing, that which occurs when people meet in person. Rather than superseding each other, the internet, phone and face-to-face contact all intertwine to create and nurture social bounds. 'The more people saw each other,' Mok and her co-researchers found, 'the more they spoke on the phone.' Indeed 'despite the advancement in telecommunications face to face contact has increased substantially'.[28] The omnipresence of virtual friends and instant online communication has not at all lessened the need for the hybrid, unpredictable encounters that only highly populated cities can bring.

Though the train, the aeroplane, the phone and the web have grown in conjunction with hyper-dense megacities, there is one technology that has succeeded in dispersing the metropolis; that, of course, is the automobile. The technology of suburbia is the car. 'No other invention has altered urban form more than the internal combustion engine,' wrote Kenneth Jackson in his great study of American suburbia, *Crabgrass Frontier*.[29] Cars need the space that tightly packed cities can't provide. Not only roads, with multiple lanes to drive, but also—even more crucially—parking lots and garages. Urbanist Edward Glaeser spells out the implications in detail:

Nine square feet of road is plenty for a pedestrian walking down Fifth Avenue, and on a busy day, a walker will put up with much less. The Honda Accord, a modest-size car, takes up about a hundred square feet on its own. If that car is going to have a couple of feet around it and several lengths ahead of it, its space needs can easily increase to three or four hundred square feet of highway. The fortyfold increase in space that accompanies the shift from walking to cars explains why so much of the land in car-based cities is given over to highways. And cars don't use up space only when they're hurtling down the asphalt. They also require space when they are standing still.[30]

'Modern sprawl,' Glaeser concludes, 'is the child of the automobile.'[31] Cars are inherently antithetical to urban concentration; they are 'anti-city' machines. The automobile, writes Lewis Mumford, 'annihilates the city whenever it collides with it.'[32]

Nowhere was the revolutionary impact of the car felt more profoundly than America. By 1908 Ford's Model T brought the motor vehicle to the masses. Ford promised to 'build a car for the great multitude' that was 'big enough for a family' but cheap enough so that it could be purchased by anyone making a decent salary to 'enjoy with his family the blessing of hours of pleasure in God's great open spaces.'[33] 'There was nothing like it before in history', writes Kunstler; 'a machine that promised liberation from the daily bondage of space.'[34] The passion for car ownership was supported by deliberate government policies. General taxation was used to bolster private transportation through the massive funding of roads and highways. This state subsidy of new roads produced a new urban form. Cars opened up vast spaces off the old networks of public transportation where cheap land was plentiful. As larger homes became increasingly affordable the American government bolstered the dream of home ownership through the development of new financial mechanisms to pay for them. As Andrew Kirby and Ali Modarres write in their 2010 special issue on suburbia, in America, 'The postwar suburbs constituted a completely innovative social experiment, in which Federal programs brought about explosive levels of construction and migration to new subdivisions. Highway construction and mortgage loans completely altered the way in which homes were produced and how Americans consumed them.'[35] The 'centerless city'[36] pioneered in California soon become a model for the entire nation. By the end of the twentieth century, the automobile had transformed America into a society defined by its garages, drive-throughs, shopping malls and suburban communities. As Robert Fishman has written, 'If the 19th century could be called the Age of Great Cities, post-1945 America would appear to be the Age of Great Suburbs.'[37]

The culture of suburbia

Urban plans, government policy and technological determinacy each played a role in the city's outward spread. Yet, there is also a crucial cultural impetus to the story of suburbia. In his captivating book *Bourgeois Utopia*, author Robert Fishman explores this history in fascinating detail. The suburbs, argues Fishman, particularly as they have developed in England and America, are the collective creation and architectural emblem of the modern middle class, 'its greatest and most lasting achievement ... The true center of any bourgeois society, is the middle class house. If you seek the monuments of the bourgeoisie, go to the suburbs and look around.'[38]

Suburbia, Fishman shows, arose as a deliberate contrast to the intense intermixing of the pre-modern city, a hybrid space where people lived where they worked, and men and women, young and old, rich and poor actively intermingled. In the pre-modern city, enterprise occurred in the home and business was a family affair. The grocer lived above the shop, and the banker counted money in the parlour. 'The typical merchant's house was,' according to Fishman, 'surprisingly open to the city. Commercial life flowed in freely, so that virtually every room had some business as well as familial function. From the front parlor where customers were entertained and deals transacted, to the upper stories where the apprentices slept and the basement where goods were stored, there was little purely domestic space.'[39]

In pre-modern societies a combination of physical proximity and vast social distance allowed rich and poor to live side by side. 'One of the paradoxes of urban history,' writes Fishman provocatively, 'is that the extremely unequal cities of the eighteenth century tolerated a great measure of close physical contact between rich and poor, whereas the more "equal" cities of the nineteenth and twentieth century were increasingly zoned to eliminate such contacts.'[40] In the earlier metropolis there was no district devoted to a single function or class. 'The wealthy might, at best, occupy large town-houses that fronted on the principal streets,' Fishman explains, 'but the poor inevitably crowded into the narrow alleyways and courtyards that existed literally in the backyards of the rich.'[41] This radical intermingling of class, it is worth noting, is precisely the situation of Shanghai today.

In Europe, this began to change in Manchester, the city at the heart of the industrial age, when the newly emerging middle class sought to distinguish itself from its own recent past. In nineteenth-century Manchester, the suburbs became the 'universal remedy'[42] for the frequent and intimate contact between classes—'a closeness that the bourgeoisie had come to fear'. Eager to separate themselves from the ranks of the poor out of which they themselves had just risen, the new middle class established a pattern of clearly distinct zones: an urban core; an intermediate factory zone; and a residential suburbia. The suburbs are propelled by both fear and desire, Fishman argues, and are defined primarily by what they exclude: 'all industry, most commerce except for enterprises that specifically serve a residential area, and all lower class residents (except for servants)'.[43] Suburbia, as the central stage for bourgeois life is, therefore, intrinsically paradoxical, 'reflecting the alienation of the middle classes from the urban-industrial world they themselves were creating'.[44]

The middle-class desire for clearly marked boundaries soon infiltrated private life. Eager to differentiate itself from the working class, from which they had only recently arisen, the new social group strived to separate work from the domestic sphere. Before the industrial age, family members were deeply immersed in the life of the city. The family was an economic unit and women and children formed a vital part of the workforce. The invention of suburbia created a necessary distance from this economic model, coinciding with the creation of a nuclear family that was removed and 'protected from the free flow of strangers that constitute urban existence'.

This culture of suburban domesticity was strengthened by the Evangelical movement, which saw urban life as immoral, and preached that 'salvation depended on separating the woman's sacred world of family and children from the profane world of the metropolis'. By the eighteenth century, Fishman tells of 'a new intensity in the relations between mother, father and children'. The family turned inwards, focusing 'on mutual intimacy and child rearing'.There was spectacular innovation 'in young people's clothes, toys, books, sports, music and art especially designed for the first time to suit children's interests and promote their happiness'. 'The eighteenth century did not invent love between children and parents,' Fishman concludes, 'but it flourished then (at least amongst the bourgeoisie and gentry) as never before. Where children had been ignored, harshly punished, or treated as small adults, the eighteenth century English bourgeoisie saw childhood as a specific stage in life that requires special protection and love.'[45]

Middle-class culture, then, placed a heavy emphasis on a sacred and separate domestic sphere that was especially well suited to the suburbs. This culture was so successful at propagating itself that by the end of the twentieth century it was not the life of the urbanite but rather the suburban home, the main stage for the closed and interior space of the family, that had gained a position at the centre of the modern world and reshaped the visions of the future metropolis. America, as the undisputed leader of the politics, economics and culture of globalisation, had become a 'suburban nation'. This implied not only a particular way of building cities, but also, more crucially, a way of life. Suburban culture with its lawns and fences, soccer games and strip malls had become, at least in the Western world, fundamental to the culture of modernity.

Suburban Shanghai

What then of Shanghai? Is the growth of this twenty-first century megacity following a similar path towards dispersion? Are the same patterns of suburban sprawl being reproduced? Is the current outward spread of the city compelled by the same technological and socio-economic motivations? Most importantly, does the newly emerging Chinese middle class share the dream of suburbia? Do they desire the same spacious homes and manicured lawns? Will issues like safety and schooling, convenience and crime play out in a similar fashion? In short, will the modernity that is currently being forged in China's new cities replicate the same forms of exclusion and domesticity, the same patterns of class and family life, the same extensive blueprint of the built environment, that fuelled the growth of the suburbs elsewhere?

Until the 1980s cities in China were strictly separated from the countryside. Maoist policies insisted on a sharp division between urban and rural dwellers. This ensured that, until just a few decades ago, urban centres in China were tightly compacted, demarcated with discrete boundaries that distinguished them clearly from the surrounding farmlands. Indeed the term 'suburb', write Zhou Yixing and John Logan in their contribution to *Urban China in Transition*, 'typically referred to agricultural towns outside of cities'.[46]

This rigid distinction between the city and its outside was coupled during the Mao years with a deliberate neglect of the urban landscape, which resulted in a remarkably dense metropolis. By the time Shanghai was allowed to participate in the era of openness and reform, the city was packed. Locals who lived in Shanghai during this period tell of streets crowded almost to the point of impassability and buildings, especially houses, crammed full. Families of multiple generations lived together in impossibly tight spaces. Buildings that were designed as single family homes were carved and re-carved. In the typical *shikumen* homes the extra landing at the top of the staircase—a convenient place for storage—became the dwelling place for an entire family. Still today Shanghai is a relatively dense city. According to research by Dutch urbanist Harry den Hartog, 'some parts of the central city have densities of more than 50,000 residents per km^2 (more than ten times that of Amsterdam)'.[47]

In the 1980s and 1990s, at the beginning of Shanghai's recent rise, urban congestion was viewed as one of the city's most critical problems. Planners, who urgently sought a solution, started to build up, but also, to spread out. In order to decongest the core, people needed to be relocated to the edges. The movement of industry from the core to the periphery actually began as early as the mid-twentieth century. 'Already in 1959,' writes den Hartog, 'Shanghai started to build industrial districts and satellite cities on its fringes or beyond.' Places like Minhang and Wujiang were built in a socialist realist style and—with a nod to Howard—included a green belt that was designed to form a border with downtown. Yet throughout the 1960s, 1970s and into the 1980s, though a few new factory towns continued to be built, all system-atic plans for suburban growth were halted due to the tumultuous upheavals brought by the Cultural Revolution. Until it reopened its doors after Mao's death, Shanghai, like all Chinese cities, was primarily organised by the *dan-*

wei system (large work units that organised housing, schooling, hospital care and other social services for their employees). These *danwei*s were, for the most part, located inside the urban core. 'In Shanghai nearly 60 per cent of the state-owned factories were located in the central part of the city, and almost 70 per cent of industrial workers worked and lived there in 1982.'[48] By the end of the 1980s, however, a new, and this time urgent and comprehensive, wave of industrial relocation had begun. The scale and speed of this urban transition was massive. Among the many districts to be utterly transformed was Baoshan, which is administered by the Baoshan Steel Corporation, one of the city's largest SOEs (State Owned Enterprises); Jiading, which specialises in the auto industry; and the new university town of Songjiang, which houses seven new campuses and more than 100,000 students, instructors and personnel.

The transfer of industry away from the city centre where land is most valuable occurred simultaneously with a mass relocation of residential buildings. The old, dense network of housing that constituted the inner landscape of Puxi, came to be seen as an obstacle to the development of the core. In Shanghai, each new high-rise, subway stop or shopping mall thus involves, first of all, the people already living there, who are standing in the way of the potential development, being persuaded—or forced—to move out. Most of the old residents living downtown, especially in the most desirable locations, were Shanghai natives. Their mass migration from the centre to the edges is expressed by a sardonic joke among locals who insist that it is now only the outer fringes of the city that are truly Shanghainese. Inside the inner ring road, in the downtown core, they say, the language is English since that's where all the foreigners settle. Between the middle and inner ring road, where investors from all over China come to purchase property, the language is Mandarin (or *Putonghua*, the common tongue). *Shanghaihua*, the local dialect, is only used outside the inner ring road, on the far outskirts of town.

Relocation

The centrifugal movement that populates the outskirts of Shanghai, then, is not most commonly driven, as it was in America, by a voluntary outward spread to suburbia, but rather by the directed force of relocation. This issue of forcibly shifting people from one place to another is one of the most contentious in contemporary China. Undoubtedly there are those who welcome the move. Shanghai's old run-down homes (or 'shabby sheds', as they are often called) are difficult places to live. Spaces are tiny and cramped— cold and dark in winter, and stiflingly humid in the heat. Kitchens—and more importantly bathrooms—are shared and there is often little running water. Walls are thin and the cosy neighbourhood feel, while offering certain benefits, can also be intensely irritating. There is virtually no possibility of privacy. Many are eager for the opportunity to trade in their small spaces downtown for a new, roomy apartment in the suburbs.[49]

Nevertheless, complaints are common, bitter and growing increasingly fierce. The new communities are too remote, far from work and family, and lack all the conveniences of daily life. Land deals are riddled with corruption. Compensation is often disputed and there is no real recourse to justice. Since so much property was seized during the Cultural Revolution, those that are compensated often have only a dubious claim on ownership, and renters, most often poor migrants, are offered nothing when their homes are destroyed.[50]

Throughout China the issue of relocation is now commonly coupled with stories of terror and violence: Grandmothers being bulldozed in their homes, families being forced out at midnight, lawyer-activists being locked away. Author Yu Hua sees in relocation evidence that Mao's famous slogan, 'a revolution is not a dinner party', still holds. Urbanisation produces 'large scale demolitions' that make Chinese cities look as though they 'have been targets of a bombing raid', he writes. Scenes of 'utter devastation' betray 'a developmental model saturated with revolutionary violence of the Cultural Revolution type'.[51] The homes of those who refuse to budge are known as 'nail houses'. They remain even after everything around them has been destroyed. In the lead up to 2010 World Expo one was left standing in a torn-down area near Shanghai's old city. The woman of the house could be spotted, sweeping her front gate amidst the rubble, like a character in some absurdist play. She would rant at passersby, railing against the injustice of the compensation package that she refused to accept.

In China 'chai' (拆), the character meaning torn down or disassembled, is one of the primary signs of city life. Throughout the city it is spray-painted in red on the sides of old buildings in half-demolished neighbourhoods that are about to be torn down. The symbol has become so ubiquitous that the Chinese, who take a notorious delight in puns, now refer to their country as 'Chai—Na'. 拆is a potent visual marker for the high-speed intensity of urbanisation and has become a popular motif in art shows. It even featured in the children's cartoon *Xi Yang Yang* (China's state-supported Mickey Mouse), when the enemies of the hero 'pleasant sheep', wanted to use their land for an amusement park, and stamped the sheep village for destruction.

Increasingly, however, families, neighbourhoods and sometimes whole villages are fighting back against property seizures they deem unfair. Many district governments and developers now see the process of moving people too troublesome and expensive, and many projects stall or even fail because the process of relocation is too difficult. This is particularly true in Shanghai and it is arguably the case that—in the downtown core at least—the era of mass relocation has, for the most part, come to an end.

Speculation

A second highly localised factor crucial to the growth of Shanghai's suburbia is the highly lucrative market in real estate. In Shanghai discussing housing prices is like talking about the weather. With high saving rates and few channels for investment, the Chinese buy apartments like others buy gold. Buildings are viewed as just a place to park your money and a huge number sit empty. Locals say that they serve as a home to the ghosts. Buying is fuelled by speculation, which so far has proved immensely profitable. People are so accustomed to prices moving in only one direction that in 2011, when developers in the suburbs of Jiading sought to slash prices to attract buyers, the existing customers got together and rioted. In the meantime there is a huge gap at the bottom of the market where demand far outstrips supply. With prices increasing exponentially, first-time buyers find it almost impossible to enter the market. In 2010, a new term *fang nu*, meaning mortgage slave, entered the popular lexicon. The problem is especially acute for men since, in Shanghai, owning a home is generally seen as a prerequisite for luring a bride. Popular culture captured the complex obsession with housing in a hit TV serial called *Wo Ju* (or Snail House). The show, one of the most realistic dramas to ever play on Chinese television, told the story of two sisters who lived in a fictional town made to resemble Shanghai. Much of the drama centred on the attempt to buy an apartment. One sister's desperate search for housing led her to have an affair with a corrupt official. Most viewers thought it was a pretty clever strategy. Before the first season was over, the government got nervous and the show was banned.

Underlying the revolutionary transformation in the built environment, then, is the enormous force of the property market. The market began in 1988 with the passing of the Land Management Law, now encoded in the constitution, which separated ownership rights from use rights. Since the late 1980s property inside the cities has been available to be bought and sold for a fixed period of time (from twenty years for commercial properties to seventy years for residential ones). This marketisation of land—all of which is owned by the government—has introduced enormous profits into the building of cities and is critical to the Chinese model of state capitalist growth.

In conjunction with the establishment of the land-leasing market, the government simultaneously began selling off public housing to private tenants. In this initial period, homes were sold at highly favourable rates. Most Shanghainese—who are notoriously shrewd at business—bought as many as they could afford. Two decades later—despite all the warning signs of a bubble—the investment had paid off enormously. Besides a few short, not very sharp dips, prices have risen at astounding rates; by 2010 housing in Shanghai was almost as expensive as cities like New York and London, despite the fact that most residents in Shanghai still earned only a fraction of the typical wages of the developed world. Housing purchases that were made in the late 1980s and 1990s when the market was just starting to open and prices were still very cheap help to explain an apparent economic mystery of Shanghai. How can it be that people whose wages are so relatively low can have such enormous purchasing power and high saving rates? It is stunning, considering the average salary, to see so many Shanghai residents treat technology as fashion, buying a new phone with every season, spending exorbitant amounts on luxury goods and crowding into the city's innumerable restaurants. This is only possible because so many residents have cashed in on the property boom, buying homes often without mortgages. Shanghainese have money to spend because so many own their own places (or at least have parents who do). Real estate has become the basic economic foundation of the city. Shanghai's economy, it can thus be argued, is based fundamentally on the project of building Shanghai.

Once established, the market in land quickly came to dominate China's politics, causing a fundamental shift in the Chinese state. The decentralisation of the political landscape it engendered challenges, as was noted in the discussion of Pudong, the common perception that urbanisation in China is being led by 'state centred growth'. Since land is intrinsically territorial it tends to empower local and district authorities. While the central government owns all land in China, explains Thomas Campanella, 'responsibility for the management and administration of urban land was decentralized in the reform era to local municipalities—and this included authority to lease development rights to that land'.[52] Local governments spread ever-outwards, eagerly selling land for development, and using the money to pay for infrastructure, which in turn increases the value of the land. Everyone wants in on the game and there is lots of room for multiple players: government on every level, state-owned development companies, entrepreneurs—many from the greater Chinese region—as well as regional and local entrepreneurs. Suburban growth, then, is a manifestation of political as well as spatial decentralisation.

In other parts of the world suburban communities have grown up gradually. Infrastructure has tended to come first, with towns emerging slowly around it. But things work differently here. As a result Shanghai's new towns are locked in a dead end cycle that is extremely difficult to escape. No one is willing to open a store or provide a service when there are so few people around. But few are willing to move when there are no stores and services close by. A prime example is a huge new project in Zhujiajiao where a large community is filled with model units that have been renovated to house imagined 'model citizens'. The designer pads—with poured concrete bars, sleek lighting and sunken tubs—are meant for artisans who could use them as live-work space. The idea is to turn the whole town into a functioning congregation of artist-entrepreneurs. The developer sought to jump start the process by reserving some units to be sold under market price and stated his willingness to help with mortgages if buyers promise to move there and make the town their home. The aim is to try and establish rules to guard against speculation, since the barrenness it brings so often leads to the death of the town. It is a struggle, however, to find the right concept that will lure in this ideal, still virtual population. Should the village be a place for corporate getaways, an artist retreat, a tourist centre? Would a big weekend farmers' market entice? What about a special place for wedding parties? How about an old age home?

Twentieth century modernity, led by the middle class of America, chose life in the suburbs as the sought-for ideal. The city's dispersion has been so complete that theorists like Fishman argue that communities on the edges have created a new urban form:

The most important feature of postwar American development has been the almost simultaneous decentralization of housing, industry, specialized services and office jobs; the consequent breakaway of the urban periphery from a central city it no longer needs, and the creation of a decentralized environment that nevertheless possesses all the economic and technological dynamism we associate with the city. This phenomenon is not suburbanization but the creation of a new city.[53]

Will China share in this new creation? So far it seems doubtful. While relocation and land speculation push the population outward, as yet there is little evidence of a true suburban culture taking root. Few seek to flee the urban core. Chinese tend to love the hustle and bustle of city life and the convenience of downtown living is highly valued. Housing prices are highest inside the inner ring road and, unlike most cities in America, in Shanghai many of the most sought-after schools are downtown. Professional families who own villas in the suburbs tend to prefer their much smaller apartments in the city. When asked about their suburban property many will claim that they intend them as weekend homes, but they rarely, if ever, go. Homes are renovated and furnished but many just sit there, gathering dust. In China, as Thomas Campanella notes, 'there has been no rampant street crime to run from, nor any deep-rooted philosophy of anti-urbanism to coax urban flight. The city in China has never been stigmatized the way American cities were in the postwar era.'[54] The inner city has problems, of course: traffic, pollution and the high price of housing are common complaints. 'But even if the air is cleaner and there are more trees and open spaces on the suburban fringe, the city is still the star about which things orbit, the political and administrative hub of the metropolitan universe. Unlike American suburbs, those in China are literally *sub*-urban: that is subordinate to the city.'[55] Those suburban areas that work best, moreover, are the ones that are most like cities, places like central Qingpu or the old town of Songjiang, which have crowded streets and alleys and lively, dense downtown shopping hubs. Even the suburbs themselves are, at least by American standards, not very suburban, as Campanella points out:

Chinese 'villa' complexes (*bie shu qu*), strikingly similar to gated McMansion-type developments, began appearing on the outskirts of major cities in the early 1990s. But far more numerous in China are gated housing estates of clustered mid-to-high-rise apartment buildings, which have become the basic unit of suburban sprawl in China. This is, of course, sprawl with Chinese characteristics—much denser and much more 'urban' than anything in suburban America.[56]

In her profile of the well-known author Wang Meng featured in *Tide Players*, Jianying Zha writes of China's inherent aversion to the suburbs. Wang, she writes, describes his many visits to America by noting the intense self-regard and the loneliness of American life. He is struck, in particular, by the solitary individual who lives in a big house or on a ranch in the middle of nowhere. The Chinese, he observed, are not fit for such a way of life. Wang admits to finding solitude unbearable and gets homesick easily. 'China has all kinds of problems ... but it doesn't have loneliness and boredom, because Chinese life is always *renao*! *Renao* (热闹) means, literally, hot and noisy.'[57]

Perhaps attitudes will change and sometime in the not too distant future neighbourhoods on the metropolitan edges will reach a tipping point. Maybe the new middle class will choose suburbia yet. Car ownership, the key pre-requisite, is increasing exponentially and once people own cars they tend to avoid the intense congestion of the urban core. It is also possible, however, that the property bubble will pop and speculative buying will no longer mask the desolate nature of these suburban zones. In neo-modern Shanghai, however, even failure is uncertain. Derelict cities, most notoriously Detroit, have shown us what happens in America when urban zones collapse. In Shanghai, however, we still don't know what it looks like when cities wane. In China the ultimate shape of urban failure is still largely unknown. Indeed, it is possible that some form of malfunction—which invariably opens new possibilities—is precisely what is needed for Shanghai's edges to finally come to life.

8

THE FLOATING CITY

Neal Stephenson's science fiction novel *The Diamond Age* contains one of the most fully elaborated portrayals of Shanghai futurism. The book is set in the twenty-first century and depicts a world entirely transformed by a revolution in nanotechnology. The colossal technological mutation has caused a radical transformation in the socioeconomic landscape. Nation States have disappeared. The only territories left that matter are hyper-dense urban concentrations. At the centre of the novel is Shanghai.

In Stephenson's vision, the city has been virtually cut off from the rest of China, which is being ravaged by a Boxer-like rebellion led by a group called 'the Fists', whose deeply regressive aim is to search out and destroy the 'nanotech feeds'. Shanghai's Old City has undergone a cultural implosion and now forms its own separate district, which is exclusively Chinese and is ruled by strict adherence to Confucian law. Outside these borders, however, Shanghai has continued on its trajectory as a modern, cosmopolitan metropolis. The city forms part of a new entity called the 'Chinese Coastal Republic' and is oriented ever more outwards, towards the sea. With *The Diamond Age*, Stephenson thus allows, at least virtually, for Shanghai to finally fulfil its (not so) unconscious desire and follow the SARs of Hong Kong and Macau in unleashing itself from the country and becoming its own autonomous entity that plugs directly into the rest of the world.

The story is set in a nanotech landscape, in which a 'causeway' links Shanghai to a cluster of artificial islands that hovers just offshore. These belong exclusively to certain tribes—or phyles—the groups that form the basis of the new social order. Instead of being brought together by a shared ethnicity or a loyalty to the state, people gather according to a shared culture. It was realised, reflects one of the main protagonists, describing the evolution of the new socio-political arrangement, that 'while people were not *genetically* different they were *culturally* as different as they could possibly be'.[1]

The wealthiest of these phyles, called the neo-Victorians, live in a community suspended 'a mile above sea water' that looks out over the buildings of the old urban landscape. They call their home Atlantis/Shanghai. All the other phyles freely traffic in the 'Pudong Economic Zone', where every tribe has its own skyscraper. In this sense the city is unchanged, it remains, as it is today, a nucleus for drifters passing through.

Stephenson's vision of twenty-first century Shanghai is pervaded by flood. Everything is waterlogged in the 'Yangtze's sodden delta', and much of the action takes place on beaches, boardwalks and boats. Narrow ravines crisscross Pudong's 'floating mediatronic skyscrapers'. The only way for the city to escape submergence is by becoming airborne:

The nanotechnological trick of making sturdy structures that were lighter than air had come along just at the right time, as all of the last paddies were being replaced by immense concrete foundations, and a canopy of new construction had bloomed above the first-generation undergrowth of seventy and eighty story buildings. This new architecture was naturally large and ellipsoidal typically consisting of a huge neo-rimmed ball impaled on a spike, so Pudong was bigger and denser a thousand feet above the ground than it was at sea level.[2]

In the fictional site of a waterlogged, waterborne city, Stephenson offers a conception of the future metropolis that functions not as a territory for permanent settlement but, instead, as an inherently unsettled plane upon which peoples and cultures traverse. In this dream of tomorrow, it is the metropolis itself that floats. Though he never mentions them, Stephenson's imagined metropolis, which functions as host to a continuous flow, resonates with China's vast 'floating population' and the singular form of urbanisation that the movement of their lives produce.

The periphery

The trip from downtown Shanghai is a long one. Up to an hour and a half on subways and buses. The way is marked by the radical heterogeneity of the urban periphery: giant megamalls and gated villa communities; forests of high-rises; Disneyfied theme parks and tourist attractions; and new development zones filled with an industrial core that has now been relocated to the

156

city's outer shell. The infrastructure is astounding. Beautifully paved roads with well-marked signs in English and Chinese rival the richest neighbourhoods of the developed West.

The brand new bus is equipped with bilingual announcements (though there are few foreigners in the area, the voice announces each bus stop in English). The city bleeds into the countryside as the rural encroaches on the urban (and vice versa). Just off the main highway, traces of the old water-towns remain. Farmers grow their vegetables in patches of muddy earth. Agricultural land mutates into an urban street lined with dilapidated apartment buildings that host small ground floor businesses: a mattress shop; a video arcade; garages advertising 'modern machine parts' where people stop to fix their scooters; and shops stuffed with random odds and ends. Outside, rows of street snacks and vegetable stalls serve the newly-urbanising population. Just off the main roads, the streets revert back to canals. Here, in the outer reaches of the metropolis, is the frontline of history. This is how a city arrives.

Shanghai's edges are home to millions of migrant workers who flock to the megacity from all over China. Statistics vary, but a commonly cited figure is that out of Shanghai's population of approximately twenty-five million, more than nine million are migrants. Though far from home, these new sojourners tend to cluster according to region, replicating their village communities in the micro-neighbourhoods of the vast urban space. In the villages and small towns of Anhui, Hunan or Sichuan the pattern is the same. One person leaves first, finds a job, and then recruits family and friends. They work in the nearby factories and industrial parks, as entrepreneurs in the informal economy or as cleaners and babysitters in the gated villa communities and new high rises, that they also help build.

To live, many rent spaces in homes that, not too long ago, housed the old farmers of the area. Today, few locals are interested in cultivating this once rural land. All the young have moved on or been relocated elsewhere. Only the aged remain. Shrewdly, they have all become landlords, taking advantage of a new mode of income brought by the most recent urban residents. Their homes are carved up, divided into rooms which can be rented for hundreds of renminbi each. In the outlying district of Minhang, 'New Citizen Life', a migrant-run NGO, rents out what was once a community hall for local seniors to use as a gathering space for young mothers and their children. A place that not long ago housed only the old, now, once again, belongs to the young.

If developers have trouble filling their latest gated compounds, if the new suburban complexes remain empty and unused, it is because the planners of

Shanghai's edges are failing to take adequate account of the true population of the periphery. Throughout Shanghai there exists an enormous divide between luxurious empty homes and people seeking accommodation at the low end of the market, but the problem is especially acute at the fringes. This is because the relocation of people from the urban centre is only a small fraction of the suburban population. Far more influential are the waves of people floating in from the outside.

An urban planet

The world today is undergoing a mass process of urbanisation on a scale and speed greater than we have ever known. We are becoming, for the first time in history, a mostly urban species. Cities, as urbanist Mike Davis points out, 'will account for virtually all future world population growth'.[3] Megacities (cities of more than eight million) are sprouting everywhere. More spectacular has been the growth of 'hypercities', giant entities of twenty million inhabitants or more.

Almost all of this growth is happening outside the West. 'Ninety five per cent of this final buildout of humanity,' writes Davis, 'will occur in the urban areas of developing countries.'[4] Nowhere is the process more intense than in China. 'China is urbanising at a speed unprecedented in human history,' he notes, 'adding more city dwellers in the 1980s than did all of Europe (including Russia) in the entire nineteenth century.'[5] Those on the move in China today are part of the largest migration in human history 'three times the number of people who emigrated to America from Europe over a century'.[6] In its study of China's urbanisation, McKinsey Global foresees China adding more than 350 million people to its urban population by 2025, and creating 221 cities with over a million people (Europe has thirty-five) and twenty-three cities with a population of over five million. It predicts a change from 572 million city dwellers in 2005 to 926 million in 2025. By 2030 it forecasts that China's urban population will reach the one billion mark.

This process of mass urbanisation recalls the period between the mid-eighteenth and early twentieth century when, in a little over a century, most people in Europe and America left the countryside to make a new life in the city. Author Doug Saunders calls this the 'first great migration'. It was, he writes, 'the greatest surge of rural to urban migration the world has ever seen'.[7] This tremendous movement from the farms to the cities of Europe and America coincided with both industrialisation and economic take-off, and thus laid the foundations for Western modernity with its very particular understanding of time. It is at this point in history, argues author Martin Jacques, that 'the new mentality—the orientation towards change and uncertainty, the belief that the future will be different from the past—slowly moves from the preserve of a few elites to eventually infecting the psyche of the entire population'.[8]

It is tempting to presume that the echo between yesterday and today, between the developed and developing world, is a mere repetition, in which past conditions and experiences are simply reoccurring in another time and place. Yet, implicit in this assumption is the belief that the processes of urbanisation, despite differences in culture, time and space, are necessarily, intrinsically, the same. The underlying supposition, states Jacques succinctly, is that 'there is only one way of being modern'.[9]

Western culture has been extremely successful at framing modernity within the context of its own narratives. Ideas that equate modernisation with westernisation are exceedingly widespread. As a result, there is an implied consensus 'that China will eventually end up—as a result of its modernisation, or as a precondition for it, or a combination of the two—as a Western-style country ... [and] that, in its fundamentals, the world will be little changed by China's rise'.[10]

Among the most critical components of the Western expression of modernity is, as has been argued, its teleological understanding of time. Though the greatest of modernist artists and writers immersed themselves in the tumultuous process of modernisation itself, there was almost always an end point that haunted—or beckoned—up ahead. When considered within the context of cities, this teleological narrative presumes what Liisa Malkki has called, in another context, 'a metaphysics of sedentarism,'[11] which assumes that the process of urbanisation will culminate, ultimately, in settlement. Under this conception China will be modernised once the flow of urbanisation has ceased. Poor peripheral neighbourhoods, which function as transitional zones, will eventually, either be formalised and integrated into the urban core or else fail, and be permanently locked outside. When the movement has reached its limit, when all have become urbanised, when everyone is finally settled, then the future will have arrived. At that point a 'developed', and 'modern' China will reach an end-point similar to Western-style modernity, and the world will not 'be so different from the one we inhabit now'.[12]

Inside China many have shared this belief. From the Qing reformers through the May Fourth movement, the idea has been prevalent that to be modern is inevitably to adopt a Western understanding of time. The current 'China Model,' which is rooted in Marxist-Leninism is, at its core, embedded in this a Western formulation of a linear chronology that is governed by a relative futurism, in which an idealised tomorrow waits, as a destination point on the road up ahead.

When subjected to this temporality, contemporary modernity (modernity 2.0) is locked in a fatal repetition, in which the future is bound to unfold just as it has in the past. Yet the possibility of this recurrence is unlikely:

Western modernity—or modernity as we have hitherto known it—rests, on a relatively small fragment of human experience. In every instance, that experience is either European or comes from Europe, sharing wholly or largely the cultural, political, intellectual, racial and ethnic characteristic of that continent... But as other countries, with very different cultures and histories, and contrasting civilisational inheritances, embark on the process of modernisation, the particularism and exceptionalism of the Western experience will become increasingly apparent.[13]

In contemporary China the process of urbanisation is ongoing. Unlike with past flows of urban migration, the metropolis, so far at least, acts not as an end-point, but is, instead, entwined in a relentless flow between city and countryside which shows little signs of abating any time soon. The city, then, is not necessarily a place of permanent encampment but may rather function as a hub or anchor for a floating population that remains perpetually uprooted. This drift complicates the idea of the city as a fixed and stable terminus. New York, as the epicentre of twentieth-century modernity, was a migrant city, but Shanghai has always been a city of sojourners, determined by people permanently on the move. The future the city creates rests on these floaters and their continuous, transitional flow.

Slums

A stark counterpoint to the suburban dream of a bourgeois utopia made up of villas, lawns and parking garages is the increasing sprawl of shanty-towns that have spread across the urban periphery. This nightmare apparition is compellingly captured by the dystopian vision Mike Davis recorded in his book *Planet of Slums*. 'The majority of the world's urban poor no longer live in inner cities,' writes Davis. 'Since 1970 the larger share of world population growth has been absorbed by slum communities on the periphery of Third World cities.'[14]

Whereas the classic slum was a decaying inner city, the new slums are more typically located on the edge of urban spatial explosions. The horizontal growth of cities like Mexico, Lagos or Jakarta, of course, has been extraordinary, and 'slum sprawl' is as much of a problem in the developing world as suburban sprawl in the rich countries.[15]

Planet of Slums examines the ongoing production of a new hinterland, 'now adjacent to fields, forest or desert [that] may tomorrow become part of a dense metropolitan core'. In the growing urban landscape of the developing world—in Asia, Africa and Latin America—a thick forest of makeshift housing sprawls outward like a 'giant amoeba'[16] consuming the city from the outside in. 'The urban edge is the societal impact zone,' Davis darkly declares, 'where the centrifugal forces of the city collide with the implosion of the countryside.'[17] Davis recognises the echoes of yesterday in today's great waves of urbanisation, but his reminiscences show not a trace of romantic nostalgia. For Davis 'the peasant flood' of the twenty-first century is a horrific 'back to Dickens' rerun of the worst of what once was. 'The dynamics of Third World urbanisation both recapitulate and confound the precedents of nineteenth and early twentieth century Europe and North America.'[18] What results is the emergence of 'a shantytown world encircling the fortified enclaves of the urban rich':

The cities of the future, rather than being made out of glass and steel as envisioned by earlier generations of urbanists, are instead largely constructed out of crude brick, straw, recycled plastic, cement blocks and scrap wood. Instead of cities of light soaring toward heaven, much of the twenty-first century urban world squats in squalor, surrounded by pollution, excrement and decay.[19]

There are those who challenge Davis' bleak outlook, questioning his characterisation of poor urban neighbourhoods as slums. Ananya Roy, in her call for a new geography that would reshape global metropolitan studies, is critical of the dismissive bias of the term. 'While global cities, mainly in the First World, are seen as command and control nodes of the global economy, the cities of the global South are scripted as megacities, big but powerless. Off the map, they are usually assembled under the sign of underdevelopment, that last and compulsory chapter on "Third World Urbanization" in the urban studies textbook ... They are the megacities, bursting at the seams, overtaken by their own fate of poverty, disease, violence, toxicity. They constitute the "planet of slums," with its "surplus humanity" and "twilight struggles"'.[20] Tom Angotti, in an essay entitled 'Apocalyptic Anti-urbanism', echoes this critique of Davis' rhetoric that invariably leads down the 'blind ally' of despair. His essay begins with a quote from V. S. Naipaul: 'A stranger could drive through Miguel Street and just say "Slum!" because he could see no more. But we who lived there saw our street as a world, where everybody was quite different from everybody else.'[21]

This observation of Naipaul's is given theoretical weight by Jane Jacobs who famously argued in *Death and Life of Great American Cities*, that so-called slums had great internal vibrancy. Since then, city lovers have been extremely wary of the label. To declare and dismiss whole communities as slums is to help pave the way for the often violent and unjust process of slum clearance (a process that Davis also condemns).

The term 'slums', has long been reviled because it de-values communities and helps rationalise giant urban renewal plans that result in the displacement of poor people. Once the places where they live are tagged as dysfunctional, crime-ridden, generators of evil, they become targets for removal, often with violence. Noted activist Mel King remarks, 'When I was at college, I learned that I lived in a "slum"… somebody else defined my community in a way that allowed them to justify the destruction of it.'[22]

Journalist Robert Neuwirth, who travels among the borderland communities of the developing world, finds much to admire in the patched-together neighbourhoods produced by the newly urbanised. In these dense networks of informal housing, so often scavenged and self-built, there is great tenacity, ingenuity, entrepreneurship and hope. The urban poor have invented an ingenious form of 'pirate urbanisation,' he argues, and it is this world of 'shadow cities' where the true dream of the future metropolis lies.

Doug Saunders names these poor neighbourhoods on the outskirts of town 'Arrival Cities' in order to emphasise their role as transition zones between rural and urban life. Shantytown neighbourhoods on the urban perimeter may seem like slums, he writes, with their 'shambles of thrown together houses', 'dirt laneways' filled with the 'cacophony of commerce', rubbish and waste seemingly piled everywhere and 'chaos of vehicles' that navigate the narrow streets. Yet, to condemn them as static encampments fails to recognise the essentially fluid nature of these critical urban forms. Arrival Cities, Saunders contends, are primarily determined by the functions that they serve. By bridging the gap between city and the countryside, their existence helps bring villagers into the urban sphere. Peripheral shantytowns are based on a series of networks whose links reach back out into the home village and also further into the core of the established city. They thus work—when successful—as machines of integration, allowing the city's marginal population to eventually make the metropolis their home. 'Here, on the periphery,' he writes, 'is the new centre of the world.'[23]

Urban economist Edward Glaeser also writes in defence of city slums. In his book *Triumph of the City*, in a chapter entitled 'What's Good about Slums?', Glaeser challenges the common presumption that the existence of widespread urban poverty is the sign of 'a great crises of the megacity'. Poor urban neighbourhoods, he asserts, indicate precisely the opposite, illustrating by their very existence the fact that megacities are welcoming places of opportunity for poor people to live. 'Cities don't make people poor; they attract poor people,' he writes. 'The flow of less advantaged people to cities from Rio to Rotterdam demonstrates urban strength, not weakness.'[24] A city's population tells you what a city has to offer, he reasons. 'If lots of poor people flock to a certain place', this 'shows that it is a relatively good place to be poor.' We should worry more, Glaeser concludes provocatively, 'about places with too little poverty.'[25] Zones where everyone is well off are simply places that have failed to attract, or have actively cast away, those that are least fortunate.

Urban villages

In the first decade of the twentieth century, throughout Shanghai's 'golden age', vast shantytowns grew up on urban edges as rural migrants, fleeing poverty and war, flooded into the city to settle. 'During the Republican period (from 1911–1949),' writes Hanchao Lu in his evocative history of the city, 'hundreds of thousands of urban poor lived in Shanghai shantytowns.'[26] Unlike in twentieth-century America, these were 'never inner city slums'. Instead 'squatter communities in Shanghai [were] always peripheral' situated on the 'outskirts of the foreign concessions'.[27] The largest shantytown was Yaoshuilong, a dense zone along Suzhou creek about five miles northwest of the Bund. Yaoshuilong was known as 'lotion lane' due to a large lotion factory located in the area. By the 1940s, it had 4,000 straw shacks and housed 16,000 residents.[28] Lu describes the slum housing of the period in its various stages of decay. Migrants would come to Shanghai by boat, travelling along the Grand Canal. Upon arrival they would dock their vessels along Suzhou creek and use them as homes. Once the boats became too decrepit to stay afloat, they would drag them to the bank and transform what was left into makeshift huts which were known by the deceivingly romantic name *gundilong* (or rolling earth dragons).

The best form of makeshift housing was the *penghu* (straw huts), which though dark, wet and windowless, and without good access to power and water, were a step up from the other forms of housing with which slum dwellers made do. Yaoshuilong was built up during the 1920s. Twenty years later two other large shantytowns emerged: Fangualong, near the Shanghai railway station which housed about 20,000 people and Zhaojiabang, now a central multi-lane road at the outer limit of the French Concession, which was then a silted-up creek that served as a wretched home for thousands of refugees that swarmed into the city fleeing the civil war. By the 1940s, shantytowns encircled the city. 'From the plate glass windows of the skyscrapers in the bustling downtown area, virtually wherever one looked one's eyes fell on "the Orient's most scrofulous slums". It is proper to say that, like the Bund skyline, the shantytowns were a symbol of modern Shanghai.'[29]

Today, shantytowns in China are known as urban villages (*cheng zhong cun*). The name designates singular places that have emerged out of China's unique transition from rural to urban life. These 'slums with Chinese characteristics' are located outside the core of the metropolis, in places where the countryside remains, though the city has grown all around. They are built on agricultural land and are still designated 'rural' even though they are situated in the midst of the city, surrounded by rising skyscrapers. As pockets of village authority within the municipality, *cheng zhong cun* largely function outside the strict controls of urban planning and administrative regulations. Farmers, who have the right to the land, build up their houses on their own, carve them up and rent them to migrant workers.[30] Throughout the past decades of China's rise these informal neighbourhoods have functioned as a vital source of affordable housing for the new urban poor. Some are crime-ridden, desolate places, but others have developed successful, thriving communities and a few have become quite rich. Urban villages exist outside the realm of planning and often escape the country's strict administrative control. They have, therefore, been highly controversial and the target of widespread campaigns. Many have been torn down. On the outskirts of Beijing, Guangzhou, Chongqing and other large cities, something resembling squatter communities can still be found. Yet, they exist only in pockets. Unlike the vast shantytowns that surround other mega-cities of the developing world, in China slums do not dominate the suburban landscape.

There are very few urban villages left in Shanghai. The poor, rather than settling in sprawling shantytowns, tend, whether in the inner city or in the suburbs, to squeeze into existing neighbourhoods, slicing up space so as to find tiny rooms within which to live. Those that work on building sites use the prefabricated housing that the developer provides. Factory jobs often come with a dormitory. Others depend on Shanghai's long tradition of hyper-density, which subdivides space again and again to fit more and more people in. True to the urban tradition, which created extra capacity by splitting up what is already there, today's migrants sleep in the back of shops, in the basements of buildings, in the corridors or in other micro-spaces that have been chopped out for their use.

As a result, contemporary Shanghai functions much like the pre-modern city, in which the rich still live in extremely close proximity to the poor. In the downtown lane houses of the old French Concession, renovated luxury homes sit next door to houses carved into apartments that house multiple families. In the Embankment Building, a historic apartment overlooking Suzhou creek, floors are split in two. On one side old Shanghainese, along with an increasing number of foreign tenants, enjoy beautiful high-ceilinged apartments with vast windows overlooking the water. On the other side of the hallway, cramped rooms originally designed as maid's quarters now house tightly packed migrant communities. Every year, during the New Year season, when so many urban dwellers return to their villages, it is not only the suburbs that feel the impact of the annual return migration. People living downtown also experience—especially during the holiday's golden week—a sudden quietness (interrupted only by the mad eruptions of fireworks) that blankets the city as so much of the urban core empties of its migrant population.

While many celebrate China's striking lack of shantytowns, there are those that argue the country is making life harder on its poor by denying them the rights to dwell in these marginal neighbourhoods. Qin Hui, a professor at Beijing's Tsinghua University and a well-known public intellectual, has criticised the government for demolishing informal housing without adequate compensation and for acting in the name of development when they knock down the makeshift homes that migrants build with their own hands. 'Only one precedent comes to mind for what we do to our poor, and that is how the white imperialists in South Africa treated the black population under apartheid,' he has said.[31] Since migrants have no access to low-cost public housing, which is all reserved for municipal residents, 'local governments could at least allow them to build their own housing in some designated areas in cities'.[32] Qin Hui acknowledges that granting people the freedom to build their own houses will almost certainly lead to the slum-like neighbourhoods so starkly visible in other cities of the developing world. Yet, he doesn't think of this as a problem:

It is no shame for big cities to have such areas. On the contrary, Shenzhen and other cities should take initiatives to build cheap residential areas for low-income residents including migrant workers who want to stay in the cities where they work ... By building those areas, big cities could show more consideration for low-income residents, and provide them with more welfare.[33]

From as early as the 1950s, the Shanghai municipality has been determined to destroy and revamp the city's historic shantytowns and there have been repeated waves of slum demolition alongside the mass construction of public housing. Many thousands have been relocated. Suzhou creek is being cleaned up and revitalised and Zhaojiabang Lu is now a major city street with high-rise shopping malls, parkland, fancy office towers and expensive apartments. This overt campaign to tear down all makeshift communities has been coupled with a fierce intolerance of squatters, migrant congregations and informal settlements. This has been facilitated by the government's unequivocal ownership of land. The squatter communities of Neuwirth's 'pirate urbanisation' depend upon open areas where the claims on land are vague and contestable. The culture of squatting is also alien to the commerciality of Shanghai, where housing the poor as well as the rich has always been in the job of the market.

Most importantly, however, Shanghai's lack of shantytowns is a result of China's distinctive mode of contemporary urbanisation. In China, internal migrants—a growing surge hundreds of millions strong—are known as the 'floating population'. The name designates the fact that much of China's rural population is becoming urbanised, while remaining essentially mobile. They have left the countryside, but are not yet permanently settled in the city. This quasi-urban population floats throughout the country, stopping where there is money to be made. When they are sick, or tired, or the economy is uncertain, or they want to celebrate the holidays or they just need a break, they go back home to stay for a while at the village where they are from. Many have family—both parents and children—left behind. This 'circulatory migration', as it has been called, stems from the *hukou* (or household registration) system, a bureaucratic control, which underlies the contemporary process of urbanisation in China and makes it unique.

Hukou

China has a very long history of recording information about its population, mostly for the purposes of taxation and farmland allocation. Registration records exist from as early as the Zhou dynasty, and the *baojia* system, which dates back to the Song dynasty, is often pointed to as a precursor to today's bureaucratic population controls.

Yet, while documentation of the populace has a long historical precedence, the present *hukou* system arises from the particularities of contemporary history. It was implemented in the winter of 1958, and arose as a response to the specific conditions of the time. Throughout the 1950s there were large-scale spontaneous migrations across China as peasants sought jobs in the city and tried to escape the poverty of village life. In the ten years after communist victory, thirty million labourers poured into the cities to find employment, causing China's urban population to leap from 10.64 per cent of the total in 1949 to 18.41 per cent in 1959.[34] The establishment of the *hukou* system coincided with the Great Leap Forward and in its first years internal migration continued to intensify as millions fled to the urban centres hoping to break free from the policies of collective farming, which was resulting in widespread famine in the countryside.

Fearing chaos in the overstretched cities, Mao's government aimed to reinsert control over what had come to be known as this blind flow (*mang liu*) of rural labour. The development strategy of the planned economy, which he adopted, was based on fixing the population in place, allowing movement only when the state directed it towards key industrial targets. The idea was to create an 'unequal exchange' in which a surplus of low-cost agricultural goods would feed a high-speed industrial growth. 'Between 1961 and 1963, 50 million rural migrants were deported from the cities to the countryside, and the *hukou* went into full effect.'[35]

The *hukou* system requires that all citizens be registered at birth. One's *hukou* records a place of birth but also, more crucially, marks one as a rural or urban dweller. For the past fifty years, this distinction between agricultural and non-agricultural *hukou* type or classification (*hukou leibie*) has been at the heart of population management in China. *Hukous* are determined by birth and are the gift (or curse) of inheritance. By far the simplest way to get a Shanghai *hukou*, for example, is to be born in Shanghai to parents who are Shanghainese. Changing *hukous*, especially *hukou* type, is exceedingly difficult, even today.

In the era of the planned economy, the *hukou* system was very successful at locking the population in place. Those with an urban *hukou* lived in accordance with the Soviet-style work unit (or *danwei*) system. They were given state-subsidised food, housing, employment and welfare benefits (including health care and retirement pensions). Farmers, or those with a rural *hukou*, on the other hand, were given access to land and were tasked with growing their own food. Since government policies prohibited all private markets, surplus produce could not be sold. For those with an urban *hukou* all food staples—grain, oil, cotton, milk and meat—were available only through state rations.[36]

The same situation held true for both jobs and housing. Without a free market in food, labour or property, survival in the cities for those with a rural *hukou* was next to impossible. While life for urban dwellers was completely managed by the state, rural dwellers were anchored to the countryside. This severe restriction of non-planned migration resulted in a contraction of China's urban population from 18.4 per cent in 1959 to 17.9 per cent in 1978.

The era of openness and reform (*gaige kaifang*) has not made radical changes to the *hukou* system, but it has rendered it increasingly irrelevant. As restrictions were lifted and markets in food, labour and housing began to appear, people started to move. Author Leslie Chang tells the story concisely:

In the late 1970s, reforms allowed farming households to sell part of their harvest on the market rather than supplying it all to the state. Agricultural production soared. Suddenly, food was available in local markets across the country, and rural residents could survive independently in the cities for the first time. A 1984 government directive permitted farmers to settle in small towns; to be on the move was no longer a crime. Migration picked up speed, and by 1990, the country had sixty million migrants, many of them drawn to the booming factories and cities on the coast.[37]

Migrants who left the countryside in search of work lived in cities without the proper registration. At first this could be dangerous, since though work, food and shelter were not hard to come by, anyone who was caught in the urban centres without the proper papers could be detained and sent back. This changed in June 2003 with the detention and subsequent murder of Sun Zhigang, a twenty-seven-year-old graphic designer from Hubei Province. Sun, who was working in Guangzhou, failed to produce his temporary residence and identification card when police stopped him. He was treated as a vagrant and detained in a repatriation centre. Though young and healthy he died in custody. His death was met with an enormous media uproar, especially on the internet, which was just then emerging as an important social force in China. As a result the policy of 'custody and repatriation' was abolished. In the same year, 'the State Council, China's cabinet, issued a comprehensive document calling migration key to the country's development. It banned job discrimination against migrants and advocated better working conditions for them and schooling for their children.'[38]

This gradual easing of restrictions has continued over subsequent years and the number of migrant workers has surged. 'In factories, restaurants, construction sites, elevators, delivery services, house cleaning, child raising, garbage collecting, barbershops and brothels, almost every worker is a rural migrant.'[39] Today migrants are free to live in cities and even have some access to some social benefits. The Chinese government now accepts—and to some extent even encourages—a mobile population.

Migration was an accidental consequence of economic reforms. Though unplanned and unpredicted, a mobile population is essential to China's economic growth (as it is to capitalism everywhere). 'If the migrant workers are stopped,' said one government official, 'there would be at least stagnation in the coastal areas. At worst, the economy of the coastal area would collapse, causing the national economy to collapse.'[40] China's rise and the movement of its people are two sides of the same coin. As the *Economist* magazine wrote in an article aptly entitled 'We like to move it move it', 'The story of migration... is the story of modern China.'[41]

Urban revolution

The future, of course, is unknown. Only fools or fanatics offer certain predictions. The one potential exception to this rule is in the area of demographics. Large-scale patterns in where and when populations grow or shrink is the surest bet we have about the world that is to come. One such pattern is that people who live in cities tend to have fewer children. The fact that the majority of the world's population is now becoming urbanised should, therefore, result in a check in global population growth in the coming decades. The most commonly cited figure in this regard is that world population will peak in 2050 at around ten billion and after that stagnate and, eventually, decline. As a result of these trends it is highly possible that the current wave of urbanisation is, as author Doug Saunders argues, the 'last great migration.' By the middle of the twenty-first century, he writes, population growth will cease to be a global concern:

For the first time in history humans will stop being more numerous each year, and the prospect of a Malthusian population crises will end. This will be a direct product of urbanization: because of migration, smaller urban families will outnumber large rural ones, and, in turn, the flow of money, knowledge and educated return migrants from the arrival city back to the village will push down birth rates in rural areas ... After urbanisation is accomplished, average family sizes around the world will fall below 2.1 children and the problems of crowding and competition for resources will be replaced with the much more sustainable (though still challenging) problems of a non-growing population.[42]

In 2007, the vital threshold was crossed and, for the first time, more people on the planet lived in cities than in the countryside. To mark the occasion, the scholar William McNeill wrote an article entitled 'Cities and their Consequences', which explores the profound and far-reaching effects of the relationship between urbanisation and human reproduction. Cities, argues McNeill, are 'demographic sinkholes'. Due to the massive cost and inconvenience of raising children in urban settings, cities 'seldom reproduce themselves'.[43] In small villages, on the other hand, where the majority of human beings have spent most of their history, having children has never been a substantial drain. On the contrary, farmers need enough offspring to help till the fields and even when quite small, kids can start pitching in.

'From a very early age children began to contribute to family income by undertaking tasks within their powers—gathering berries and other kinds of wild-growing foods, and herding geese and other small animals, for example.'[44] In China there is a saying 'another child is just another pair of chopsticks'. The ease and economic benefits of child-rearing makes village life extremely 'hospitable to human reproduction'. In cities, on the other hand, children have ceased to be an economic benefit and have become instead an economic burden. As all parents know, the cost of education, books, toys, clothes and high tech gadgets all quickly spiral, leading to the paradoxical situation that the richer you are, the more expensive your children become.

Equally influential is the practical difficulties in squaring city life with raising small children. Village existence was based on a rigid division of labour along strict gender lines. This enabled women to care for small children while still attending to their daily tasks. The city liberates us from these roles, but with this freedom comes great challenges. When both parents work finding adequate childcare is difficult. Extended families tend to dissolve, and parents must painfully balance quality and cost as preschools, daycares and babysitting become the only options. 'The underlying reality,' writes McNeill, 'is that we have not found any satisfactory substitute for village communities as nurturers of the young (and sustainers of the old).'[45] In places where children are both more expensive and also less economically useful, people start growing older with fewer kids. As a result cities start to shrink. Without migration, then, urban life cannot sustain itself. Cities need the constant flow of migrants to survive.

The process of urbanisation, then, transforms human culture in the most profoundly intimate of ways. 'Few readily appreciate how deep stabilities of village life were planted,' writes McNeill, 'or how recently those stabilities have been uprooted.'[46] The move away from the countryside destroys the rooted, organic, sedentary society that humans have always known. In the rural communities of self-sustainable villages, life's patterns and codes were all prescribed. 'Custom cushioned personal interactions of every kind within each village, and however hard the work or variable the return, everyone knew what was expected of him at every stage of life in all ordinary situations.'[47] Your job, when and whom you marry, how your children will be raised, your role in the family and the wider social world was determined from birth. With the freedom of the metropolis all this is undermined. In the modern urban world, as Marx so famously wrote, 'all that is solid, melts into air'. A young girl from the Chinese countryside leaves her home in the village to work in a factory on the coast. Once there she is introduced to all the possibilities a city can offer. Soon she is utterly transformed, refusing to accept that her choices in life are already settled; that her destiny is already written. Migrant workers, writes author Leslie Chang:

use a simple term for the move that defines their lives: *chuqu* to go out … To come out from home and work in a factory is the hardest thing they have ever done. It is also an adventure. What keeps them in the city is not fear but pride: To return home early is to admit defeat. To go out and stay out—*chuqu*—is to change your fate.[48]

Floaters

The Chinese diaspora—at over sixty million—is one of the largest in the world. On the edges of the mainland (Hong Kong, Taiwan, Singapore) many now eschew strict national ties, instead constructing new transnational identities. They adopt what theorist Aihwa Ong has called a 'flexible citizenship',[49] comfortably holding numerous passports so as to better facilitate a hybrid existence that traverses both countries and continents. Inside China, those with enough means emulate this transient culture, moving family and capital across a variety of places. This same nomadic lifestyle, albeit amongst a very different class, is, as we have seen, adopted by millions of China's internal migrants. Yet, much like the wandering Jew, the Chinese tendency to roam is coupled with the contradictory impulse—a fierce attachment to home. In Chinese culture, rootedness, the deep bond to one's *lao jia* (native town), is a crucial part of life and also of death. The still living tradition of 'corpse walking' speaks to the fervent migrant wish to be buried at home, among one's ancestors.[50] This sentiment is expressed, as author Li Zhang writes in his book *Strangers in the City*, in 'the widely accepted Confucianist saying *antu zhongqian* (to be attached to one's native land and unwilling to leave it)'.[51]

The flip side of the enormous value attributed to native place is the fact that those who do leave home are often treated with contempt. In his book *Soul Stealers* Philip Kuhn details how itinerant people and wanderers in late imperial China were widely perceived as being ghostlike and subject to a widespread witch-hunt, in which they were accused of stealing souls. Writing about the contemporary period, Li Zhang enumerates the various negative connotations that still accumulate today:

Mobile people (*liumin*) tended to be associated with destructive images such as *wu* (witches), *gui* (ghosts), *jianghu pianzi* (swindlers) and *youqi* (wandering beggars). In Chinese, the word *liudong* (floating) has two different meanings: one is to be lively and unencumbered; the other is to be rootless, unstable, and dangerous. This double meaning opens the image of floaters to multiple interpretations. The dominant discourse tends to invoke and oversimplify the negative meanings by emphasising their relationship with residual terms such as *liumin* (vagrants, homeless people), *liukou* (roving bandits), *liumang* (hooligans), *liucuan* (to flee), *liudu* (pernicious influence), *liuwang* or *liufang* (exiles), and *mangliu* (an unregulated flow of people), which is a transposition of the sounds in the derogatory term *liumang* (hooligans).[52]

With the loosening of restrictions and the rise of the market economy, the great wall that has divided urban and rural China is now filled with holes. Those who choose to leave the countryside and find work in the city, however, still face great difficulties. Citizens with a rural *hukou* lack access to social welfare in the form of health care, unemployment insurance, senior services etc., which are all reserved for official urban residents. In addition to these extra living costs there are other vital barriers to permanent settlement.

One of the most serious is in the realm of education. Until quite recently only those with a Shanghai *hukou* were admitted into Shanghai public schools. The children of migrant workers relied instead on a private, grass-roots network of schools that grew up piecemeal to serve the migrant community. These were often expensive, had inadequate facilities, untrained teachers, and lacked textbooks and other material. Starting in 2010 the Shanghai city government enacted a policy of integrating migrant children into the public school system. The regulations sought to both assert control on the exterior status of the floating population and to provide some measure of quality control. The grassroots schools were closed, sometimes quite violently. (In one widely publicised case a principal set herself on fire to protest against the shutting down of the school.) The demand for migrant schooling greatly outstripped official supply and in many cases, once the grassroots networks were shut down, there was simply no schooling available. Those public schools that do take migrants (though it is supposedly against the law, not all do) are crowded and admittance requirements are becoming increasingly strict. As a result many migrant children are forced to accompany their parents to work or to spend time at home alone.

For those that are accepted in the local system there are still other problems. Many schools have special migrant classes, which are consciously taught at a lower level since migrant parents (who often work long hours) are not able to oversee the rigorous homework regime or send their kids to extra classes as local parents do. More importantly there is a systemic discrimination against the floating population, rooted in the *gaokao*—the college entrance examination, to which all higher education in China is rigidly tied. While migrants are being integrated into Shanghai's primary system, few can attend high school in the city due to a law that ties the entrance examination to the place where one's *hukou* is registered. To take the test, migrant children—even those born and educated in Shanghai—must return to their 'home village'. The test itself lasts only a few days but migrant schoolchildren need to prepare in their home town for at least a year. The *gaokao* is not standardised nationally, so students who plan to take the examination in a particular region must be familiar with local text books and curriculum, which can vary substantially from place to place. Shanghai, for example, has its own curriculum, which places at least a relative stress on creativity, diversity and openness. This enlightened system can be damaging to migrants who have to return to their villages where the education system is more traditional and the *gaokao* more rigid. Once they have finished middle school, migrant kids who have grown up in the city thus face a difficult choice: they can go back and be educated in their home village—a place they may be totally alienated from; they can quit school and try to find work; or they can go to a vocational school. The latter sounds a promising solution and is the one most promoted by municipal governments, but the majority of vocational schools have terrible reputations (as prisoners for teenagers) while the best ones, which offer highly skilled training in a high-end trade, are often reserved only for the Shanghainese. An increasing number of migrant teenagers pass the time by just hanging out on the streets.

Social commentators in China warn that these frustrated youths, cut off from the opportunities of the metropolis, to which they only semi-belong, are a grave threat to China's stability. Second-generation migrants (those born after the beginning of opening and reform) are quite different from their parents, who grew up as poor peasants, and found jobs in the city as an escape from village life. This older generation pride themselves on their ability to *chi ku* (eat bitterness). Though they have led rough lives, in the move away from the countryside, they have seen their prospects improve. Both stoic and pragmatic, these first-generation migrants accept their fate of being both of the city and outside it. Their children's experiences, however, are not at all the same. For those who have been raised in the city, ties to their 'home village'—a place they only go on holidays to visit their grandparents—are frayed. Many are already urbanised and feel that the city, not the village, is their home.

The alternative strategy of leaving children behind to be raised in the villages is also enormously problematic. As the divide between village and city life grows sharper, migrant families have begun to feel the disadvantages of separation. Parents and children are strangers to each other and

173

become deeply alienated when they only see each other once a year. Young parents who leave their children to be brought up by grandparents worry about their own lack of influence. They fear that the generation gap has widened and the old are now incapable of preparing the young for the world that is to come. They want to help educate their kids in what they themselves are learning. When you are of the city, you want your kids to be too.

Changing spending patterns suggest to some that floaters are beginning to put down roots. Unlike their parents, the younger generation of migrants is less likely to save and send their wages back home. Some spend their entire salaries on clothes, motorbikes and other high tech gadgets. Taking credit—once unheard of—is becoming increasingly common. The new behaviour has sparked a heated debate. On the one hand, young people are being criticised for being self-centred and living beyond their means; on the other hand, this cavalier spending can be taken as a sign of optimism and hope.

Many in China believe that the era of floating is coming to an end. Calls for *hukou* reform have grown louder and more frequent. In March 2010 a coordinated newspaper campaign published thirteen simultaneous editorials arguing for the abolishment of the *hukou* system. Since then cities across China have experimented with a wide variety of reforms. Inside the party, attempts to create a nationwide social security net along with land reform in the countryside (policy changes that, if taken together, would render the *hukou* restrictions obsolete) are under constant debate and some form of *hukou* reform is seen as central to the urbanisation strategy of the new regime. 'A floating population cannot be permanently sustained,' says scholar Qin Hui, expressing an opinion widely shared; 'residence in the city is inevitable.'[53]

Circular migration

Nevertheless, questions remain. If the *hukou* system were to suddenly disappear, would it necessarily bring an end to the peculiarities of China's urbanisation? Would those that are now divided between rural and urban life sever their ties with the village and plant their roots in the city? Would the shantytowns familiar from other developing cities inevitably appear? Would the wanderers all settle down?

When approached historically, it becomes clear that the answer to these questions is, at the very least, uncertain. The *hukou* system accentuated pre-existing tendencies in the relationship between city and countryside, but it did not invent them. The marginalisation of the rural population certainly pre-exists the *hukou*. 'There is no question that *hukou* has reinforced urban-rural divides, engendered a two-track migration system, and relegated peasant migrants to the bottom rung of society,' writes researcher C. Cindy Fan. 'Yet, the roots of Chinese peasants' and peasant migrants' marginality are deep, historical and complex.'[54]

In contemporary Shanghai everyday insults are tied to the countryside. Those who are unsophisticated are described as *tu* (earthy) and the word for peasant, *nongmin*, is laden—at least when used in Shanghai—with negative connotations. A *nongmin* is a country bumpkin, uncivilised and incapable of mastering the intricacies of city life. Indeed, for the Shanghainese anyone who is not of the metropolis, the *waidiren*, outsiders from elsewhere in China, are burdened by the obvious deficiency of not being urban enough. This prejudice, as historian Hanchao Lu explains, has always been an inherent part of the city's identity. Poor rural refugees were treated as 'urban outcasts' as soon as they began to flow into Shanghai. The zones they occupied—straw shack shantytowns on the outskirts of the city—testified to this marginal status. These rural immigrants, writes Lu, were the 'uninvited outsiders' who 'by virtue of their poverty, suffered social discrimination' and were 'denied entrance to the life of the inner city'.[55] Lu compares this situation to the racial divides in America. 'The shanty squatters in Chinese cities reflected something quite different,' he writes, that is 'the gulf that separated rural from urban China.'[56] The depth of the urban-rural gulf was such that rural migrants, even those who had lived in the city for decades and had no plans to leave, did not develop clear 'Shanghai identities'. They were physically in Shanghai but to some degree they had not yet entered the city—psychologically they remained outside, 'hardly regarding themselves as "urbanites"'.[57]

This hybrid identity, of being both of the city and outside it, extended throughout the social classes. Middle class and wealthy migrants to the city frequently identified as sojourners, simultaneously embracing a Shanghai identity while retaining strong native place links. On the one hand, and 'almost as a rule', maintains Lu, a 'new immigrant to the city would soon be proud of being not just a city person but a "Shanghai person" or "Shanghairen"'. 'To compare Shanghai with the hinterlands,' writes Lu quoting Wang Xiaolai, a leading entrepreneur of the time, 'is to compare paradise and hell.'[58] Yet, while the people of Shanghai were proud to call themselves *Shanghairen*, they were not always ready to totally identify themselves with the new metropolis. The village home was used as a type of social security, and native place ties (which were associated with urban guilds) became vital to the business and work of urban sojourners. 'Since the people of Shanghai were mostly immigrants, ties to one's native place were acknowledged as a social norm... One's hometown or village was not only a place to be buried but also a place that modern Shanghainese, as well as others, regarded as a home to which one could return.'[59] The people of Shanghai, then, embraced a dual identity. 'They happily saw themselves as Shanghainese, [but] also liked to maintain every possible tie to their native place.'[60]

Today's floating population exhibits precisely this type of fractured identity. They live and work in the city but keep ties to a countryside home for security. From this pragmatic arrangement, they have developed a lifestyle of 'circular migration' that maximises income and minimises risk. In maintaining a home (along with a plot of land) in the village and leaving the young, old and sick behind, China's internal migrants are able to tap into resources both in the city and in the countryside. The strategy of 'earning in the city and spending in the village' takes full advantage of the urban-rural cost differentiation, maximises employment opportunities, enables families to diversify their income and reduces expenses in the migration destination.[61]

After studying the modern nomadism of today's migrants a number of scholars urge that the urbanisation debate in China consider alternatives to the permanent migration paradigm. 'Obtaining an urban *hukou* alone,' writes C. Cindy Fan:

does not seem to have jump-started peasants' social and economic mobility. At the same time, there is plenty of evidence to show that peasant migrants may not want to stay permanently in the city. Circulation from and to the village home and among places of migrant work, and return migration, have in fact enabled peasants to straddle the city and countryside and benefit from both.[62]

In an article entitled 'Beyond Hukou Reform' theorist Yu Zhu elaborates the idea:

many local urban governments, especially those of medium-sized and small cities, have made great efforts to reform the [*hukou*] system, which has been regarded as the central mechanism underlying the unsettled nature of the floating population, in the hope that they will settle down in the cities and be fully integrated into China's urbanisation process ... However, the response of the floating population to the *hukou* reform has been surprising. It has been reported that in many places, most members of the floating population are not enthusiastic about transferring their rural *hukou* to the urban one, although they are offered the opportunity to do so ... In Shijiazhuang City, the capital city of Hebei Province, a radical reform in the *hukou* system was implemented from August 2001 to June 2002; however, the results show that only about 30% of the floating population has transferred their *hukou* to the city. Such a situation raises two issues. First, it seems that *Hukou* status is a far cry from the complete explanation of the temporary pattern of the floating population; second, if the majority of the floating population do not have the intention of changing their *hukou* status, this implies that circulating still served the interests of the responding migrants better than settling down in the cities.[63]

Doug Saunders devotes one section of his book *Arrival Cities* to Shenzhen, one China's oldest Special Economic Zones and among the most dynamic metropolises in the world. He titles the section 'Arrested Development: A City Without Arrival'. Saunders begins by telling the story of a couple searching for housing in the city. They cannot afford to live together and look instead for rooms in separate dormitories, which is a good way to save money. 'They both enjoy the lively bustle and high wages of Shenzhen,' Saunders reports, 'and would love to find a way to move here permanently, but they've realised it's almost impossible to put down roots in any lasting way.'[64] For Saunders this is a sign that in Shenzhen something has gone terribly wrong. As evidence, he points to the large labour shortages in China's coastal cities. Despite sharp increases in wages, workers have been flooding out, heading to inland cities closer to their home villages. After the 2008 financial crisis two million workers failed to return. What Shenzhen lacks, argues Saunders, is the possibility of permanent migration. Without offering its migrants the promise of purchasing a home, bringing their family or building a small shop, restaurant or even starting a factory, the fate of Shenzhen is doomed to be that of a failed transitional zone; 'a wound that will not heal, a place nobody can call home'.[65]

It is true that, from about 2006 onwards, China's coastal cities have suffered a labour shortage in those sectors usually dominated by migrant workers (factory workers, domestic staff, restaurant servers etc.). Yet, the shortage, which is felt most acutely in the months following the New Year holiday, is not due to a decline in the overall trend of rural to urban migration in China. Instead, it is a by-product of the endurance of a floating population that is increasingly able to pick and choose zones of temporary migration according to which place offers the best wages and working conditions. Rather than come to Shanghai and Guangdong, where living costs are exceedingly high, many migrants are now finding work in the much cheaper second- and third-tier cities, which are closer to home. The fact is that it is 'circulation, not moving for the purpose of staying, that defines rural-urban migration in China', and the great Chinese metropolises are feeling the effect. 'While second generation migrants and family migration is on the rise',[66] the dominant form of urbanisation, concludes Fan, consists of a permanently unsettled population that travels between the 'home' village and various cities offering work. 'Circular migration is no longer just a temporary solution but has become a long term practice of many rural Chinese. It has firmly established itself as a way of life, perhaps even a culture, throughout China's countryside.'[67] In China, then, urbanisation coincides with mobility and arrival exists in transition. 'Experienced migrants have already mastered the art of circularity and their children are following their footsteps and joining the flows.'[68] Perhaps, then, in China's new modernity, it is not only a once rural population that will need to adapt to new cities, but also the new cities that will need to adjust to a population that continues to float.

The relationship between rootedness and flow has a long and complex history in China and this deep ambivalence has had a tremendous impact on the culture. In the north, nomadic conquerors came down in waves, battling an intensely territorial state (which they themselves helped create). The southern coast, on the other hand, bred a maritime culture marked by commercial dynamism, entrepreneurial risk and an offshore mentality that was sharply distinct from the inward-looking, land-locked, power that dominated from above. Shanghai especially has been, and always will be, defined by its own particular hybrid relationship between movement and place. On one hand, Shanghai is a cosmopolitan, polymorphous metropolis that plays welcoming host to its continuously shifting, transient population. It is also a city that is entrenched in a very local language and culture of which it is fiercely proud. It is at once intensely global—in some ways more connected to Paris and New York than to the towns and cities of China—and also firmly rooted in the fabulously rich cultural geography of the Jiangnan region, of which it is a part. This contradictory fusion, as scholar Frederic Wakeman notes, made the Shanghai sojourner unique:

Traditional Chinese sojourners (*youyu*, 'travelers in residence') were simply people to be mentioned in the district gazetteer or else were exiles who had sought temporary shelter and succor. The very term suggested a transient local identity, as though the 'real' existence of traditional sojourners had to be kept in some other part of the empire where the family graves were kept and where one eventually had to return ... Shanghai sojourners (*luhu*, 'travelers in Shanghai') were also transients from somewhere, but the term in this case did meaningfully emphasize the place where they sojourned: Hu, or Shanghai. It thereby summed up the central ambiguity of sojourning in this particular metropolis. Shanghai sojourners were more than persons passing through; they were denizens. Their stay was on the way to becoming permanent residence, where their loyalties fluctuated strategically between attachment to native place and the announcement of new identity as Shanghairen (Shanghai people).[69]

Shanghai's productive tension between the singular and localised, the heterogenous and hybrid, is playing itself out with delicious results in the city's food culture (everyone's favourite obsession). At issue is whether the true Shanghai cuisine is *benbangcai*, the local cuisine that is determined by the particular tastes of the Shanghainese, or *haipaicai*, which is born instead out of intermixing and radical, continuous contamination. In his book *Culinary Nostalgia* Mark Swislocki contends that at the heart of the *haipaicai-benbangcai* debate is the quintessential Shanghai question: is it locals or migrants who define the city's soul?

On the relation between *haipaicai* and *benbangcai* (local cooking) ... There is an implicit idea that local Shanghai food culture has such a powerful hold on the palates of city residents that it has forced chefs who cook non-Shanghai cuisine to modify their repertoire accordingly. Yet, local Shanghai cuisine, which itself is thereby represented as not having the same qualities of adaptation, innovation, and fusion is not identified by the *haipaicai* discourse as definitive of urban culture more generally. This paradox reflects a tension in terms of ideas about the sources of the cultural identity of the city. At stake is what one means when one is talking about, and identifying a character to the culture of, Shanghai. Does the crucial element of Shanghai culture lie with locals, who have watched their city be transformed during the past century and a half by several waves of migration from all parts of China? Or do these migrants themselves, by virtue of the ways that they adapt to Shanghai and its multicultural environment, define the city's character and identity?[70]

Shanghai (literally translated as 'on the sea') is a city that is both anchored and unmoored. It is at once solidly and exclusively entrenched in a particular historical, cultural and geographic location and also, simultaneously, the welcoming host to a myriad of wandering populations. It is precisely the friction between these two seemingly contradictory states that constitutes the city's modernity. Shanghai's continued vitality is not directed towards a future in which these tensions have all been resolved. Instead, it is more likely that Shanghai, as Stephenson foresaw, will reconfigure the very idea of a future city as a place where one can be both absolutely at home and, at the same time, forever adrift.

9

SHADOW MARKETS

Just across the ferry from Pudong with its hypermodern spectacle of super-tall skyscrapers lays one of the city's oldest neighbourhoods. Situated to the south-east of Yuyuan, the touristy 'Old City' with its Ming-style replicas and *tzachkas* shops, it spreads out towards the river's edge. The entire area is slated for redevelopment and much has already been destroyed. Scattered amidst the half-demolished structures, however, some buildings remain: red wooden houses that date back to the turn of the twentieth century; tall homes with makeshift add-ons exhibiting the layers of time; traditional *shikumen* with their decorative doorways; and half-torn edifices that still retain their elaborately carved balconies, window frames and roofs.

Wandering through the neighbourhood, the streets soon give way to alleyways too narrow and chaotic for cars. Here the streets are for the people. In this crumbling zone of the metropolis, pedestrian only by default, one gets an immersive experience in the intense dynamism of Shanghai's micro-commercial culture. This is the site of the former fabric market, which has now been cleaned up and relocated to sanitised malls a few blocks away. Here, remnants spill into the streets. Outdoor stalls are stuffed with buttons, zippers and rolls of material of all kinds. Turn a corner and the fabric vendors give way to a vegetable market. Peddlers set out their carts or blankets and display their wares: vegetables, live chickens sold from their cages, complacent ducks that sit in their buckets watching as their brethren are weighed, slaughtered and sold, the requisite vats of fish, frogs and snakes. Close by, a street dentist practices his trade. His stand—a selection of pictures of horribly mangled mouths and teeth moulds—is nothing more than a foldout table. The barber nearby needs only a mirror and chair.

181

These street traders are just a small part of Shanghai's immense and wildly heterogeneous underground economy. Participants include domestic workers, mostly migrants from the countryside who clean, cook and care for both young and old, as well as the waiters in restaurants and workers in beauty salons. There is an entire system of informal transport or 'black taxis', which range from motorised rickshaws, unmarked cars and motorbikes to cabs that actually look legitimate but whose official registration, licences and meters are frauds. In Shanghai, the shadow economy is an intrinsic part of the mid-autumn festival, which celebrates autumn's first full moon. Holiday ritual centres on eating round, heavy cakes that few actually enjoy (*yuebing* or mooncakes are the Chinese equivalent of Christmas cake). This fact, plus their hefty price tag (a box of moon cakes is typically 200 RMB and up) has resulted in the widespread trafficking of cake coupons in the weeks leading up to the festival. Other offshoots of traditional culture include itinerant vendors of ghost money and a second hand 'gift market' specialising in the useless plates and paperweights, which form the necessary accoutrements of *guanxi*. Far more valuable are the peddlers of recycled materials who come to your home, weigh your 'goods' and pay to take away your rubbish. They ride through communities with loudspeakers calling out *kongtiao, diannao* (air conditioner, computer), a familiar urban singsong that signals the second-hand trade in used electronics and household appliances. Items discarded by city folks are either sold to factories to be used as scrap or taken directly to the countryside where—if still operational—they will be purchased by less discerning customers. The vast array of fake goods, watches, bags, CDs and DVDs are also, of course, an intrinsic part of the hidden economy. At the top end of the market, pirated goods are not even fake at all, but rather the run-off extras produced by factories that manufacture famous brand-named goods for export. These end-of-the-line goods are typically sold out of the factories' backdoor and then resold in the domestic market. Today, this business model thrives on the immensely popular e-commerce site 'taobao' where scores of online stores form an online grey market that trades in clothes, appliances and toys.

The most visible part of Shanghai's grey economy, however, is street food, which, just like skyscrapers, forms a critical component of any global megacity. During the era of the planned economy, it was the lack of an open food market that, more than any other factor, locked the population in place. Without the ration tokens supplied by the state, people couldn't eat. Today migrants from all over the country hawk their regional delicacies, creating a cacophony of street food that contributes substantially to the cosmopolitan culture of Shanghai.

For many years, the back-gates of East China Normal University hosted one of the most bountiful snack clusters in the city. Handmade carts, rigged up with coal or gas, cook pastries and skewers of all kinds, stinky tofu, fried noodles, 'pot-sticker' dumplings and *baozis* stacked high in bamboo steamers. In the early morning the *bing* sellers come to create their egg crepe combinations that celebrity chef Jean Georges has called the best breakfast in the world. In winter fragrant sweet potatoes are sold out of makeshift metal barrels. During the hot months, pieces of jackfruit, durian and fresh coconuts are for sale. One student favourite was the spicy chicken lady, who sold her delicacies in makeshift paper bags. Her hand-made cart consisted of a couple of wooden drawers for cash, a place below to store ingredients and a burner at the top. The vendor is a single mother. Her husband, she said in an interview conducted in 2012, died a decade ago and her son, an army veteran, came to help out at the stall when things got busy. She had a daughter still at school and claimed an average of over 2,000 RMB per month, enough to have bought a small apartment nearby. For a while a couple selling squid set up a three-wheeled bike across the road, a valuable spot they inherited from a friend. Their prices ranged from 3 RMB for a tentacle to 10 RMB for a whole squid. At the table's edge sat an array of bottles filled with various spices, which they claimed, along with their iron grill, were a specialty from their hometown of Harbin. The woman had a hard face and chain-smoked. The man was softer and mostly silent. They wore matching white chef hats, meticulously starched. In Harbin they had worked selling vegetables in the wet market, but life was too hard. 'It's too cold there,' the woman explained, 'your spit is frozen before it hits the ground.'

In the narrative of development that is based on a linear and directional conception of time, the shadow economy is invariably eventually erased. As society modernises along the path of progress the informal economy becomes subsumed by the formal. The shadowy darkness of the 'traditional' markets is transformed and absorbed by the bright, transparent light of the modern economy. 'The widely held view of those who work in and study urban economic development,' write Jamie Alderslade et al. in their study of the informal economy for the Brooking Institute, is that 'the more "advanced" a city's economy becomes, the more inevitable the shift of economic activity from informal to formal spheres. Based on this assumption, "backward" Third World cities will generate more informal economic activity than their more "advanced" urban counterparts in more developed countries trends.'[1]

In Shanghai there are many powerful forces that advocate this view. In the decades of its hypergrowth, there is no question that the city has been disciplined and reined in. In just the past ten years, the large fake market on Xiangyang Lu, the flower market on Shanxi Lu, the insect, bird and fish market on Tianyaoqiao Lu and the famous street food market on Wujiang Lu, all immensely popular street markets, have been shut down. The hawkers have closed up shop or relocated elsewhere and the areas that once hosted an animated street life have all been sanitised. The 'clean up' process was rendered starkly visible in the lead up to the 2010 World Expo. Officials decided that the area near the China Pavilion just outside the Expo grounds, which once teemed with street food and was famous for its wide variety of regional snacks needed to be cleaned up. At first, in keeping with the supposed experimental nature of the 'Better City, Better Life' campaign the municipal government toyed with the idea of licensing street vendors, even going so far as to build special carts for them to use. In the end, however, they were deemed too uncivilised and the traditional street foods were replaced with the more 'modern' alternative of bad imitation French *boulangeries*. This same metamorphosis, in which cheap, local food is superseded by more expensive Western-style fare, has also occurred on Taikang Lu outside Tianzifang. The colourful street once boasted *baozi* and *bing* stands, a wet market and a hawker selling deep fried fowl. People would gather in the evening to buy the birds by weight and stand on the kerb as the family dinner was sizzled and spiced. (The fast convenience of street food, as scholar Irene Tinker notes, is particularly appealing to working-women, a distinctly urban population.) Today, most of these stands have been replaced by fancy gelato parlours and coffee shops. In recent years, even the back gate of East China Normal University is being placed under control, and the *bing* and squid sellers, the fruit vendors, even the spicy chicken have all but disappeared.

Bearing witness to this process, it is apparent that the transition from the informal to the formal economy, from shadow to light, is not a natural, gradual progression, but rather an intense and often violent struggle. The typical strategy, writes journalist Robert Neuwirth, is to 'criminalize the chaotic marketplace that [has] defined the cities of the developing world'.[2] In Shanghai the struggle is played out through daily battles between street vendors and *chengguan* (city inspectors), who are only loosely related to the municipal authorities. *Chengguan* are not part of the official police, and are generally made up of former state employees who receive little if any training, and have a general reputation for hooliganism. While *chengguan* do not have the power to make arrests, they are allowed to seize vendors' carts, confiscate all their goods and administer some fairly steep fines. Spend time among the hawkers and you see their constant fear. Suddenly the word *chengguan* is uttered in a secret whisper and, in a panicked instant, a whole market can pack up and start running. If caught alone, individual vendors have little choice but to quietly surrender. A man selling roasted potatoes is stopped at the crosswalk. He tries to run but his cart topples over and all his vegetables spill out on the street. A flower hawker desperately pleads his case while a crowd watches in sympathy, but he is surrounded, the *chengguan* lift his cart into a truck and drive away. Sometimes, however, the seizures turn into skirmishes and occasionally riots break out.

High-level attempts to destroy the informal bottom-up commercialism of the street reveals, as historian Fernand Braudel teaches, the emphatically anti-market nature of capitalist development. To quote from a Braudellian-inspired essay by the Cybernetic Culture Research Unit:[3]

The more 'developed' a society becomes the less comfortable it is with market environments. When compared to uncluttered boulevards and shops—especially exclusive ones—markets are not very 'nice'. Bourgeois ('civil' or 'polite') society is unanimous in condemning the dirt, noise, and disorder of concrete markets, even when it espouses a measure of confidence in abstract market principles. The state is encouraged to adopt wide-ranging responsibility for protecting 'the public' from markets, using the tools of regulation, policing, and urban planning, which are enforced in the name of safety and hygiene.[4]

This 'anti-market capitalism,' dominated by big business married to the state, insists on a rigid segmentarity between the privatisation of wealth and a well-ordered public sphere. It was precisely the enforcement of this divide that, according to libertarian blogger Ian B, led to the demise of Old Nichol, the largest and most famous market in Victorian London. Old Nichol is most often remembered as a slum, 'but the list of occupations that were carried on within Old Nichol's cramped confines reads like a Victorian trade directory. There were furniture makers, satin weavers, cats'-meat sellers, ivory turners, French polishers, watercress hawkers, cobblers, omnibus-washers and dozens more.'[5] The area was demolished in a clean-up campaign and the country's first council housing—The Boundary Estate—was built in its place. Yet out of over 5,000 Old Nicholites, only eleven ended up moving into the new council flats. 'Not allowed their old population density, they couldn't afford the rents and the council regulations meant they couldn't carry on their trades—essential to these people who were not just poor but working poor. Instead, they simply had to move on to other slums in Dalston and Bethnal Green...' Implicit in the clean-up of Victorian London, which involved a shift away from informal housing and street markets (the slum) was a 'palpable horror of the poor and in particular, of the "petty capitalism" that sustained them'. The 'costermonger and hawkers and small underclass production businesses had to be done away with, and replaced with something more acceptable to higher class tastes'.[6] It is worth noting that this critique of the 'clean up' of modern England finds a contemporary parallel in the work of Yasheng Huang, who argues that China's market-driven, grassroots, bottom-up development of the early 1980s was substantially crushed in the 1990s, and replaced by the cumbersome, bureaucratic state capitalism of what he despairingly calls the 'Shanghai model'.

Nevertheless, despite the strong and determined forces allied against it, Shanghai's shadow economy persists. Its resilience, determined ingenuity and black humour are illustrated best by the deeply ironic underground market in tax receipts, one of the most subversive and widespread manifestations of Shanghai's quasi-hidden economy. In order to better track the formal trade in goods and services, and to compensate people fairly, China has developed an official system of tax vouchers, which are known as *fapiaos*. Taxi cabs offer *fapiaos* directly to their customers, but in restaurants and supermarkets you have to ask specifically to transform pay stubs into official receipts. Landlords and businesses often demand more money for providing a *fapiao*. These valuable payment records have, quite unsurprisingly to anyone familiar with China, spawned their own rampant underground. It is common knowledge that fake *fapiaos* can be purchased, usually for under 10 per cent of their stated value. One lawyer investigating the illicit trade collected a thick brick-like stack of faxes that his office had received from companies offering fake *fapiaos*. At the low end these consisted of little more than a hastily scribbled phone number. Fake *fapiao* companies at the high end of the market, however, have developed their own elaborate branding designs, the most sophisticated of which are shamelessly based on pirated versions of the official logo of the tax office itself.

The shadow economy, then, perseveres through a tenacious ability to both be everywhere and yet still remain obscure. Its continued existence functions as an implicit but powerful rejoinder to the evolutionary narrative of modern development.

In a talk on 'Megacity Mumbai' urbanist Rupali Gupte argued that models of the city are typically based on the Western experience, which, for the past few decades, has been dominated by stories of postindustrial decay. The contemporary focus of urbanism, therefore, has been on dying centres in need of rejuvenation and renewal. Yet, during the past twenty years, while many cities in the West have spun into decline, the Asian metropolis has been on a takeoff trajectory that has made them more vital than ever before. In the case of Mumbai at least, the transformation from city to megacity cannot be explained by population growth. In fact, according to Gupte, Mumbai's population has remained surprisingly stable. What has changed is the nature of work. This mutation, according to Gupte, is less about density than intensity. Mumbai, like Shanghai, has become a city filled with street-level entrepreneurs, many of whom operate in a shadow economy where the line between the formal and the informal is deliberately blurred. It is precisely this blur, Gupte contends, that allows entry into the edges of the city. The micro-entrepreneurs of the shadow economy tend towards complex and innovative occupancy patterns that are extremely difficult to track (Gupte illustrated this point with an example of a store housed within a store). In Shanghai it is common to see a single space used for a variety of purposes depending on the time of the day. Urban planners have few tools to map or analyse these hybrid, multiple and highly productive arrangements. What is crucial about these critical urban spaces, as Gupte rightly stressed, is that they enable an extremely high level of transactions per unit. The most important vector in mapping the Asian megacity, therefore, is not the density of population but, rather, the intensity of economic transactions.

Planners, who rarely factor in the economic dynamism of the shadow economy, often favour projects that harden urban boundaries, reducing the blurred zones necessary for the markets of the economic underground to thrive. Rather than maximising transaction capabilities, they are drawn to large-scale, resource-intensive developments in which transaction capabilities are low. Our current models of urban futurism, Gupte concluded, suffer from a paucity of imagination. Visions are too often caught between extremes in which the future proceeds along a single linear line. Between the high gloss mega-towers of a rigid corporate utopianism, however, and the sprawling hopelessness of the planet of slums, lies a real metropolis, with its hybrid spaces, fantastical mixtures and multiple temporalities that is emerging in a host of unpredictable ways. The ubiquity of informal markets, then, is both part and symbol of the alternate modernity brewing in Shanghai, and is an intrinsic element of the future that it is helping to create.

Theorising the informal

In academic discourse British scholar Keith Hart is credited with the 'discovery' of the informal economy. Hart coined the term after a research trip to Accra, Ghana in the early 1970s, where he went to study the Frafras, a north Ghanaian group who were migrating to cities in the south and forming a large urban sub-proletariat. At the start of his influential essay 'Informal Income Opportunities and Urban Employment in Ghana', Hart asks: 'Does the reserve army of urban unemployed and underemployed really constitute a passive, exploited majority in cities like Accra, or do their informal economic activities possess some autonomous capacity for generating growth in the incomes of the urban (and rural) poor?'[7] During his fieldwork, Hart found a very large urban population untouched by wage employment as well as a 'chronic imbalance' between income from wage labour and the basic costs of everyday life.[8] To meet this gap, the urban poor had created a whole plethora of work outside official sources—from backyard farming, to street trading, to hustling of all kinds. 'Petty capitalism, often as a supplement to wage-employment,' he wrote, 'offers itself as a means of salvation. Denied success by the formal opportunity structure, these members of the urban sub-proletariat seek informal means of increasing their incomes.'[9] Following Hart, and similar work done by the International Labour Organization (ILO) in Africa during the same period, scholars began to recognise that contrary to the traditional narratives of progress, informal markets showed no signs of disappearing from the 'growing metropolis' of the developing world.

For obvious reasons the informal economy is extremely difficult, if not impossible, to quantify. Researchers use a variety of methods including inspection of tax audits, labour markets, currency demands, electricity consumption, neighbourhood surveys and complex calculations involving discrepancies in income and expenditure. Standard definitions are also highly elusive. Most researchers distinguish between an illicit economy (in which the products and services are themselves illegal) and an underground economy that trades in 'otherwise licit goods and services'.[10] While street traders, including vendors of all types, barbers, cobblers, tailors, entertainers and rubbish collectors, are the most visible of informal workers, the shadow economy also includes jobs in small factories and workshops, services in restaurants and beauty salons, repair men and women, casual day labourers on farms and construction sites, and domestic workers of all types.

Though the inherent ambiguities make it hard to prove for certain, there is a growing consensus that the informal economy is not only highly pervasive in the developing world but also an increasingly integral feature of developed economies. This is particularly so since the recent restructuring of work, with the virtual collapse of jobs-for-life and the subsequent increase in much more casual, nonstandard arrangements. 'The twentieth-century norm—the factory worker who nests at the same firm for his or her entire productive life—has become an endangered species,'[11] writes journalist Robert Neuwirth, who has done extensive research on the economic underground. Alongside this increasing instability in the workplace is the trend towards horizontal networks rather than vertical bureaucracies, and the growth of outsourcing, piecework and short contracts, all tendencies that coincide well with unregulated work. Moreover, the grey market often serves as a cushion in periods of economic hardship. After the financial crisis of 2008/2009, Neuwirth reports, informal work was found to be 'an important financial coping mechanism'. When salaried labour is scarce, people often turn to a strategy of self-reliance by becoming 'off the books' micro-entrepreneurs. According to expert Martha Chen the informal economy as a significant generator of jobs and income, 'can no longer be considered as a temporary phenomenon. Despite early predictions of its eventual demise, the informal economy has not only grown worldwide but also emerged in new guises and unexpected places.'[12] Neuwirth details those that are involved from people 'who grab some extra cash by selling their excess possessions in lawn or garage sales or even on eBay' to 'a storeowner who entices you to make a purchase by offering not to charge sales tax if you pay in cash', to freelance construction labourers who are hired by contractors on a job-by-job basis.[13]

In his book *Stealth Nation* Neuwirth seeks to show that the shadow economy not only exists at a local level but is also deeply global. The unlicensed traders, he writes, have always been the earliest globalisers. 'Without documentation or approval or any assistance from their governments, they have created a bootstrap circuit of global trade unrecognized by governments and uncelebrated by economists.'[14] The opening pages of his book tell of a street market in Brazil where hawkers sell bracelets, backpacks, sunglasses and plastic toy spidermen. The products are 'made in China, imported to Paraguay, smuggled across the border into Brazil, and trucked down to Sao Paulo.' In the world of back-door trade routes, traffic is particularly intense between China and Africa. Neuwirth tracks clothes, machinery, mobile phones and motorcycles as they make their way from Guangzhou to Lagos. This growing trade has brought an enormous population of Africans to settle in the southern coastal city. 'Though the official Guangzhou statistical agency puts the number at thirty thousand, other observers have suggested that there could be as many as three hundred thousand Africans living in the city.'[15]

In his exploration of this 'global back channel', Neuwirth rejects the dominant discourses on the subject. The early 'dualist approach' (associated with Hart and the ILO) is based on too rigid a divide between the formal and the informal, which grants the grey economy too marginal a role. While the structuralists, who emerged later, offer a corrective by viewing the black and white economy as intrinsically intertwined, their approach to this inter-relationship, which sees it as essentially exploitative, misses the vibrancy, aspirations and optimism of the 'world underneath'. In order to think outside these dominant frameworks, Neuwirth advocates scrapping the term 'infor-mal' altogether and offers a new term, 'System D', instead. The expression is based on a 'slang phrase pirated from French-speaking Africa and the Caribbean'. The D stands for '*debrouillards*', a word that stands for 'self starting entrepreneurs who work outside the bureaucracy and regulations of the state'.[16]

There is another economy out there … Its edges are diffuse and it disappears the moment you try to catch it. It stands beyond the law, yet is deeply entwined with the legally recognized business world. It is based on small sales and tiny increments of profit, yet it produces, cumulatively, a huge amount of wealth. It is massive yet disparaged, open yet feared, microscopic yet global. It is how much of the world survives, and how many people thrive, yet it is ignored and sometimes disparaged by most economists, business leaders, and politicians. You can call it System D.[17]

According to Neuwirth's calculations 'the billions of underground trans-actions around the world', which are performed by 'dozens, hundreds, thou-sands, millions' together amount to a total value of close to ten trillion dollars. Its enormous scale demands attention. For Neuwirth and the others who share his concerns it makes no sense to speak of development without talking about the shadowy economic sphere that, at least according to the evolutionary story, was supposed to be eradicated by advancing the momen-tum of economic growth:

System D is growing faster than any other part of the economy, and it is an increasing force in world trade … This spontaneous system, ruled by the spirit of organized improvisation, will be crucial for the development of cities in the twenty-first century … Given its size, it makes no sense to talk of development, growth, sustainability, or globalization without reckoning with System D.[18]

Hernado De Soto and the legalist approach

Peruvian economist Hernando De Soto shares Neuwirth's admiration for the tenacity and entrepreneurship of the urban poor. In his book *The Mystery of Capital* he states his position forcefully:

The grimmest picture of the Third World is not the most accurate. Worse, it draws attention away from the arduous achievements of those small entrepreneurs who have triumphed over every imaginable obstacle to create the greater part of the wealth of their society. A truer image would depict a man and a woman who have painstakingly saved to construct a house for themselves and their children and who are creating enterprises where nobody imagined they could be built. I resent the characterization of such heroic entrepreneurs as contributors to the problem of global poverty. They are not the problem. They are the solution.[19]

Yet, despite De Soto's respect for the makeshift communities and self-made micro-businesses that power the underground economy, he is a strong proponent of formalisation, believing that it is only as the informal is made formal that the poor can share in the fruits of the capitalist system. 'Capitalism is essentially a tool for poor people to prosper,' he contends.[20] The tool is only able to function, however, if the assets of the poor—their informal homes and businesses—cease to be hidden and are fully incorporated into a transparent economic system.

De Soto's position is taken, alongside the dualists and the structuralists, as one of three key scholarly approaches to the problem of the shadow economy. His ideas, outlined in his 1989 book *The Other Path*, define what has come to be called the 'legalist school'. In the book De Soto, along with a team of researchers, carefully examine the informal housing, trade and transport rampant during the rapid and mass urbanisation of Peru. Among the most important contributions of *The Other Path* was to record, in precise detail, the enormously high cost and cumbersome bureaucracy involved in both gaining access to the formal economy and, even more importantly, in remaining inside it. The difficulties in navigating state laws and bureaucracy, the book argues, force people to operate in a system that is external to the law. Legal compliance is so burdensome, maintains De Soto, that many people 'economically speaking are better off when they violate the laws than when they respect them'.[21] Workers in the informal economy 'want to engage in the same activities as formals but, since the legal system prevents them from doing so, they have had to invent ways of surviving outside the law'.[22]

While living and working underground can be a useful strategy for those who cannot afford the costs of formality, De Soto nevertheless insists that informality too involves tremendous costs. Life in the shadows necessitates a colossal waste of resources. Informals devote enormous energy in avoiding detection and punishment, they cannot easily advertise their goods and services, and don't benefit from any of the institutional advantages of capitalism like credit or shares. They must find alternative means of enforcing contracts and spend a huge amount of time and money building trustworthy relationships. In the end, De Soto concludes, an economy based on 'law-

SHANGHAI FUTURE

breaking is not, on balance, desirable', as it invariably results in 'declining productivity, reduced investment, and lack of technological advance'.[23]

According to De Soto the crucial factor that excludes people from the formal, legal economy is the absence of secure and reliable property rights.[24] Private property, he insists, is essential to efficient modern economic development, not only because of the asset itself (the poor, De Soto is careful to explain, actually have substantial resources), but because of the legal representation of that asset, which allows an owner to leverage property as capital. In the capitalist system this access to the representation of property, through land records and titles, is the central mechanism through which capital is produced. Without it, De Soto contends, there is no way to extract the potential from one's holdings and enter the system of credit and trade that enables an escape from poverty. 'The value of property rights, which relate not only to houses, cars, machinery or merchandise but also to rental agreements, foreign currency certificates and their free convertibility, and all sorts of credit,'[25] is their capacity to formalise capital assets.

Not only do property rights allow the holder to make use of their assets as collateral in securing loans, they also, and more importantly, encourage investment and innovation. A feeling of security greatly enhances the desire to increase the value of one's possessions. 'What property rights, contracts, and extra-contractual liability do is reduce uncertainty for people who want to invest.' This is especially important for innovation, 'the riskiest investment', which is fostered by a sense of confidence in the institutions of capitalism. Without these, De Soto believes, it is extremely difficult for economies to grow.

In societies with legal structures that enforce contracts and protect property people tend to be more innovative, more productive, and more prepared to run greater economic risks. Are we inhabitants of underdeveloped countries genetically or culturally incapable of saving, innovating, taking risks, or running industries? Or are these 'causes' of development not the causes at all, but in fact development itself?'.[26]

In the mass migration of peasants to cities and in the squatter communities and grey markets of the newly urbanised, De Soto sees the reflections of a previous age. More precisely, he argues that Peru's situation in the 1980s parallels the economic system of mercantilism, which dominated Europe from the sixteenth to the eighteenth century. Peru, De Soto writes, 'is a predominantly mercantilist system which has little to do with a modern market economy'.[27] Mercantilism, as De Soto describes it, was a policy through which the economy was controlled by a privileged business elite that was married to the state. It was a period 'of widespread state intervention in the economy', he writes, which was 'characterised by the close ties that existed between an ever-present state and a privileged and exclusive entrepreneurial clique'.[28] Mercantilism, then, rests on the 'belief that the economic welfare of the State can only be secured by government regulation of a nationalist character'.[29]

During the industrial age, when European peasants first began to flood into this heavily regularised and highly bureaucratic urban environment, crises ensued. Neither the private nor the public sector, which were bogged down by 'institutional rigidity and excessive administrative obstacles' could create jobs fast enough to absorb the arriving immigrants. As a result, 'informals began to proliferate'. To start with, city dwellers 'despised the work done by these people outside the guilds and the system. Since it was the only feasible alternative, however, informal activity spread quickly.'[30] Conflict was sweeping and often fierce as formal traders did their best to get rid of the new imposters. Street disturbances and legal battles were commonplace. Many informal business operators tried to avoid state control and the oppression by the guilds by moving 'to outlying towns or established new suburbs (informal settlements) where state supervision was less strict and regulations more lax or simply inapplicable'.[31]

Though they began in the shadows, however, over time the new street traders succeeded in completely revolutionising the socio-economic order. Informality, writes De Soto, 'grows as a reaction to mercantilism and hastens its demise… As formal businesses were gradually stifled by taxes and regulations and informals openly defied the law and voiced dissatisfaction at being pushed to the margins, the stage was set for collapse.' Eventually, the competition proved to be too much and the formal businesses at the city centre could no longer ignore the increased efficiency of the markets that were proliferating at the edges. The privileges of the guilds and the heavy-handed authoritarian bureaucracy thus went into decline and the state, eager to retain social relevance, adopted a 'legal system that was adapted to the realities of a diverse and pluralistic society, widespread popular entrepreneurship, and an economy that was rapidly evolving technologically'. The state was thus able to 'reduce the level of informal activity, control violence, and gradually dispel uncertainty'. In this way, 'the mercantilist institutions were eliminated', paving the way for the emergence of the 'modern market economies of the West'.[32] In retelling this developmental history, De Soto urges nations like Peru to follow this 'deliberate path, which will enable us to escape from backwardness and advance toward a modern society'.[33]

Back alley banking

The progressive narrative of the legalist school, in which a modern economy emerges through the gradual adoption of transparent, contract-based capitalist institutions supported by the rule of law, may have been true for Europe. It also may apply to Peru. China, however, is veering off script. The dynamism of the Chinese economy has been powered in large part by a hugely energetic private sector (in the 1990s the private sector expanded to the point of producing one-third of China's GDP).[34] This growth, however and contrary to the theories of De Soto, has occurred despite a lack of property rights and almost entirely without access to formal credit.

Instead, the private sector in China is funded by an extensive and multifaceted ecosystem of informal finance that operates outside capitalist institutions and their legal frameworks. Kellee Tsai, a scholar at John Hopkins University, estimates that throughout the era of opening and reform, informal sources have accounted for up to three-quarters of private-sector credit.[35] 'The vast majority of private financing mechanisms reside beyond the scope of permissible economic activity,' she writes. 'Private entrepreneurs are violating official laws and regulations to finance their businesses. They are banking creatively behind the legal lens of the state.'[36] The result is that China, as researchers Franklin Allen, Jun Qian and Meijun Qian contend, offers 'an important counterexample to the findings in the law, finance, and growth literature'.[37] The country enjoys one of the fastest growing economies, despite the fact that its legal and financial systems are not well developed by existing standards. In order to explore this seeming contradiction, Allen, Qian and Qian compare growth in the formal and informal sector. What they find is that 'with much poorer applicable legal and financial mechanisms, the informal sector grows much faster than the formal sector, and provides most of the economy's growth'.[38]

Tsai's book *Back Alley Banking* details the shadow banking system in all its heterogeneous variety. Her research shows how informal finance in China is impacted by differences in region, gender and class. Among the assorted forms of back alley banks are parasitic institutions that feed of the official loans in the formal financial sector; institutions of rotating credit; private money houses; pyramid investment schemes; pawnshops; and probably most commonly of all, a culture of mutual help. The state itself recognises a distinction between this lending among intimate relations known as *minjian* (popular, folk or of the people) and *siying* (or private lending) much of which is illegal. According to some studies, in small firms in China (especially in the start-up phase), 'more than 90 per cent of the initial capital came from the principal owners and their families and friends'.[39]

Back alley banking exists, primarily, for a negative reason. Namely, state banks don't lend to private entrepreneurs. Tsai quotes the response of one small business owner when asked about the possibility of a loan from the formal sector. 'Are you crazy?,' she said. 'Private entrepreneurs can't get loans from banks! ... A state bank would not give me a loan if Chairman Mao himself rose from the dead and told me to give him one.'[40]

During the Mao era all private banking was banned. Reforms introduced by Deng Xiaoping prompted substantial liberalisation of the banking system. Nevertheless, the state banks still loan almost exclusively to state-owned companies. 'As of the end of 2000,' Kellee Tsai reports, 'less than 1 per cent of loans from the entire national banking system had gone to the private sector.'[41] This despite the fact that 'in terms of capital-industrial output ratios, collectively-owned and privately owned firms are on average more than twice as productive (for every $1 invested) as SOEs'.[42] Partly, this is a result of political pressure. The government fears widespread unemployment, and maintaining a tight control of lending is one of the best mechanisms for supporting state-directed policy goals. Banks know to loan to SOEs in industries that the centre has officially targeted as developmental priorities. In addition to government pressure, other important factors include the general suspicion of entrepreneurs and the widespread lack of experience in dealing with the private sector. Banks feel safer loaning to state-owned enterprises, partly because bad loans are often forgiven, and, also because many bankers simply have no idea how to process an individual a loan.

Without support of formal institutions, private entrepreneurs have been forced to find alternative sources of capital. This has been made easier by the deep tradition of informal finance in China. 'Pawnshops run by Buddhist monasteries,' Tsai tells us 'date back to the middle of the Six Dynasties (317–589).' Co-operative loan societies proliferated in the Tang Dynasty (618–907) as did rotating credit associations in the late Qing and early Republican.[43] The world of hidden finance has flourished not only in the mainland but also throughout the Chinese diaspora. As William Cassidy writes in an article entitled 'Fei Chien, or Flying Money', 'Apart from a historical distrust for banks among the Chinese, the [underground banking] system grew out of political turmoil, Communist takeovers in many countries where the Chinese reside, and constant harassment of expatriate Chinese in nearly all the countries where they are present in significant numbers.'[44]

By tapping into a long history and planet-wide networks, China has created a mode of grassroots financing that does not require the formal security of private property and the assurances that the state will act as third-party enforcer of contracts and deals. Rather, the shadow banking system operates through kinship ties, local networks and shared identities. In these informal social institutions, the cultural norms of shame and face, which are based on reciprocity, trust, reputation and relationships govern financial transactions. Research shows that these substitutes sometimes do better than standard channels and mechanisms. In back alley banking, says Tsai 'taken-for-granted norms and habits condition transaction as if they were protected under an explicit system of property rights'.[45]

The Wenzhou model

Nowhere has the world of underground finance found a more supportive home than in Wenzhou, a city in Zhejiang province, a few hours south of Shanghai. Due to its rugged, mountainous terrain Wenzhou has a long history of isolation. The relative independence of the place is evidenced by the autonomy of its language. According to research by Kristen Parris, 'a 1955 report stated that only 5 per cent of Wenzhou's population understood Mandarin, and that the Wenzhou dialect was understood only by those living within a 34-mile radius of the city radio system'.[46] Left to their own devices, the city became extremely adept at evading control from the centre. This grassroots culture was combined with an intense commercial instinct—Wenzhou people are known throughout China for their keen business senses and innovation, as well as their sharp management skills. These factors, along with easy access to the sea, have made Wenzhou a notorious hub for smuggling. In recent times, the city's age-old link to the black economy has become ever stronger.

Wenzhou's shadow economy was repressed during the Mao era, but it re-emerged with gusto as soon as the Cultural Revolution drew to a close and the restrictive policies of the Communist era began to relax. As early as the late 1970s, a whole host of underground factories and labour markets were already springing up in Wenzhou. When China's economy opened in the 1980s these numbers exploded. 'In 1979 there were already an estimated 1,844 micro-entrepreneurs in the area,' writes Tsai; 'three years later the number had multiplied eleven times, to 20,363 entrepreneurs'.[47] Wenzhou's entrepreneurs excel in family-run back-room factories that specialise in small-scale enterprise. The city thrived off tiny off-the-books businesses that manufacture low-end products for export. Wenzhou produces a huge percentage of the world's lighters, small knickknacks and everyday household goods. The focus is on the things that the large state-owned factories ignore. 'Wenzhou's consumer industry,' writes researcher Alan Liu, 'grew truly "in the crevices of China's industrial structure"'.[48]

The underground economy of Wenzhou has been funded, almost entirely, from back alley banking. 'It was private lending that made grassroots entrepreneurship and expansion possible.'[49] Supported by permissive local officials, Wenzhou developed a dynamic ecosystem of shadow banking. Households pooled their money into underground lending syndicates and private money houses operated around the clock. 'By the mid 1980s local economists estimated that 80 to 95 per cent of the capital flows of Wenzhou were tied up in informal finance.'[50] The high-octane shadow economy of Wenzhou enjoyed enormous success. The city is widely lauded as the home of private entrepreneurship in China and, as private businesses boomed, people got very rich. From 1980 to 1988 the proportion of industrial output by private firms in Wenzhou increased from 1 per cent to 41 per cent.[51] In the same decade the average income of Wenzhou peasants went from being among the lowest in the nation, to 50 per cent above the national average.[52] Today the city is famous for its multimillionaires.

China's growth is often attributed to the strong controls of a state-led capitalism. The 'Wenzhou model'—a term that was promoted in the mid-1980s by officials in Shanghai[53]—shows that the dynamism of China's economy, however, owes just as much, if not more, to the small-scale bottom-up entrepreneurship of a private sector that has been, by necessity, hidden from view. 'Capitalism with Chinese Characteristics', then, is not solely the product of a market that conforms to the dictates of the party/state. Rather, in the shadows of state-directed capitalist development are the back rooms and back alleys of Wenzhou, propelling China's high speed acceleration.

More recently, however, the 'Wenzhou model' has come under threat. For over a decade, cash-rich Wenzhou businesspeople have been fuelling real estate speculation in Shanghai. In 2011, when the Chinese market began to feel the effects of the global financial crisis, the real estate market started to slow. The underground banking system of Wenzhou faced a credit crunch. For months newspapers were filled with stories of broke Wenzhou bosses fleeing the country in the dead of night. Some committed suicide. Many took this as a sign that the whole of the Chinese economy was in trouble and there were urgent calls for reform. In October of that year premier Wen Jiabao made a high-profile visit to the city and in an attempt to quell the crisis the

State Council announced a package of policies including tax breaks and easier access to loans from state banks for small enterprises nationwide.[54]

Yet, despite these efforts, formalising the informal is not easy. Even if, as Kellee Tsai points out, the government develops the institutional capabilities to lend to the private sector they will still, invariably, leave out substantial numbers of creditworthy entrepreneurs. Still others will deem it profitable to stay below the radar. Historically, all attempts at reining in underground activity in China have met with a passive, but highly effective resistance. Chinese businesspeople are notoriously good at getting around the rules. In China 'legislative fiat should not be confused with legislative compliance', warns Tsai.[55] Instead, economic life is more often governed by a cat and mouse game, consisting of circuits of innovation and regulation. As activities are shut down or brought into the light, businesses find ways to reconfigure and continue their activities. In the end, writes Tsai, 'The stubborn persistence of informal interactions and informal finance is how China's economic miracle has been financed. Not the establishment of state-run commercial banks.'[56]

The informal economy, with its street hawkers and household lenders has not given way to the bright transparency of formal institutions. Instead, the continued persistence of shadow markets shows that, contrary to thinkers like Marx and Weber, modern capitalism is not marching towards a rational, highly bureaucraticised machine, which arrives as the inevitable culmination of history. Rather, in China's new cities, at least, the dynamic perseverance of *baozi* sellers and back street lenders relentlessly disrupts this narrative of inevitable advance.

The disruptive potential of innovation from below

The theorist most attuned to this entrepreneurialism of the street is economist Joseph Schumpeter, who saw capitalism as a biological organism, an entity in a constant state of becoming. 'The essential point to grasp,' he wrote in *Socialism, Capitalism, Democracy*, 'is that in dealing with capitalism we are dealing with an evolutionary process. Capitalism is by nature a form or method of economic change and not only never is but never can be stationary.'[57] Schumpeter's 'evolutionism', however, differs fundamentally from the progressive theories of Marx, whose dialectical unfolding presumes that all the elements of a system are there from the start. Instead, for Schumpeter, capitalism does not unfold according to a preset dialectic but rather grows unpredictably through its hunger for the new. 'The fundamental impulse that sets and keeps the capitalist engine in motion,' he states, 'comes from the new consumer goods, the new methods of production or transportation, the new markets, the new forms of industrial organization that capitalist enterprise creates.'[58] In Schumpeter's theory of capitalism, explains the journalist Thomas Friedman, 'innovation replaces tradition and the present—or perhaps the future—replaces the past.'[59]

The agent of this constant mutation is the entrepreneur. Operating at the edges of the system, the entrepreneurial function creates ruptures of change by replacing old arrangements and hierarchies with those that are unfamiliar and unknown. Schumpeter famously names this process 'creative destruction'. 'Industrial mutation—if I may use the biological term,' he writes in a frequently cited passage, 'incessantly revolutionizes the economic structure from within, incessantly destroying the old one, incessantly creating a new one. This process of Creative Destruction is the essential fact about capitalism.'[60]

China's recent growth (its ability to position itself as factory to the world) is one such industrial mutation. The country's remarkable ability to produce stuff cheaper than ever before has not only slashed prices in the developed world (the Walmart phenomenon), but also opened vast new markets in Asia, Africa and Latin America. China's rise has shown that the true markets of contemporary globalisation are not just the wealthy few of the developed world or even the growing middle class, but, rather, to quote management guru C. K. Prahalad, 'the billions of aspiring poor who are joining the market economy for the first time'.[61] The expansive networks of China's shadow economy—whether the street food of Shanghai, the trade in motorcycles between Guangzhou and Lagos, or the huge export of low-end goods pouring out of Wenzhou—are serving not just the cosmopolitan elite but rather what Prahalad has termed the 'bottom of the pyramid', a vast global population of urban poor. Taken together this grassroots, bottom tier economy 'represents a multitrillion-dollar market'[62] and has the potential to produce global, revolutionary change, particularly in the field of high-tech. Bottom-up street markets are capable of far more than plastic Spiderman toys, and low-end batteries. Contrary to common perceptions, the poor have substantial consumer power, and are generally eager to embrace new technologies. China's migrant workers, for example, spend a huge amount of money on their cell phones. 'The bottom of the pyramid,' writes Prahalad 'is waiting for high-tech businesses such as financial services, cellular telecommunications, and low-end computers. In fact, for many emerging disruptive technologies (e.g., fuel cells, photovoltaics, satellite-based telecommunications, biotechnology, thin-film microelectronics, and nanotechnology), the bottom of the pyramid may prove to be the most attractive early market.'

In an essay entitled 'The Great Disruption', Clayton Christensen, Thomas Craig and Stuart Hart expand on this theme. Businesses ignore the bottom end of the market at their peril, they write. Disruptive technologies 'have plunged many of the best companies into crises and, ultimately, failure'.[63] The big mistake of 'well managed' companies, they warn, is to assume that it is only developed markets which appreciate and are willing to pay for technological innovation. 'Good companies' tend to focus all their attention on the demands of their 'best' customers (that is those who will pay most for the latest product). As a result they spend the majority of their time and money researching those products that are highest on the value chain, which will satisfy their most demanding, and profitable, consumers. A management strategy that is strictly geared to high-end markets, however, can only result in the production of what Christensen calls 'sustaining technologies', that is, technologies that are designed to improve the performance of already established goods.

Disruptive technologies, on the other hand, emerge from experimentation at the lowest end of the market where the large, 'best' companies are simply not looking. Generally 'worse' than the technologies they are designed to replace, they are not intended as improvements of existing products, but act instead as a means of incorporating a whole new market that previously didn't exist. Because they are new, these technologies are impossible to measure by market research. When Sony introduced the Walkman, to use just one phenomenally successful example, no one was asking for hand-held stereos because Sony thought of them first. The attempt to meet the demands of existing customers, by concentrating on the high end of the market, often proves disastrous when it comes to determining future trends. Insulated from the information on the ground, large, successful companies ignore innovations at the lowest tiers of the market, and thus became desensitised to the emergence of their most dangerous competitors: the new products, production processes, markets, supply sources and business organisations that flow in subliminally from the edges of the capitalist world. The introduction of the PC, a classic disruptive technology, managed to damage and even destroy many of the mainframe giants. It never made sense for IBM to market software in the 1970s because the profits from hardware were so much higher. When disruptive technologies do appear in a zone that is already occupied, 'they usually perform worse at the beginning than mainstream products and are thus not of interest to high-end customers'.[64] They also tend to 'have lower profit margins and do not have as wide a market as mainstream products'.[65] It is this which gives them the potential to disrupt and—creatively—to destroy.

Disruptive technologies create major new growth in the industries they penetrate—even when they cause traditional entrenched firms to fail—by allowing less-skilled and less-affluent people to do things previously done only by expensive specialists in centralized, inconvenient locations. In effect they offer consumers products and services that are cheaper, better, and more convenient than ever before.[66]

Shanzhai

China's word for disruptive technology is *shanzhai*, which translates literally as 'mountain village' or 'mountain stronghold'. The term has strong subversive connotations denoting a zone that operates exterior to the law. *Shanzhai* belongs to the rebellious side of Chinese culture, and is therefore associated with *Outlaws of the Marshes*, one of China's four great classic novels, which tells the story of bandits that operate outside official control. The origins of the term, according to writers Sheng Zhu and Yongjiang Shi, stem 'from the medieval period when illegal products were produced far away in a remote mountain village'.[67] In contemporary (originally Cantonese) slang *shanzhai* refers to the cheap knock-off goods produced by small, low-quality factories in southern China. As a concept and practice it is rooted in the fiercely autonomous SEZ culture of Guangdong. *Shanzhai*, many note, sounds a lot like Shenzhen.

From the start *shanzhai* differed in a small but significant ways from the familiar piracy of counterfeit Gucci watches and Louis Vuitton bags that proliferate in the new Chinese metropolis. Unlike these standard knock-offs, *shanzai* products don't try to hide that they are copies. Instead, 'Hi-phone', 'Nikia' and 'Motopola' cellphones seem to take a comic pride in the fact they are fakes. At first *shanzhai* referred almost exclusively to mobile phones, a device that has a special affinity with disruptive technology in the developing world. *Shanzhai ji* (bandit phones) came into existence in 2005, the year that Mediatek, a semiconductor design company from Taiwan, introduced an innovation that significantly reduced the cost and complexity of producing mobile phones. Edward Tse, Kevin Ma and Yu Huang in their study 'Shanzhai: A Chinese Phenomenon' report on Mediatek's transformative breakthrough as follows:

In 2005 Taiwanese firm MTK developed a new JSTPC 1,1 46 'total solution chip'. For the first time, an independent company was able to provide a single chip, which would give a similar operating platform and comprehensive functionality to that used by OEMs and supplied by many major chip providers. It meant the cost of developing a mobile phone from the ground up was no longer prohibitively expensive.

Developers could create their own product, without having to fund costly R&D or face the threat of legal action for infringing intellectual property rights.[68]

In 2007, the industry got another boost when regulators stopped insisting that companies needed a licence to manufacture cellphones. Since then *shanzhai* phones have mushroomed, capturing an enormous share of both the domestic market and also of emerging markets in Asia, Africa, the Middle East and South America. *Shanzhai* companies like G'Five have grown into some of the largest producers of mobile phones in the world, posing what may well be a lethal challenge to famous brands such as Nokia, Motorola and Samsung. Many businesses with humble *shanzhai* origins, write Tse, Ma and Huang, are now becoming formidable market disrupters and, in many cases, market leaders. Apple has taken the top end of the market, argues Shanghai-based analyst David Li. *Shanzhai* will take care of the rest.

With the proliferation of *shanzhai* products in both China and abroad, *shanzhai* manufacturers are slowly making the shift from imitation to innovation. The mutation was not intentional. Due to *shanzhai's* uniquely rapid production cycle, companies have been forced to innovate simply because the branded companies are too slow to come up with new products to copy. When there is nothing left to counterfeit, quips Li, you have to try to come up with something new. Indeed their incredible speed is one of the key characteristics of *shanzhai* producers. 'Whilst its legitimate counterparts need months or even years to bring out a new product, *shanzhai* companies,' write Sheng Zhu and Yongjiang Shi, 'can go from concept to delivery in a matter of weeks, if not days.' According to their website G'five has more than 300 handset models in place and is capable of launching two new models every week. This accelerated pace demands innovation. Years ago the iPhone Mini could be spotted in Shanghai's digital markets despite the fact that the product was not something Apple had produced. The 'copy' was as real as it gets. The iPhone Mini, moreover included 'features Apple is yet to announce in its smartphone: an FM radio player, dual-SIM card support, Java, external storage via miniSD and video recording, to name just a few'.[69] Today companies need only speculate on a product, and the *shanzhai* version immediately exists.

As they evolve, *shanzhai* companies are inventing their own production ethos. The makers of *shanzhai* are no longer just rebelling against expensive world-leading brands, but are, instead, emerging as indigenous adaptors and innovators. Compared with the big branded names in mobile phones, small *shanzhai* businesses come equipped with 'powerful and efficient sensors'. Their speed and bottom-up networks of distribution allow them to get ideas for designs and functionality directly from agents and customers. People in rural India want a low-cost, jewel-encrusted mobile phone that displays pictures of local gods—done. Obama is wildly popular and people want a phone that displays his smiling face—no problem. 'If you can think it you can make it,' is one of the key features of *shanzhai*, state Sheng and Shi after examining numerous case studies.[70] Out of the cell phone market in the wilds of Shenzhen, then, *shanzhai* has built an anti-corporate community that is fast, flexible and willing to take risks. 'The salient quality of modern-day Chinese entrepreneurs, including *shanzhai* practitioners, is not their "me-tooism",' write Tse, Ma and Huang 'but their willingness to take chances and learn from their experiences. "Let's try it," they say. If an idea doesn't work, they abandon it and try something else.'[71]

This DIY, grassroots ethos has spread virally throughout Chinese culture. In their article on copycat culture for the *Wall Street Journal* Sky Canaves and Juliet Ye tell of 'a property developer in Nanjing, hoping to lure business and buzz, set up storefront façades with logos such as "Haagon-Bozs", "Pizza Huh", "Bucksstar Coffee", "KFG" and "McDnoald's". Images of what became known as "Shanzhai Street" spread rapidly online.'[72] 'A Beijing man,' they continue, 'repeatedly rebuffed in his attempts to appear on a popular CCTV academic program, produced his own "Shanzhai Lecture Room" show on the Internet, in which he holds forth on the heroes of the Song dynasty for a six-hour stretch.'[73] There are, writes Yu Hua 'copycat stars, TV programmes, advertisements, pop songs, Shenzhou 7 space capsules, and Bird's Nest national stadiums'.[74] To this list can be included *shanzhai* White Houses, Pentagons and Tiananmen squares.

Shanzhai culture's most notorious expression however has been in the proliferation of copycat Spring Festival galas, now a regular feature of the holiday season. CCTV's official New Year gala—a variety show with singers, sketches and comedians—was, for decades, mandatory viewing for the majority of Chinese. This made it the most watched show in China, and therefore the world. As China opened to the outside, however, the show faced growing criticism. Audience numbers were dwindling as younger generations became unwilling to watch the staid top-down entertainment produced by the state. In 2009 'for the first time in its 27-year history, the official broadcaster's show has competition when a 36-year-old wedding planner named Shi Mengqi sought to produce a Shanzhai gala and air it live on Guizhou TV as well as streaming it for free over the Internet'.[75] In the end, according to Yu Hua:

more than a dozen such copycat events were broadcast on the Internet. As Spring Festival approached, their organizers unleashed a flood of copycat advertising, send-

ing vehicles out into the streets to publicize their events, conducting news conferences in city squares, marching through downtown holding aloft wastepaper baskets
emblazoned with promotional quips. Advertising slogans for the copycat galas took
multiple forms; one, borrowing Mao Zedong's calligraphy.[76]

Today the word *shanzhai* can be used to describe anything that is non-
official, underground and inexpensive with acceptable quality. *Shanzhaiism*
has become a philosophical term denoting a Chinese style of innovation with
a peasant mind-set. *Shanzhai's* cool DIY spirit has a nationalistic pride but
it is rooted not in the strength of the state but in the flexible, creative culture
of the street. *Shanzhai* culture 'is from the grass roots and for the grass
roots', says Han Haoyue, a media critic in Beijing. It represents 'a challenge
of the grassroots to the elite, of the popular to the official, of the weak to the
strong', agrees Yu Hua. *Shanzhai* (translated as copycat) is one of the ten
words Yu Hua chooses to capture contemporary China. 'It would not be
going too far,' he writes, 'to say that "copycat" has more of an anarchist
spirit than any other word in the contemporary Chinese language.'[77]

Xinchejian

China's first hacker-space, Xinchejian, a self described community of hackers and makers, initially set up its first stand-alone shop in a semi-abandoned
warehouse on Shanghai's Anhua Lu, a narrow street lined with food stalls
and hawker stands. At home in this cyberpunk setting, founder David Li
speaks of how the bottom-up culture of *shanzhai* fuses with some of the
most future-oriented trends in high tech. Li points to the work of John Hagel
and John Seely Brown who write of a 'vibrant new way of designing and
manufacturing motorcycles that has developed in the mega-metropolis of
Chongqing'.[78] Chongqing's motorcycle industry has managed, in only a few
years, to challenge Japanese brand leaders and seize 50 per cent of the global
production of bikes. In an influential piece published by *McKinsey Quarterly*
the authors describe a distinct, loosely controlled, supplier-driven network
that speeds up time to market, cuts costs, enhances quality and 'is a prototype for disruptive innovation'. Economists at Tokyo University, who have
studied such networks in depth, call the new system 'localised modularisation.'[79] 'Localised modularisation', Li says, is just a fancy academic way of
saying hanging out in teahouses.

Like the Chongqing motorcycle makers, *shanzhai* manufacturing is based
on intense local clustering of shared technology and information. Radically
opposed to the secretive, security-obsessed culture of intellectual property,

shanzhai stems from an ecosystem of bottom-up technological growth, in which knowledge and information is distributed freely. This has little to do with any anarchist or libertarian ideal. Instead, argues Li, it has emerged out of necessity. In the world of *shanzhai* production one is forced to participate in the open ecology. Try to hoard information or designs and you are simply booted out. *Shanzhai*, Li thus contends, should be considered as the shadowy twin of 'open innovation', a concept promoted by popular theorists like Eric von Hippel and Clay Shirky who argue that 'sharism'—to use a term invented by Isaac Mao, one of China's first bloggers—is in the process of revolutionising the very idea of innovation itself.

What Li and the 'makers' of Xinchejian are most excited about is the combinatory trend that marries open innovation with distributed manufacturing and open source hardware. Xinchejian holds workshops in 3D printing and Arduino, the linux of the hardware world. With an abundance of cheap tech to play around with and more and more people eager to create, Li is confident that China will play a powerful role in new technological trends. People say China can't innovate, says Li, but companies like Seed Studio, a company based on pairing a global 'maker culture' with the *shanzhai* networks of Shenzhen have already become global leading brands.[80]

In an attempt to take hold of the future, China is investing heavily in R&D. Immense, state-backed laboratories are growing in future-oriented fields like green tech, nano-tech and bio-engineering. Yet the technology that supports the future-city will not necessarily unfold linearly, evolving in a predictable, pre-planned way. Indeed, revolutionary innovations are more likely to emerge from the distributed networks—more cyberpunk than sci-fi—through which disruptive technology is bred. Far more than cheap fake phones, the informal factories and markets of *shanzhai* production—whose influence has spread from the gritty suburbs of Shenzhen to the hackerspaces of Shanghai, where highly globalised urbanites come to play—has immense potential to unsettle what the 'world of tomorrow' might bring.

CONCLUSION

OPEN LOOPS

> *Abe: Studying up on your Mandarin?*
> *Joe: French.*
> *Abe: Why the fuck French?*
> *Joe: I'm going to France.*
> *Abe: You should go to China.*
> *Joe: I'm going to France.*
> *Abe: I'm from the future, you should go to China.*
>
> Looper, 2012

Looper, a 2012 time travel film set, in part, in Shanghai, tells the story of hit-men who are hired to execute people sent back in time to the year 2044. 'Time travel hasn't been invented yet,' says the main protagonist Joe at the start of the film, 'but thirty years from now it will have been.' In 2074 when a crime boss wants to end the contracts of his hired gunmen (who are known as 'loopers') he sends back their future selves to be killed by their younger incarnations. This is known as 'closing the loop'. (With the murder of a future self, the film playfully subverts the most common trope of time-travel narratives, which rest on the paradox of going back in time to change your fate by killing an ancestor.) Once each loop has been closed, the hit-man concerned receives a massive pay out and the opportunity to live out the rest of his life in luxury. Thirty years later time folds in on itself and the assassination takes place from the other side.

When Joe's loop closes, he flees with all his gold to Shanghai, despite the fact that he had been planning all along on France. The unexplained change of heart follows a switch in the production schedule that became embedded in the script. *Looper* director Rian Johnson had originally intended to set the film in Paris, but when Chinese distributors offered to pay to switch the location to China, Johnson agreed to rewrite the script and transplant production from Paris to Shanghai. The resulting scenes contain spectacular images of Shanghai futurism (many of which were only shown to Chinese audiences). In addition, *Looper* was able to count as a co-production, through a deal—destined to be repeated—which allowed the film to bypass foreign quota regulations and premier on the mainland. Johnson insists, however, that these pragmatic considerations did not negatively impact the film. 'In many ways Shanghai was a more natural setting for a sci-fi movie than my beloved Paris,' he admitted.[1] In the cultural imagination Shanghai and time travel are twinned.

While Joe's life in Shanghai only begins once the circle is complete, *Looper* refuses the neatness of a closed time circuit. Much of the story is set in a parallel, alternative, or coinciding time-line, in which the time-loop stays open and the future remains receptive to change.

This book is inspired by Shanghai's hunger for the future. It travels through the city's transitional zones—the new skyscrapers and heritage architecture of the urban core as well as the migrant communities and dream-like developments of the suburbs—to track the city's economy of anticipation. Through this future orientation, this palpable desire to inhabit the world of tomorrow, Shanghai, it argues, is manifesting a new modernity.

In the past, Chinese modernity has generally been conceptualised as involving the adoption of a progressive, linear time that can replace the country's older and more traditional notion of cyclic temporality. From the reformers of the May Fourth Movement to the ideology embodied in the Cultural Revolution, the dominant idea has been that modern China must accept the forward chronology of Western time: erase the old to make way for the new.

This conception of time as a unidirectional flow implies a relative notion of the future, essentially defined by its difference from the present and the past. In linear time, the future is in front of us, waiting on the road up ahead, and even as the end of the road. When viewed in terms of such a time-line, Shanghai's contemporary modernity can only ever be a re-run; the copy or repetition of conditions, actions and attitudes of a modernity that already once has been.

The modern as an historical epoch that culminated in the first half of the twentieth century, posited a future that could be projected, planned, predicted and controlled. Post-modernism emerged from the wreckage, precisely at the moment that this type of futurism collapsed. In China, however, where a developmental model based on centralised control seems to be supporting such staggering growth, the futurism of the past—that is elsewhere deemed 'retro'—appears to be making a comeback. Look closer, however, and it is clear that China's remarkable rise is not, or at least not solely, based on the top-down planning of an authoritarian state. Rather, in its yin/yang balance of shadow and light, the new modernity brewing in the contemporary Chinese metropolis pairs the bright spectacle of economic exuberance with a darker, bottom-up, unplanned and unpredictable culture that emerges from the street.

In this hybrid and multiplicitous modernity, the future—now intrinsically obscure—is no longer conceived as a destination or end point, or even clearly up ahead. Evolution from the informal to the formal, from the 'backward' to the 'advanced' (which was never natural nor inevitable) is disrupted. In Shanghai's jumble of high-rises and street markets, industrial heritage and gothically-slanted architecture, hidden lanes and suburban communities, the very processes of urbanisation and development are being transformed.

Shanghai evades a relative future by tangling the timeline. Its re-imagination of the City of Tomorrow is saturated by a nostalgia for what is to come. It is evident through the renovation of an art deco heritage that eludes historical comprehension; the reanimation of industrial zones that look back as they look forward; and the rejuvenation of an urban culture that aims to awaken an older golden age, that Shanghai's ambitions for the twenty-first century are suffused with echoes of the past. As a future city, Shanghai does not gradually arrive out of linear, evolutionary history. It (re)emerges in a temporal spiral out of which the future city reaches back to the past in order to construct itself today.

Within this time-spiral, Shanghai's 'neo-modernity' offers an escape from the devastating dilemma that has plagued China's formulation of the modern. A spiral is neither trapped by the cyclical time of a stagnant tradition nor committed to the forceful destruction of progressive linearity. Spirals are simultaneously progressive and cyclical. As the *Yijing* teaches, the spiral 'produces novelty while simultaneously returning again and again to the nascent sources'.[2] Contemporary Shanghai thus tends to the reinvention of an enormously rich cultural and philosophical heritage. 'The path was a circle,' says Joe at the end of *Looper*, 'so I changed it.'

NOTES

PREFACE: THE FUTURE IS NOT DATED

1. This question was posed in the introductory video to the exhibit 'Future City: China Prophecy' held at The Skyscraper Museum from June 2009 through April 2010. See http://www.skyscraper.org/EXHIBITIONS/CHINA_PROPHECY/china_prophecy.htm, last accessed 17 Aug. 2012.
2. Futuruma 1939, New York's World Fair, 'To New Horizons', You Tube, http://www.youtube.com/watch?v=1cRoaPLvQx0, last accessed 27 Oct. 2012.
3. Ibid.
4. See David Graeber, 'Of flying cars and the declining rate of profit', *The Baffler*, 19, http://www.thebaffler.com/past/of_flying_cars, last accessed 17 Aug. 2012.
5. Nick Land, 'A time-traveler's guide to Shanghai (Part 3)', *Urban Future*, 29 July 2011, http://www.thatsmags.com/shanghai/article/811/a-time-travelers-guide-to-shanghai-part-3, last accessed 25 Oct. 2012.
6. As stated in the acknowledgments, Nick Land is my partner. I quote him extensively, since we developed much of the thinking that went into this book together.
7. 'Michael Specter: the danger of science denial', *TED Talks*, February 2010, http://www.ted.com/talks/michael_specter_the_danger_of_science_denial.html, last accessed 27 Aug. 2012.
8. An advertising slogan for Expo 2010.
9. Daniel Brook, 'Head of the Dragon: The Rise of the New Shanghai,' *Places: Design Observer*, 18 February 2013, http://places.designobserver.com/feature/the-rise-of-new-shanghai/37674/, last accessed 2 Jan. 2014.
10. 'Shanghai rising', *Bloomberg Businessweek Magazine*, 18 February 2007, http://www.businessweek.com/stories/2007–02–18/shanghai-rising, last accessed 27 Aug. 2012.
11. Maura Elizabeth Cunningham and Jeffrey N. Wasserstrom, 'China Discovers World Expo Is No Olympics,' *YaleGlobal*, 17 August 2010.

12. Virginia Postrel, 'The lost glamour of World's Fairs', *Deep Glamour*, 27 July 2010, http://www.deepglamour.net/deep_glamour/2010/07/the-lost-glamour-of-worlds-fairs.html, last accessed 27 Aug. 2012.

13. Patti Waldmeir, 'Determined to be biggest and best', *Financial Times*, 30 April 2010.

14. Ananya Roy, 'Conclusion—Postcolonial Urbanism: Speed, Hysteria, Mass Dreams', in Aihwa Ong and Ananya Roy, *Worlding Cities: Asian Experiments in the Art of Being Global*, Oxford: Wiley–Blackwell, 2011, pp. 309–310.

15. Virginia Postrel, 'Shanghai Shangri-La?', *Big Questions Online*, 27 July 2010, http://www.bigquestionsonline.com/columns/virginia-postrel/shanghai-shangri-la, last accessed 27 Aug. 2012.

16. Nick Land, 'Time in transition', *Urban Future*, 13 July 2011, http://www.thatsmags.com/shanghai/article/777/time-in-transition, last accessed 25 Oct. 2012.

17. Nick Land, 'Calendric dominion', *Urban Future*, 30 September 2011, http://www.thatsmags.com/shanghai/article/1096/calendric-dominion, last accessed 29 Oct. 2012.

18. Cohn, Norman Cosmos, *Chaos and the World to Come: The Ancient Roots of Apocalyptic Faith*, Yale University Press, 1993, p. 227.

19. Ibid.

20. Nick Land, 'Introductions to the afterlife', *Design Ecologies*, 2, 1 (2012).

21. From the 1984 documentary *World of Tomorrow*, directed by Lance Bird and narrated by Jason Robards. The screenplay of this film was written by John Crowley, who Jeff Wasserstrom informed me is known largely for his works of science fiction and fantasy (for example, the novella *The Great Work of Time*).

22. Quoted in Nick Land, *Shanghai World Expo Guide*, Shanghai: Urbanatomy, 2010, p. 83.

23. Ibid., p. 107.

24. Bird, *World of Tomorrow*.

25. Virginia Postrel, 'Shanghai Shangri-La?', *Big Questions Online*, Tuesday 27 July 27 2010, http://www.bigquestionsonline.com/columns/virginia-postrel/shanghai-shangri-la, last accessed 27 Aug. 2012.

26. Matt Novak, '50 Years of *The Jetsons*: why the show still matters', *Paleofuture*, 19 September 2012, http://blogs.smithsonianmag.com/paleofuture/2012/09/50-years-of-the-jetsons-why-the-show-still-matters/, last accessed 25 Sep. 2012.

27. Ibid.

28. Ibid.

29. Nick Land, 29 July 2011.

30. The use of science fiction in discussions about Shanghai is fairly common (almost every visitor to the city compares the skyline of Pudong to the *Blade Runner* set). Shanghai scholar Jeff Wasserstrom, in particular often evokes the genre in writing about the city. Gibson has not visited Shanghai and the city does not feature directly in any of his fictions. However, the cyberpunk author does admit in a

preface to Greg Girard's book of photography *Phantom Shanghai* that Girard's images of a disappearing Shanghai felt, as Wasserstrom notes, like 'a place where features of the urban futures conjured up in sci-fi came to life.' See Wasserstrom, Jeffrey, 'Science Fiction Fantasies of Shanghai', *Danwei*, 31 December, 2008. http://www.danwei.org/shanghai/a_brief_history_of_shanghais_f.php

31. William Gibson, *The Gernsback Continuum*, http://lib.ru/GIBSON/r_contin.txt, last accessed 27 Aug. 2012.

32. Ibid.

33. Ibid.

34. Ibid.

35. See Andrew Field, *Shanghai's Dancing World: Cabaret Culture and Urban Politics, 1919–1954*, The Chinese University Press, 2011.

36. Marie-Claire Bergère, *Shanghai: China's Gateway to Modernity*, Stanford University Press, 2009.

37. See, for example Mark Magnier, 'China's great leap upward', *Los Angeles Times*, January 2 2005.

38. Nick Land, 'A time-travelers guide to Shanghai (Part 2)', *Urban Future*, 27 July 2011,http://www.thatsmags.com/shanghai/article/802/a-time-travelers-guide-to-shanghai-part-2, last accessed 27 Oct. 2012.

39. Lynn Pann, *In Search of Old Shanghai*, Hong Kong: Joint Publishing Co, 1982, p. 2.

40. Jeffrey Wasserstrom, *Global Shanghai: 1850—2010: A History in Fragments*, Routledge, 2008, p 6. The idea that Shanghai was simply asleep throughout the horrors of mid-twentieth century is of course a myth—though one the city likes to reinforce in the narratives it tells of itself (see, for example, the exhibits at the Shanghai History Museum where there is almost no mention made of Mao). For more on Shanghai during the Mao years see the chapters on 1950 and 1975 in Wasserstrom's book as well as Marie-Claire Bergère's *Shanghai: China's Gateway to Modernity*.

41. Simon Winchester, *River at the Center of the World*, New York: Picador, 1996, p. 64.

42. Seng Kuan, 'Images of the Metropolis: Three Historical Views of Shanghai', in Seng Kuan and Peter Rowe (eds), *Shanghai: Architecture and Urbanism for Modern China*, Prestel, 2004.

43. Nick Land, 'A time-travelers guide to Shanghai (Part 2)', *Urban Future*, 27 July 2011. http://www.thatsmags.com/shanghai/article/802/a-time-travelers-guide-to-shanghai-part-2, last accessed 27 Oct. 2012.

44. See Jeffrey Wasserstrom, 'Science Fiction fantasies of Shanghai', *Danwei*, 31 December 2008, http://www.danwei.org/shanghai/a_brief_history_of_shanghais_f.php last accessed 2 Jan. 2014; and Li Tangtang, 'A Long Love Affair', *Beijing Review*, 9 May 2009, http://www.bjreview.com.cn/nation/txt/2009–05/09/content_194750.htm, last accessed 2 Jan. 2014.

45. The building has since been refurbished as a contemporary museum of art.
46. The exhibition was given 'Chinese Characteristics' by referring to Guanzi and Feng Shui.
47. Evan Osnos 'Green Giant' *The New Yorker*, 21 December 2009. http://www. newyorker.com/reporting/2009/12/21/091221fa_fact_osnos
48. 'The redistribution of hope', *The Economist*, 16 December 2010.
49. David Brooks, 'The nation of futurity', *New York Times*, 16 November 2009.
50. Martin Jacques, *When China Rules the World*, New York: Penguin Press, 2009, p. 21.
51. Jeffrey Wasserstrom, *Global Shanghai*, p. 128.
52. Maura Elizabeth Cunningham and Jeffrey N. Wasserstrom, 'China Discovers World Expo Is No Olympics,' *YaleGlobal*, 17 August 2010.
53. Virginia Postrel, 'The lost glamour of the World's Fairs', *Deep Glamour*, 27 July 2010, http://www.deepglamour.net/deep_glamour/2010/07/the-lost-glamour-of-worlds-fairs.html, last accessed 27 Aug. 2012.
54. Mark Fisher, 'Opening remarks', *Accelerationism*, Goldsmiths College, University of London, 14 September 2010. http://backdoorbroadcasting. net/2010/09/accelerationism/, last accessed 27 Aug. 2012.
55. Virginia Postrel, 'The lost glamour of the World's Fairs'.
56. Robert Hughes, *The Shock of the New*, London: Random House, 1980, p. 9.

INTRODUCTION: THE FUTURE IS ALWAYS MODERN

1. Abbas Ackbar, 'Cosmopolitan Descriptions: Shanghai and Hong Kong', in John Hartley (ed.), *Creative Industries*, Oxford: Wiley–Blackwell, 2005 p. 274.
2. Martin Jacques *When China Rules the World*, New York: Penguin Press, 2009, p. 20.
3. Nick Land, 'Neomodernity', *Urban Future*, 22 April 2011, http://www.thatsmags. com/shanghai/article/375/neomodernity, last accessed 25 Sep. 2012.
4. Robert Hughes, *The Shock of the New*, New York: McGraw Hill, 1980, p. 10.
5. Jameson continues: 'More decisively than in the other arts or media, postmodernist positions in architecture have been inseparable from an implacable critique of architectural high modernism and of Frank Lloyd Wright or the so-called international style (Le Corbusier, Mies etc), where formal criticism and analysis (of the high-modernist transformation of the building into a virtual sculpture, or monumental "duck," as Robert Venturi puts it), are at one with reconsiderations on the level of urbanism and of the aesthetic institution. High modernism is thus credited with the destruction of the fabric of the traditional city and its older neighbourhood culture (by way of the radical disjunction of the new Utopian high-modernist building from its surrounding context), while the prophetic elitism and authoritarianism of the modern movement are remorselessly identified in the imperious gesture of the charismatic Master.' Fredric Jameson, *Postmodernism, or the Cultural Logic of Late Capitalism*, London: Verso, 1991, p. 2.

6. Personal interview, Gary Wang, May 2009.
7. Jane Jacobs, *Cities and the Wealth of Nations*, New York: Vintage, 1984, p. 221.
8. Peter Hall, *Cities in Civilization*, New York: Pantheon, 1998, p. 3.
9. Ibid.
10. Ananya Roy, 'Conclusion—Postcolonial Urbanism: Speed, Hysteria, Mass Dreams', in Aihwa Ong and Ananya Roy, *Worlding Cities: Asian Experiments in the Art of Being Global*, Oxford: Wiley–Blackwell, 2011, p. 310.
11. Marie-Claire Bergere, 'Shanghai's Urban Development A Remake?' in Peter Rowe and Seng Kuan (eds), *Shanghai: Architecture and Urbanism for Modern China*, Prestel, 2004.
12. Doug Saunders, *Arrival City*, Toronto: Alfred Knopf, 2010, p. 21.
13. Erla Zwingle, 'Cities: challenge for humanity', *National Geographic*, November 2002.
14. Saunders, *Arrival City*, p. 1.
15. 'Metropolis Now' in *Foreign Policy*, 16 August 2010.
16. McKinsey Global, *Preparing for China's Urban Billion*, McKinsey Global Institute, February 2009, http://www.mckinsey.com/insights/mgi/research/urbanization/preparing_for_urban_billion_in_china, last accessed 13 Sep. 2012.
17. Nick Land, *Shanghai World Expo Guide*, Shanghai: Urbanatomy, 2010, p. 147.
18. Jeff Wasserstrom, *Global Shanghai: 1850–2010*, Abingdon: Routledge, 2009, p. 110.
19. Nick Land, 'Introductions to the afterlife', *Design Ecologies*, 2, 1 (2012).
20. Land, 'Neomodernity'.
21. For an easily accessible example see the image at the start of Peter Hessler, *Oracle Bones*, London: Harper Perennial, 2007.
22. Wonsuk Chang, 'Reflection on time and related ideas in the Yijing', *Philosophy East and West*, 59, 2 (April 2009).
23. *Yijing*, translated by Wu Jing Nuan, Washington, D.C: The Taoist Center, 1991, p. vi.
24. Anand Girdharadas, 'A yearning for the soul of two nations', *New York Times*, 26 November 2010.

1. MASTER AND DISCIPLE

1. This image can be found in multiple locations. Here is one: http://twistedsifter.com/2011/01/picture-of-the-day-shanghai-1990-vs-2010/, last accessed 3 Sep. 2012.
2. Qizheng Zhao and Yudong Shao, *Shanghai Pudong Miracle*, Shanghai: China Intercontinental Press, 2008, p. 10.
3. Clay Chandler, 'Building Shanghai's tower of power', *Fortune Magazine*, 9 January 2008.
4. William Pedersen, 'KPF, Shanghai: skyline and streetscape', *Shanghai Skyline*

Lecture Series, Skyscraper Museum, 27 October 2009, http://www.skyscraper. org/PROGRAMS/SHANGHAI_SKYLINE/kpf.php, last accessed 4 Sep. 2012.

5. 'The families that own Asia', *Time*, 168, 8 (23 February 2004).

6. Chandler, 'Building Shanghai's tower of power'.

7. Catherine Shaw, 'Interview with Minoru Mori', *The Magazine of the British Chamber of Commerce in Japan*, December 2009.

8. Jim Frederick, 'Mori', *Time*, 11 April 2004.

9. Pedersen, 'KPF, Shanghai: skyline and streetscape'.

10. Diana Mehl, 'Collectors with panache: art and architecture', *Panacheprivee*, http://www.panacheprivee.com/Arts_Culture/Minoru_Mori_Collection.asp, last accessed 4 Sep. 2012.

11. Robert Fishman, *Urban Utopias in the Twentieth Century*, Cambridge, MA: The MIT Press, 1982.

12. Ibid., p. 182.

13. Ibid., p. 172.

14. Ibid., p. 175.

15. Ibid., p. 183.

16. Ibid., p. 188.

17. Ibid.

18. Le Corbusier's *City of Tomorrow* had various iterations: The Contemporary City of 1922; Plan Voisin of 1925; and The Radiant City of 1935.

19. Fishman, *Urban Utopias*, p. 189.

20. Ibid., p. 206.

21. Le Corbusier, *The City of Tomorrow and its Planning*, New York: Dover Publications, 1987, p. 175.

22. Chandler, 'Building Shanghai's tower of power'.

23. Thomas J. Campanella, *Concrete Dragon: China's Urban Revolution and What it Means for the World*, Princeton University Press, 2008, ebook.

24. Quoted in Fishman, *Urban Utopias*, p. 192.

25. Le Corbusier, *Radiant City*, New York: Viking Press, 1970, p. 104.

26. Ibid., p. 106.

27. Ibid., p. 104.

28. Ibid.

29. Ibid., p. 38.

30. Ibid., p. 129.

31. Rem Koolhaas, *Delirious New York: A Retroactive Manifesto for New York*, New York: The Monacelli Press, 1997, p. 82.

32. Frank Lloyd Wright, 'The vertical dimension', *The Skyscraper Museum*, October 2004–January 2005, http://www.skyscraper.org/EXHIBITIONS/FRANK_ LLOYD_WRIGHT/flw.htm, last accessed 4 Sep. 2012.

33. Paolo Soleri, *Arcology: The City in the Image of Man*, Paradise Valley, Ariz: Cosanti Press, 1969.

34. Ibid.
35. Edward Glaeser, 'How Skyscrapers Can Save the City', *Atlantic*, March 2011, http://www.theatlantic.com/magazine/archive/2011/03/how-skyscrapers-can-save-the-city/308387/, last accessed 5 Sep. 2012.
36. See http://www.mori.co.jp/en/company/urban_design/vgc.html, last accessed 5 Sep. 2012.
37. Quoted in Mehl, 'Collectors with panache: art and architecture'.
38. Ibid.
39. David Owen, 'Green Manhattan', *New Yorker*, 18 October 2004.
40. Ibid.
41. Jonathan Woetzel et al., *Preparing for China's Urban Billion*, Greater China Offices: McKinsey Global, February 2009, http://www.mckinsey.com/insights/mgi/research/urbanization/preparing_for_urban_billion_in_china, last accessed 5 Sep. 2012.
42. This is due to last until the Pingan International Finance Centre, which in 2012 was the tallest building under construction, opens in Shenzhen in 2015.
43. Gensler, *Design Update: Shanghai Tower*, http://www.gensler.com/uploads/documents/Shanghai_Tower_12_22_2010.pdf, last accessed 4 Sep. 2012.
44. See 'Shanghai Tower: a vertical, sustainable city', http://www.youtube.com/watch?v=mq5EqMkvgZM, last accessed 4 Sep. 2012.
45. Ibid.
46. Le Corbusier, *The City of Tomorrow and its Planning*, 1987.
47. Ibid., p. xxv.

2. THE ROAD VERSUS THE STREET

1. Le Corbusier, *The City of Tomorrow and its Planning*, New York: Dover Publications, 1987, p. xxiii.
2. Marshall Berman, *All That is Solid Melts Into Air: The Experience of Modernity*, New York: Viking, 1982, p. 167.
3. Le Corbusier, *The City of Tomorrow*, p. 10.
4. Ibid., p. 38.
5. Ibid.
6. Ibid., p. 12.
7. Robert Fishman, *Urban Utopias in the Twentieth Century*, Cambridge, MA: MIT Press, 1982, p. 210.
8. Peter Hall, *Cities in Civilization*, New York: Pantheon, 1988, p. 796.
9. Ibid., p. 797.
10. Ibid., p. 708.
11. Ibid., p. 723.
12. Ibid., p. 708.
13. Berman, p. 15.

14. Hall, *Cities in Civilization*, p. 719.

15. Jean-Louis Cohen, 'Factory or landscape: the street of the moderns' in *The Street Belongs to All of Us*, Paris: Au Diable Vauvert, 2007, p. 36.

16. Berman, *All That is Solid Melts Into Air*, p. 150.

17. Robert Caro, *The Power Broker: Robert Moses and the Fall of New York*, New York: Vintage, 1975, p. 5.

18. Ibid., p. 10.

19. Ibid., p. 839.

20. Ibid., p. 12.

21. Ibid., p. 838.

22. Ibid., p. 838.

23. Berman, *All That is Solid Melts Into Air*, p. 165.

24. Edward Glaeser, *Triumph of City*, New York: Penguin, 2011, p. 136.

25. Ibid., p. 134.

26. Hall, *Cities in Civilization*, p. 719.

27. Caro, *The Power Broker*, p. 849.

28. Quoted in Cohen, 'Factory or landscape', p. 42.

29. Le Corbusier, *Towards a New Architecture*, New York: Dover Publications, 1986, p. 2.

30. Fishman, *Urban Utopias in the Twentieth Century*, p. 189.

31. Ibid., p. 190.

32. Ibid., p. 190.

33. Glaeser, *Triumph of City*, p. 134.

34. Ibid., p. 134.

35. Hall, *Cities in Civilization*, p. 716.

36. Jane Jacobs, *The Death and Life of Great American Cities*, New York: Vintage, 1961, p. 3.

37. Ibid., p. 4.

38. Ibid., p. 4.

39. Glaeser, *Triumph of City*, p. 153.

40. See Jeffrey Wasserstrom, 'NIMBY comes to China' in *The Nation*, January 18 2008, http://www.thenation.com/article/nimby-comes-china, last accessed 3 Jan. 2014.

41. Evan Osnos, 'The Jasmine Revolution "Strolls into China"', *The New Yorker*, 23 February 2011, http://www.newyorker.com/online/blogs/evanosnos/2011/02/china-strolls.html#entry-more, last accessed 5 Sep. 2012.

42. Berman, *All That is Solid Melts Into Air*, p. 332.

43. See http://www.learn.columbia.edu/moses/, last accessed 5 Sep. 2012.

44. Fredric Jameson, 'Future city', *New Left Review*, 21 (May–June 2003), http://newleftreview.org/II/21/fredric-jameson-future-city, last accessed 30 Oct. 2012.

45. Theodore Dalrymple, 'The architect as totalitarian', *City Journal*, 19, 4 (Autumn

2009), http://www.city-journal.org/2009/19_4_otbie-le-corbusier.html, last accessed, 7 Sep. 2012.

46. Ibid.
47. Ibid.
48. Ibid.
49. Ibid.
50. Cohen, 'Factory or landscape', p. 47.
51. Yawei Chen, *Shanghai Pudong: Urban Development in an Era of Global-local Interaction*, Amsterdam: IOS Press, 2007, p. 101.
52. Ibid., p. 124.
53. Ibid., p. 47.
54. Thomas Friedman, 'Our one-party democracy', *New York Times*, 8 September 2009.
55. Campanella, *Concrete Dragon*, p. 81.
56. Clay Chandler, 'Building Shanghai's tower of power', *Fortune*, 9 January 2008, http://money.cnn.com/2008/01/08/news/international/Shanghai_Mori.fortune/index.htm, last accessed 7 Sep. 2012.
57. Vincent Lo, guest speaker, Shanghai FCC, 23 January 2011.
58. Daniel Brook, 'Head of the Dragon: The Rise of the New Shanghai,' *Places: Design Observer*, 18 February 2013, http://places.designobserver.com/feature/the-rise-of-new-shanghai/37674/, last accessed 2 Jan. 2014
59. Campanella, *Concrete Dragon*, p. 81.
60. Chen, *Shanghai Pudong*, p. 226.
61. Ibid., p. 48.
62. Kerrie Macpherson, 'The head of the dragon: the Pudong New Area and Shanghai's urban development', *Planning Perspectives*, 9, 1994, p. 57.
63. Ibid., p. 80.
64. Ibid., p. 78.
65. Chen, *Shanghai Pudong*, p. 55.
66. Ibid., p. 271.
67. Ibid., p. 49.
68. Ibid.
69. Ibid., p. 272.
70. See Macpherson, 'The head of the dragon'.
71. Chen, *Shanghai Pudong*, p. 93.
72. Ibid., p. 121.
73. Aihwa Ong, 'Introduction', in Aihwa Ong and Ananya Roy (eds), *Worlding Cities: Asian Experiments in the Art of Being Global*, Wiley-Blackwell, 2011, p. 10
74. Chen, *Shanghai Pudong*, p. 105.
75. Ibid., p. 218.
76. Ibid., p. 121.

77. See Constance Lever-Tracy, David Fu-Keung Ip, and Noel Tracy, *The Chinese Diaspora and Mainland China: An Emerging Economic Synergy*, Macmillan 1996.
78. Chen, *Shanghai Pudong*, p. 37.
79. Ibid., p. 222.
80. Seng Kuan, 'Images of the Metropolis: Three Historical Views of Shanghai' in Kuan, Seng and Peter G. Rowe (eds), *Shanghai: Architecture and Urbanism for Modern China*, Prestel, 2004, p. 94.
81. Ong, 'Introduction,' p. 3.
82. Clay, 'Building Shanghai's tower of power', 2008.

3. THE POWER OF SPECTACLE

1. The *jingpai/haipai* (Beijing Culture/Shanghai Culture) debate extends back over a year. For more see Lynn Pan, *Shanghai Style: Art and Design Between the Wars*, San Francisco, CA: Long River Press, 2008.
2. One branding expert told me that the cost of a luxury brand operating a store in a mall on Nanjing road is almost the same as having a giant banner advertisement. The empty stores, therefore, make sense purely from an advertising perspective.
3. The attempt to create a more civilised city for Shanghai's World Expo 2010 involved a campaign to stop people from wearing pyjamas on the street (a local habit). This provoked an interesting backlash from people who argued that outdoor pyjama-wearing was a vital part of Shanghai culture. See Gao Yubing, 'The pajama game closes in Shanghai', *New York Times*, 16 May 2010, http://www.nytimes.com/2010/05/17/opinion/17gao.html
4. The destruction wrought by spectacle can be seen, for example on Wujiang Lu, which used to be one of the best places in the city for street food and is now filled with fast-food chains.
5. James Fallows, *Postcards From Tomorrow Square*, New York: Vintage, 2008.
6. See Kerry McPherson, 'The head of the dragon: the Pudong new area and Shanghai's urban development', *Planning Perspectives*, 9 (1994).
7. Macpherson, 'The head of the dragon', p. 57.
8. Quoted in Yawei Chen, *Shanghai Pudong: Urban Development in an Era of Global-Local Interaction*, Amsterdam: IOS Press, 2007, p. 59.
9. Macpherson, 'The head of the dragon', p. 57.
10. Kris Olds, 'Globalizing Shanghai: the "Global Intelligence Corps" and the building of Pudong', *Cities*, 14 (1997).
11. Huang quoted in Olds, 'Globalizing Shanghai', p. 116.
12. Ibid.
13. Non Arkaraprasertkul, *Politicisation and the Rhetoric of Shanghai Urbanism*, http://harvard.academia.edu/NArkaraprasertkul/Papers/1179799/Politicisation_and_the_rhetoric_of_Shanghai_urbanism, last accessed 13 Sep. 2012.

14. Olds, 'Globalizing Shanghai', p. 117.

15. Thomas J. Campanella, *The Concrete Dragon: China's Urban Revolution and What it Means for the World*, Princeton: Princeton Architectural Press, 2008, ebook, p. 81.

16. 'Shanghai critique misses the point', *Shanghai Star*, 9 April 2003, http://app1. chinadaily.com.cn/star/2003/0904/vo2–3.html

17. Yasheng Huang, *Capitalism with Chinese Characteristics: Entrepreneurship and the State*, New York: Cambridge University Press, 2008, p. 176.

18. Ibid., p. 231.

19. Ibid.

20. 'The long march backwards', *The Economist*, 2 October 2008.

21. This is not to question Huang's argument. Undoubtedly China implemented economic policies that were friendly to the private entrepreneur in the 1980s that were later reversed in the 1990s.

22. This aspect of Braudel's work has been taken up more recently by materialist philosophers inspired by the work produced by Gilles Deleuze and Félix Guattari. See especially Manuel Delanda, *Markets, Antimarkets and Network Economics*, http://www.cddc.vt.edu/host/delanda/pages/markets.htm, last accessed 13 Sep. 2012.

23. Fernand Braudel, *Civilization and Capitalism: Volume 3: Perspective of the World*, Berkeley: University of California Press, 1992, p. 620.

24. Fernand Braudel, *Civilization and Capitalism. Volume 2: Wheels of Commerce*, Berkeley: University of California Press, 1992, p. 443.

25. Braudel, *Perspective of the World*, p. 631.

26. Kate Zhou, *China's Long March to Freedom: Grassroots Modernization*, New Brunswick, N.J.: Transaction Publishers, 2009.

27. A sampling of stories on *chengguang*, violence and urban unrest can be found here: http://www.economist.com/node/15806697?story_id=E1_TVRDGGJS, last accessed 13 Sep. 2012. http://shanghaiist.com/2011/04/14/showdown_ between_police_and_crowds.ph, last accessed 13 Sep. 2012.

28. Quoted in Olds, 'Globalizing Shanghai', p. 120.

29. Chen, *Shanghai Pudong*, p. 284.

30. Aihwa Ong, 'Hyperbuilding: Spectacle, Speculation and the Hyperspace of Sovereignty', in Aihwa Ong and Ananya Roy (eds), *Worlding Cities: Asian Experiments in the Art of Being Global*, Wiley-Blackwell, 2011, p. 210.

31. Drawing on the ancient commentary of Guo Xiang (AD 252–312), Hans-Georg Moeller argues that common translations of the butterfly dream misread the fable and give it a Western interpretation by adding in a constant subject—the 'I', who dreams, remembers and doubts. See Hans-Georg Moeller, 'Zhuangzi's dream of the butterfly—a Daoist interpretation', *Philosophy East and West*, 49, 4 (1999).

32. Wonsuk Chang, 'Reflections on time and related ideas in the *Yijing*', *Philosophy East and West*, 59, 2 (April 2009), p. 222.

33. Richard McGregor, *The Party: The Secret World of China's Communist Rulers*, New York: HarperCollins, 2010, p. 15.
34. Ibid., p. xvii.
35. Ibid., p. 48.
36. Ibid., p. 22.
37. McGregor, *The Party*.
38. For more on China's contemporary liberal theorists see Chaohua Wang (ed.), *One China. Many Paths*, London: Verso, 2005.
39. On China as a mafia state see, http://shanghaiist.com/2011/04/17/john_garnaut_is_china_becoming_a_ma.php
40. Expo brought an end to the great hub of DVD stores on Dagu Lu, though at least one of these has simply moved around the corner.
41. Ananya Roy, 'Conclusion', in Aihwa Ong and Ananya Roy (eds), *Worlding Cities: Asian Experiments in the Art of Being Global*, Wiley-Blackwell, 2011, p. 312.

4. GOTHIC FUTURISM

1. Leo Lee, 'The cultural construction of modernity in urban Shanghai: some preliminary explorations', in Wen-hsin Yeh (ed.), *Becoming Chinese: Passages to Modernity and Beyond*, Berkeley, CA: University of California Press, 2000, p. 32.
2. Quoted in Shaoqing Zhang, 'The supremacy of modern time: reshaping the image of China in early modern times', *Modern Art Asia*, March 2011.
3. There is of course a wide literature of the May Fourth movement, which—as any historical period—is filled with nuance and complexity. Nevertheless, most scholars agree that the adoption of a linear time-consciousness was a central tenet of this vital cultural epoch. For more on the May Fourth movevent see, for example, Vera Schwarcz, *The Chinese Enlightenment: Intellectuals and the Legacy of the May Fourth Movement of 1919*, Berkely, CA: University of California Press 1986 and Tse Tsung Chow, *The May Fourth Movement: Intellectual Revolution in Modern China*, Cambridge, MA: Harvard University Press, 1960.
4. Ibid., p. 31.
5. Shu-mei Shih, *The Lure of the Modern: Writing Modernism in Semi-Colonial China (1917–1937)*, Berkeley, CA: University of California Press, 2001, p. 49.
6. Ibid., p. 50.
7. Ibid., p. 46.
8. Lee Leo, 'In search of modernity: some reflections on a new mode of consciousness in twentieth century Chinese history and literature', in Paul Cohen and Merle Goldman (eds), *Ideas Across Cultures*, Cambridge, MA: Harvard University Asia Center, 1990, p. 114.
9. Lee, 'The cultural construction of modernity in urban Shanghai', p. 31.

10. Lee, 'In search of modernity', p. 110.
11. Hu Shih, *The Chinese Renaissance*, http://www.csua.berkeley.edu/~mrl/HuShih/ ChineseRenaissance.html, last accessed 10 Sep. 2012.
12. Lee, 'In search of modernity', p. 122.
13. Lee, 'The cultural construction of modernity in urban Shanghai', p. 31.
14. Guo Moruo, *The Nirvana of Feng and Huang*, http://eol.ntu.edu.cn/culture/ chineseculture/chineseliterature/thenirvanaofthefengandhuang1.htm, last accessed 13 Sep. 2012.
15. The Qing eventually backed the Boxers, who were ultimately defeated.
16. Quoted in Peter Hessler, *Oracle Bones: A Journey through Time in China*, New York: Harper Perennial, 2007.
17. Ibid., p. 33.
18. For a fascinating discussion of how the clock on the Custom House functioned as an icon in different historic periods see Jeffrey Wasserstrom, 'A Big Ben with Chinese characteristics: the Customs House as urban icon in Old and New Shanghai,' *Urban History*, 33,1, (2006).
19. Michael Lewis, *Gothic Revival*, London: Thames and Hudson, 2002, p. 7.
20. H. P. Lovecraft, *Supernatural Horror in Literature*, http://www.hplovecraft.com/ writings/litcrit/shil.asp, last accessed 27 Sep. 2012.
21. Ibid.
22. Ibid.
23. Ibid.
24. Carol Willis, *Raymond Hood: 'The Brilliant Bad Boy' of New York Architecture*, New York Modern Lecture Series, Skyscraper Museum, 4 March 2008, http:// www.skyscraper.org/PROGRAMS/NYMODERN/nym_hood.php, last accessed 11 Sep. 2012.
25. Rem Koolhaas, *Delirious New York: A Retroactive Manifesto for Manhattan*, New York: The Monacelli Press, 1994, p. 117.
26. Quoted in Anton Kaes, 'Metropolis: city, cinema, modernity', in Timothy Benson (ed.), *Expressionist Utopias: Paradise, Metropolis, Architectural Fantasy*, Los Angeles County Museum of Art, 1993, p. 146.
27. Lewis, *Gothic Revival*, p. 7.
28. Kenneth Clark, *The Gothic Revival: An Essay in the History of Taste*, John Murray Publishers Ltd, 1962, p. 9.
29. Wilhelm Worringer, *Form in Gothic*, New York: Schocken Books, 1972, p. 7.
30. Ibid.
31. Ibid., p. 32.
32. Ibid., p. 88.
33. Ibid., p. 105.
34. Worringer, *Form in Gothic*, p. 84.
35. Ibid., p. 21.
36. Ibid., p. 21.

37. Ibid., p. 89.
38. Ibid., p. 106.
39. Ibid.
40. Ibid., p. 81.
41. Ibid., p. 79.
42. Gilles Deleuze and Félix Guattari, *A Thousand Plateaus: Capitalism & Schizophrenia*, Minneapolis: University of Minnesota Press, 1987, p. 499.
43. David Wang, *The Monster that is History: History, Violence and Fictional Writing in Twentieth-Century China*, Berkeley: University of California Press, 2004, p. 264.
44. Ibid.
45. Hsia Tsi-an, *The Gate of Darkness: Studies on the Leftist Literary Movement*, Seattle and London: University of Washington Press, 1968, p. 159.
46. Wang, *The Monster that is History*, p. 264.
47. Lu Xun, 'The shadow's leave taking', *Wild Grass*, Beijing: Foreign Languages Press, p. 15.
48. Lee, 'In search of modernity', 1990, p. 130.
49. Shih, *Lure of the Modern*, 2001, p. 231.
50. Lee, 'In search of modernity', p. 130.
51. Wang, *The Monster that is History*, p. 276.
52. Ibid.
53. Eileen Chang, quoted in Wang, *The Monster that is History*, p. 277.
54. Hsia, *The Gate of Darkness*, p. 152.
55. Hsia, *The Gate of Darkness*, pp. 155–6.
56. Wang, *The Monster that is History*, p. 22.
57. Hsia, *The Gate of Darkness*, p. 160.
58. Luca Poncellini, 'László Hudec and the pursuit of modernity in Shanghai', *Lecture Series, Year of Hudec*, Park Hotel, 5 June 2008.
59. The phrase is Carol Willis', *Raymond Hood*.
60. Ghislaine Wood, 'The style and the age', *Art Deco 1910–1939*, National Gallery of Victoria, 2003, p. 35.
61. For detailed documentation on Shanghai's Art Deco heritage see the work of Deke Erh and Tess Johnston.
62. Nick Land, 'A time-travelers guide to Shanghai (Part 2)', *Urban Futures*, http://www.thatsmags.com/shanghai/article/802/a-time-travelers-guide-to-shanghai-part-2, last accessed 11 Oct. 2012.
63. Ghislaine Wood, 'The style and the age', *Art Deco 1910–1939*, National Gallery of Victoria, 2003
64. Ibid., p. 41.
65. Ibid., p. 39.
66. Land, 'A time-travelers guide to Shanghai (Part 2)'.
67. Ibid.

5. CREATED IN CHINA

1. Peter Hall, *Cities in Civilization*, New York: Pantheon, 1998, p. 3.
2. Ibid.
3. Ibid., p. 7.
4. Ibid., p. 284.
5. Ibid., p. 286.
6. Ibid., p. 285.
7. Ibid.
8. Nick Land, *Urbanatomy: Shanghai 2009*, Tianjin: Nan Kai University Press, 2009, p. 500.
9. Andrew Ness, 'On the waterfront: recasting Shanghai's industrial waterfront', *Surveyors Times*, p. 37.
10. Ibid.
11. Suzhou Warehouse is located at 1305 South Suzhou Creek Road.
12. Personal interview, Deng Kunyen, 2200 Yangshupu Lu, 28 May 2008.
13. Ibid.
14. Ness, 'On the waterfront', p. 38.
15. The first gallery to open in the area was Eastlink, which was set up by Li Liang, who had recently returned from Australia. He was soon joined by the Swiss-run ShanghArt and the Italian-backed Biz Art.
16. Land, *Urbanatomy*, p. 503.
17. Also influential was professor of architecture Han Yuqi of the Shanghai Institute of Technology who, along with another academic Zhang Song, edited a book called *Left Bank of the Seine of the East: The Art Warehouses of Suzhou Creek*, Shanghai: Shanghai Guji Chubanshe, 2004.
18. John Hartley (ed.), *Creative Industries*, Oxford: Wiley-Blackwell, 2004, p. 3.
19. Richard Florida, *Response*, Journal of the American Planning Association, 71, 2 (Spring 2005).
20. Richard Florida, *The Rise of the Creative Class*, New York: Basic Books, 2002, p. xii.
21. See Justin O'Connor, *Culture and Creative Industries: A Review of the Literature*, London: Creative Partnerships, 2007.
22. Michael Porter, 'The competitive advantage of the inner city', *Harvard Business Review*, May–June 2005.
23. Michael Porter, 'Location, competition and economic development: local clusters in a global economy', *Economic Development Quarterly*, 14, 1 (2000).
24. Richard Florida, 'The world is spiky', *Atlantic Monthly*, October 2005.
25. See Jane Jacobs, *Cities and the Wealth of Nations: Principles of Economic Life*, New York: Vintage, 1985.
26. Richard Florida, 'Response', *Journal of the American Planning Association*, 71, 2, Spring 2005, p. 219.

27. O'Connor, *Culture and Creative Industries*.

28. In their book on 'Worlding Cities,' Aihwa Ong and Ananya Roy stress how the use of 'inter referencing practices', in which one city acts as model for another, are vital to the ways in which contemporary Asian cities make themselves global. Aihwa Ong and Ananya Roy (eds), *Worlding Cities: Asian Experiments in the Art of Being Global*, Wiley-Blackwell, 2011.

29. Michael Keane, 'Creative industries in China: four perspectives on social transformation', *International Journal of Cultural Policy*, 15, 4 (2009).

30. Wu Qidi, 'Creative industries and innovation in China', *International Journal of Cultural Policy*, 9 (2006).

31. Ness, 'On the waterfront'.

32. Michael Keane, *China's New Creative Clusters: Governance, Human Capital and Investement*, London: Routledge, 2011, p. 2.

33. Personal interview, Tony Wang, Bridge 8, April 2008.

34. Ibid.

35. Personal interview, Daryl Arnold, The Factory, June 2010.

36. David Brooks, *Bobos in Paradise: The New Upper Class and How they Got There*, New York: Simon and Schuster, 2001.

37. Lehrer, Jonah, 'How creativity works in cities', *Atlantic Cities*, May 2012, http://www.theatlanticcities.com/arts-and-lifestyle/2012/05/how-creativity-works/1881/, last accessed 11 Sep. 2012.

38. Ibid.

39. Personal interview, Xin Gu, December 2011.

40. Clare Jacobson, *New Museums in China*, Princeton Architectural Press, 2013.

41. Xu Jilin 'Shanghai Culture Lost,' *China Heritage Quarterly* (translated by Geremie R. Barme) 22 (June 2010).

42. Ibid.

43. Jing Wang, 'The global reach of a new discourse: how far can "Creative Industries" travel?', *International Journal of Cultural Policy*, 7, 1 (2004).

44. Ai Weiwei, 'China's censorship can never defeat the internet', *The Guardian*, 16 April 2012.

45. Han Han, 'On freedom, democracy and revolution', http://zonaeuropa.com/201112a.brief.htm#009, last accessed 11 Sep. 2012.

46. Jason Lim, 'Why China won't be innovative for at least 20 more years', http://venturebeat.com/2012/03/26/why-china-doesnt-innovate/, last accessed 11 Sep. 2012.

47. Weiwei, 'China's censorship can never defeat the internet'.

48. Personal interview, Gary Wang, The Lab, May 2009.

49. Han-Teng Liao, 'Towards creative da-tong: an alternative notion of creative industries for China', *International Journal of Cultural Studies*, 9, 3 (2006).

50. Lucy Montgomery and Brian Fitzgerald, 'Copyright and the creative industries in China', *International Journal of Cultural Studies*, 9, 3 (2006).

51. Innovation in China, *Sinica: Pop Up Chinese*, http://popupchinese.com/lessons/sinica/innovation-in-china, last accessed 4 Jan. 2014.
52. Hall, *Cities in Civilization*, p. 285.
53. Ibid., p. 286.
54. Weiwei, 'China's censorship can never defeat the internet'.
55. Yu Hua, 'The spirit of May 35ᵗʰ', *New York Times*, 23 June 2011, http://www.nytimes.com/2011/06/24/opinion/global/24iht-june24-ihtmag-hua-28.html?pagewanted=all&_r=0, last accessed 13 Oct. 2012.
56. Desiree Marianini and Janek Zdziarski, 'Dancing with shackles on', http://www.danwei.org/featured_video/dancing_with_shackles.php, last accessed, 11 Sep. 2012.
57. Jane Jacobs, *Cities and the Wealth of Nations: Principles of Economic Life*, New York: Vintage, 1985, p. 221.
58. Ibid., p. 222.
59. Personal interview, Deng Kunyen, 2200 Yangshupu Lu, 28 May 2008.
60. Ibid.

6. NEO-HAIPAI

1. Ben Wood, 'Preserving Shanghai: modernizing urban identity', *Shanghai Skyline Lecture Series*, 24 November 2009, http://www.skyscraper.org/PROGRAMS/SHANGHAI_SKYLINE/shanghai_skyline.php#five, last accessed 11 Sep. 2012.
2. Ibid.
3. Ibid.
4. Ibid.
5. Ibid.
6. An Interview with Benjamin Wood, Moving Cities, http://movingcities.org/interviews/benjamin-wood_cre/, last accessed 2 Jan. 2014.
7. Ibid.
8. Ibid.
9. Ibid.
10. Jeffrey Wasserstrom, *Global Shanghai, 1850–2010*, Routledge, 2009.
11. Marie-Claire Bergère, 'Shanghai's urban development: a remake?' in Seng Kuan and Peter Rowe (eds), *Shanghai: Architecture and Urbanism for Modern China*, Prestel, 2004.
12. Hanchao Lu, *Beyond the Neon Lights: Everyday Shanghai in the Early Twentieth Century*, Berkeley: University of California Press, 1999, p. 13.
13. I helped edit *Urbanatomy*'s 2008 guide and was a main contributor to the guide in 2009.
14. Nick Land, *Urbanatomy: Shanghai 2009*, Tianjin: Nan Kai University Press, p. 17.
15. Lynn Pan, *Shanghai Style: Art and Design Between the Wars*, San Francisco: Long River Press, 2009, p. 8.

16. Ibid., p. 10.
17. Ibid., p. 6.
18. Ibid., p. 8.
19. Marie-Claire Bergère, *Shanghai: China's Gateway to Modernity*, Stanford University Press, 2009 p. 242.
20. Xu Jilin, 'Shanghai Culture Lost,' *China Heritage Quarterly* (translated by Geremie R. Barme) 22 (June 2010).
21. Pan, *Shanghai Style*, p. 27.
22. Pan, *Shanghai Style*, p. 202.
23. For richly detailed account see historian Robert Bickers' *The Scramble for China: Foreign Devils in the Qing Empire (1832–1914)*, Penguin Books, 2011.
24. Quoted in Samuel Liang, 'Where the courtyard meets the street: spatial culture of *Li* neignbourhoods, 1870–1900', *Journal of the Society of Architectural Historians*, 67, 4 (December 2008), p. 485.
25. Ibid., p. 484.
26. Nick Land, *Lilong*, unpublished, 2011.
27. Lu, *Beyond the Neon Lights*, p. 16.
28. Ibid., p. 313.
29. Land, *Lilong*.
30. Ibid.
31. Liang, 'Where the courtyard meets the street', p. 494.
32. Ibid., p. 209.
33. Pan, *Shanghai Style*, p. 16.
34. Lu, *Beyond the Neon Lights*, p. 243.
35. Pan, *Shanghai Style*, p. 5.
36. Ibid., p. 491.
37. Ibid., p. 482.
38. Samuel Liang, 'Where the courtyard meets the street', p. 501.
39. Pan, *Shanghai Style*, p. 15.
40. Quoted in Wan-Lin Tsai, *The Redevelopment and Preservation of Historic Lilong Housing in Shanghai*, thesis, Philadelphia: University of Pennsylvania, 2008, http://repository.upenn.edu/cgi/viewcontent.cgi?article=1115&context=hp_theses, last accessed 12 Sep. 2012.
41. Ibid.
42. Personal interview, Wu Meisen, 'Tianzifang', June 2009.
43. Ibid.
44. Ibid.
45. Ibid.
46. Ibid.
47. Ibid.
48. Liang, 'Where the courtyard meets the street'.
49. Pan, *Shanghai Style*, p. 32.

7. DREAMS FROM THE EDGES

1. Jonathan Watts, 'Shanghai surprise… a new town in ye olde English style', *The Guardian*, 2 June 2004.
2. Harry den Hartog, *Shanghai New Towns: Searching for Community and Identity in a Sprawling Metropolis*, 010 Publishers, 2010, p. 164.
3. Harry den Hartog, *Shanghai New Towns: Searching for Community and Identity in a Sprawling Metropolis*, Rotterdam: 010 Publishers, 2010, p. 26.
4. In Shanghai's eleventh five-year plan (2006–2010) The One City Nine Towns Development Plan was put on ice. Instead suburban growth is now concentrated on a few key locations: Jiading, Songjiang, Qingpu-Zhujiajiao, Pudong and the deep sea harbour at Lingang.
5. Den Hartog, *Shanghai New Towns*, p. 88.
6. Ibid.
7. Ibid.
8. Ibid.
9. Dieter Hassenpflug, 'European Urban Fictions in China', http://www.espaces-temps.net/document6653.html, last accessed 12 Sep. 2012.
10. Ibid.
11. Den Hartog, *Shanghai New Towns*, p. 218.
12. Ibid.
13. Ibid., p. 194.
14. Hassenpflug, 'European urban fictions in China'.
15. Ibid.
16. Peter Hall, *Cities of Tomorrow: An Intellectual History of Urban Planning and Design in the Twentieth Century*, Oxford: Wiley-Blackwell, 2002.
17. Quoted in Hall, *Cities of Tomorrow*, p. 16.
18. Robert Fishman, *Bourgeois Utopias: The Rise and Fall of Suburbia*, New York: Basic Books, 1989, [e-book].
19. Howard Kunstler, *Geography of Nowhere*, New York: Simon & Schuster, 1994, p. 37.
20. Lewis Mumford, 'The Garden City and modern planning', in Ebenezer Howard, *The Garden Cities of To-morrow*, Cambridge MA: MIT Press, 1965, p. 29.
21. Quoted in Fishman, *Bourgeois Utopias*.
22. Ibid.
23. Ebenezer Howard, *The Garden Cities of Tomorrow*, MIT Press, 1965, p. 48.
24. Fishman, *Bourgeois Utopias*.
25. Mumford, 'The Garden City and modern planning', p. 35.
26. H. G. Wells, *The Probable Diffusion of Cities, Anticipations*, London: Chapman & Hall, 1902, p. 16.
27. Diana Mok, Barry Wellman and Juan Carrasco, 'Does distance matter in the age of the internet', *Urban Studies*, 47, 13 (2010).

28. Ibid.
29. Kenneth Jackson, *Crabgrass Frontier: The Suburbanization of the United States*, New York: Oxford University Press, 1987, p. 188.
30. Edward Glaeser, *Triumph of Cities: How Our Greatest Invention Makes Us Richer, Smarter, Greener, Healthier, and Happier*, Penguin Group USA, 2011, pp. 177–8.
31. Ibid., p. 167.
32. Quoted in Jackson, *Crabgrass Frontier*, p. 270.
33. Ford Model T, *Wikipedia*, http://www.en.wikipedia.org/wiki/Ford_Model_T#cite_note-6
34. Kunstler, *Geography of Nowhere*, p. 86.
35. A. Modarres and A. Kirby, 'The suburban question: notes for a research program', *Cities*, 27, 2010.
36. Jackson, *Crabgrass Frontier*, p. 265.
37. Robert Fishman, 'The end of suburbia: a new kind of city is emerging—the technoburb', *LA Times*, 2 August 1987.
38. Fishman, *Bourgeois Utopias*.
39. Ibid.
40. Ibid.
41. Ibid.
42. Ibid.
43. Ibid.
44. Ibid.
45. Ibid.
46. Yixing Zhou and John Logan, 'Growth on the edge: the new Chinese metropolis', in John Logan (ed.), *Urban China in Transition*, Oxford: Blackwell, 2008, p. 140.
47. Den Hartog, *Shanghai New Towns*.
48. Zhou, and Logan, 'Growth on the edge', p. 36.
49. For insight into contradictory tensions embedded in this issue see Sylvie Levey's wonderful documentary 'Waiting for Paradise'.
50. See Qin Shao, *Shanghai Gone: Domicide and Defiance in a Chinese Megacity*, Rowman and Littlefield, 2013.
51. Yu Hua, *China in Ten Words*, New York: Pantheon, 2011.
52. Thomas Campanella, *Concrete Dragon: China's Urban Transition and What it Means for the World*, New York: Princeton Architectural Press, 2008, ebook, p. 195.
53. Fishman, 'The end of suburbia'.
54. Campanella, *Concrete Dragon*, p. 199.
55. Ibid., p. 200.
56. Ibid., p. 202.
57. Wang Meng, *Tide Players: The Movers and Shakers of a Rising China*, New York: The New Press, 2011, p. 213.

8. THE FLOATING CITY

1. Neal Stephenson, *The Diamond Age: or, a Young Lady's Illustrated Primer*, New York: Bantam Dell, 1995, p. 20.
2. Ibid., p. 369.
3. Mike Davis, *Planet of Slums*, New York: Verso, 2006, p. 2.
4. Ibid.
5. Ibid.
6. Leslie Chang, *Factory Girls: From Village to City in a Changing China*, New York: Spiegel & Grau, 2008, p. 12.
7. Doug Saunders, 'The first great migration: how the West arrived', in Doug Saunders, *Arrival City: How the Largest Migration in History is Reshaping our World*, New York: Pantheon, 2011.
8. Martin Jacques, *When China rules the World: The End of the Western World and the Birth of a New Global Order*, New York: Penguin, 2009, p. 20.
9. Ibid., p. 9.
10. Ibid., p. 12.
11. Liisa Malkki, 'National geographic: the rooting of peoples and the territorialization of national identity among scholars and refugees', *Cultural Anthropology*, 7, 1 (1992).
12. Jacques, *When China rules the World*, p. 9.
13. Ibid., p. 11.
14. Davis, *Planet of Slums*, p. 37.
15. Mike Davis, 'Planet of slums', *New Left Review*, 26 (March–April 2004).
16. Ibid., 2006, p. 3.
17. Ibid., p. 46.
18. Ibid., p. 11.
19. Ibid., p. 19.
20. Ananya Roy, 'Conclusion', in Aihwa Ong and Ananya Roy (eds), *Worlding Cities: Asian Experiments in the Art of being Global*, Wiley-Blackwell, 2011, p. 308.
21. Tom Angotti, 'Apocalyptic anti-urbanism: Mike Davis and his "Planet of slums"', *International Journal of Urban and Regional Research*, 30 (2006).
22. Ibid.
23. Saunders, 'The first great migration', p. 11.
24. Glaeser, p. 9.
25. Ibid., p. 71.
26. Hanchao Lu, 'Creating urban outcasts: shantytowns in Shanghai, 1920–1950', *Journal of Urban History*, 25, 1 (1995).
27. Ibid.
28. Ibid.
29. Hanchao Lu, *Beyond Neon Lights: Everyday Shanghai in the Early Twentieth Century*, Berkeley: University of California Press, 2004, p. 109.

30. See Daan Roggeveen, *How the City Moved to Mr. Sun*, Sun Publishers, 2013.
31. Qin Hui, 'China's slums: when will the poor get a break?' *Economic Observer*, 8 April 2011, http://www.eeo.com.cn/ens/biz_commentary/2011/04/08/198295.shtml, last accessed 12 Sep. 2012.
32. Ibid.
33. Ibid.
34. Peter Mackenzie, 'Strangers in the city: the hukou and urban citizenship in China', *Journal of International Affairs*, 56, 1 (2002).
35. Ibid.
36. Hukou remained linked to food rationing up until 1994.
37. Chang, *Factory Girls*, p. 12.
38. Ibid., p. 13.
39. Ibid., p. 12.
40. Mackenzie, 'Strangers in the city'.
41. *Economist*, 'We like to move it move it', 25 February 2012.
42. Saunders, 'The first great migration', p. 26.
43. William McNeill, 'Cities and their consequences', *The American Interest*, 2, 4 (March/April 2007).
44. Ibid.
45. Ibid.
46. Ibid.
47. Ibid.
48. Chang, *Factory Girls*, p. 12.
49. Aihwa Ong, *Flexible Citizenship: The Cultural Logics of Transnationality*, Durham NC: Duke University Press, 1999.
50. See Liao Yiwu, *The Corpse Walker: Real Life Sories: China from the Bottom Up*, Anchor: 2009.
51. Li Zhang, *Strangers in the City: Reconfigurations of Space, Power, and Social Networks Within China's Floating Population*, Stanford Cal: Stanford University Press, 2002, p. 33.
52. Ibid.
53. Qin Hui, 'China's slums: when will the poor get a break?'.
54. C. Cindy Fan, *China on the Move: Migration, the State, and the Household*, New York: Routledge, 2008, p. 172.
55. Lu, *Beyond Neon Lights*, p. 116.
56. Ibid., p. 117.
57. Lu, 'Creating urban outcasts'.
58. Lu, *Beyond Neon Lights*, p. 49.
59. Lu, *Beyond Neon Lights*, p. 50.
60. Lu, *Beyond Neon Lights*, p. 53.
61. See Fan, *China on the Move*.
62. Fan, *China on the Move*, p. 171.
63. Yu Zhu, 'China's floating population and their settlement intention in the cities: beyond the Hukou reform', *Habitat International*, 31 (2007), p. 66.

64. Saunders, 'The first great migration', p. 59.
65. Saunders, 'The first great migration', p. 63.
66. Fan, *China on the Move*, p. 164.
67. Fan, *China on the Move*, p. 163.
68. Fan, *China on the Move*, p. 168.
69. Frederic Wakeman and Wen-hsin Yeh (eds), *Shanghai Sojourners*, Berkeley: Institute for East Asian Studies, University of California, 1992, p. 6.
70. Mark Swislocki, *Culinary Nostalgia: Regional Food Culture and the Urban Experience in Shanghai*, Stanford, CA: Stanford University Press, 2008, p. 232.

9. SHADOW MARKETS

1. Jamie Alderslade, John Talmage and Yusef Freeman, 'Measuring the informal economy one neighbourhood at a time', *The Brookings Institution Metropolitan Policy Program*, September 2006, p. 6.
2. Robert Neuwirth, *Stealth of Nations: The Global Rise of the Informal Economy*, New York: Pantheon, 2011 [e-book].
3. The CCRU is a research unit that was most active in the late 1990s at the University of Warwick, UK. I was one of the founding members. www.ccru.net
4. Cybernetic Culture Research Unit, *Markets on the Periphery*, http://www.ccru.net/archive/markets.htm, last accessed 13 Sep. 2012.
5. Ian B, 'Poor people were libertarians, once', Counting Cats in Zanzibar, 21 April 2010, http://www.countingcats.com/?p=6584, last accessed 12 Sep. 2012.
6. Ibid.
7. Keith Hart, 'Informal income opportunities and urban employment in Ghana', *The Journal of Modern African Studies*, 11, 1 (1973), p. 61.
8. Ibid., p. 62.
9. Ibid., p. 67.
10. M. Castells and A. Portes, 'World underneath: the origins, dynamics, and effects of the informal economy', in A. Portes et al. (eds), *The Informal Economy: Studies in Advanced and Less Developed Countries*, Baltimore: John Hopkins University Press, 1989, p. 1.
11. Chen, Martha, *Rethinking the Informal Economy: Linkages with the Formal Economy and the Formal Regulatory Environment*, http://www.un.org/en/ecosoc/meetings/2006/forum/Statements/Chen's%20Paper.pdf
12. Neuwirth, *Stealth of Nations*.
13. Ibid.
14. Ibid.
15. Ibid.
16. Ibid.
17. Ibid.
18. Ibid.
19. Hernando De Soto interviewed in Daniel Yergin, 'The new rules of the game',

Commanding Heights: The Battle for the World Economy, William Cran, producer, Public Broadcasting, InVision Productions, Heights Productions Inc., 2003.

20. Ibid.
21. Hernando De Soto, *The Other Path: The Economic Answer to Terrorism*, New York: Basic Books, 1989 [e-book].
22. Ibid.
23. Ibid.
24. This point is further developed in De Soto's highly influential book *The Mystery of Capital: Why Capitalism Triumphs in the West and Fails Everywhere Else*, New York: Basic Books, 2003.
25. De Soto, *The Economic Answer to Terrorism*.
26. Ibid.
27. Ibid.
28. Ibid.
29. Ibid.
30. Ibid.
31. Ibid.
32. Ibid.
33. Ibid.
34. Kellee Tsai, *Back Alley Banking: Private Entrepreneurs in China*, Ithaca N. Y.: Cornell University, 2002, p. 258.
35. Ibid., p. 37.
36. Ibid., p. 10.
37. Franklin Allen, Jun Qian and Meijun Qian, 'Law, finance and economic growth in China', *Wharton Financial Institutions Center*, 2002.
38. Ibid.
39. Franklin Allen, Jun Qian and Meijun Qian, 'China's financial system: past, present, and future', 2004, http://fic.wharton.upenn.edu/fic/papers/05/0517.pdf, last accessed 12 Sep. 2012.
40. Tsai, *Back Alley Banking*, p. 2.
41. Ibid.
42. Allen et al., 'China's financial system'.
43. Tsai, *Back Alley Banking*, p. 26.
44. William Cassidy, 'Fei chien, or flying money: a study of Chinese underground banking', *National Criminal Justice Reference Service*, 1990, p. 1.
45. Tsai, *Back Alley Banking*, p. 261.
46. Kristen Parris, 'Local initiative and national reform: the Wenzhou model of development', *The China Quarterly*, 134 (1993), p. 243.
47. Tsai, *Back Alley Banking*, p. 123.
48. Alan Liu, 'Wenzhou model of development and China's modernization', *Asian Survey*, 32, 8 (1992), p. 703.
49. Li Jia, 'When Wenzhou sneezes', *News China*, December 2011, http://www.

newschinamag.com/magazine/when-wenzhou-sneezes, last accessed 13 Sep. 2012.

50. Tsai, *Back Alley Banking*, p. 16.
51. Liu, 'Wenzhou model of development and China's modernization', p. 703.
52. Ibid., p. 699.
53. Ibid., p. 704.
54. Li, 'Wenzhou model of development and China's modernization'.
55. Tsai, p. 22.
56. Ibid.
57. Joseph Schumpeter, *Capitalism, Socialism, and Democracy*, 2nd ed., New York, London: Harper & Brothers, 1947, p. 82.
58. Ibid., p. 83.
59. James Surowiecki quoted in Thomas Friedman, *The Lexus and the Olive Tree*, New York: Anchor Books, 2000, p. 11.
60. Schumpeter, *Capitalism, Socialism, and Democracy*, p. 83.
61. C. K. Prahalad and Stuart L. Hart, 'The fortune at the bottom of the pyramid', *Strategy & Business*, 26 (2002).
62. Ibid.
63. Clayton Christensen, Thomas Craig and Stuart Hart, 'The great disruption', *Foreign Affairs*, March/April 2001, http://www.foreignaffairs.com/articles/56851/clayton-christensen-thomas-craig-and-stuart-hart/the-great-disruption, last accessed 13 Sep. 2012.
64. Ibid.
65. Ibid.
66. Ibid.
67. Sheng Zhu and Yongjiang Shi, 'Shanzhai Manufacturing—an alternative innovation phenomenon in China', http://connected-marketing.tumblr.com/post/2689 7090180/shan-zhai-manufacturing-an-alternative-innovation, July 10, 2012, last accessed 13 Sep. 2012.
68. Edward Tse, Kevin Ma and Yu Huang, 'Shan Zhai: a Chinese phenomenon', Booz & Co. http://www.booz.com/media/file/Shan_Zhai_A_Chinese_Phenomenon_en.pdf, last accessed 13 Sep. 2012.
69. Brendon Chase, 'Shanzhai ji: all you need to know about fake phones', 2009, http://www.cnet.com.au/shanzhai-ji-all-you-need-to-know-about-fake-phones-339297258.htm, last accessed 13 Sep. 2012.
70. 'Shanzhai manufacturing—an alternative innovation phenomenon in China'.
71. Tse, Ma, Huang, 'Shan Zhai: a Chinese phenomenon'.
72. Sky Canaves and Juliet Ye, 'Imitation is the sincerest form of rebellion in China', *Wall Street Journal*, 22 January 2009, http://online.wsj.com/article/SB123257138952903561.html, last accessed 17 Oct. 2012.
73. Ibid.
74. Yu Hua, *China in Ten Words*, New York: Pantheon, 2011, [e-book].

75. Canaves and Ye, 'Imitation is the sincerest form of rebellion in China'.

76. Hua, *China in Ten Words*.

77. Ibid.

78. John Seely Brown and John Hagel, 'Innovation blowback: disruptive management practices from Asia', *The McKinsey Quarterly*, 1 (2005).

79. Ibid., p. 38.

80. These connections are explored in detail by Hacked Matter, a research hub founded by Li, researcher Silvia Lindtner and myself. See www.hackedmatter. com

CONCLUSION: OPEN LOOPS

1. Helen Pidd, 'Sci-fi blockbuster *Looper* achieves Chinese box office first', *The Guardian*, 1 October 2012, http://www.guardian.co.uk/film/2012/oct/01/looper-sci-fi-blockbuster-china, last accessed 11 November 2012.

2. Wonsuk Chang, 'Reflection on time and related ideas in the *Yijing*', *Philosophy East and West*, 59(2) April 2009.

INDEX

Abbas, Ackbar 2
abstract expressionism 18
Accra, Ghana 187–8
aeroplanes 141–2
After Cubism 21
Ai Weiwei 103, 104, 105
Albert Speer & Partners 136
Alcock, Rutherford 117
Alderslade, Jamie 183
All that is Solid Melts Into Air 31
Allen, Franklin 194
Amazing Stories xxi
Ambrosia restaurant, Shanghai 82
American Radiator building, New
    York 84
Angotti, Tom 161
Anhua Lu, Shanghai 204
Anhui Province, China 157
anti-market capitalism 185
anti-urbanism 38–41, 152, 161
Anting New Town, Shanghai 135–8
antu zhongqian 171
Anyang, Henan 72
apartheid 165
Apple 202
Arab Spring 39
Arcologies 25
Arkaraprasertkul, Non 55
Arrival Cities 176

Art Deco 1910–1939 84
Art Deco xvii, xxii, 6, 73, 80, 82,
    84–5, 99
Arts and Crafts Museum, Shanghai 82
Asia Reality Company 83
Asian Financial Crisis (1997) 112
Asimov, Isaac xvii
Athens, Greece 8, 89
Atkins Consultancy 131, 137
Austro-Hungarian Empire 82
authoritarianism 4, 5, 7, 36–7, 42–5,
    58, 103–6, 209
Autogyros xii

Back Alley Banking 194
Ballard, James Graham xxiii
baojia system 166
Baoshan, Shanghai 147
Batman 76
Battle of Shanghai 91–2
Baudelaire, Charles Pierre 34
Baudrillard, Jean 135
Bauhaus 83, 136
Beaux-Arts 82
Beijing, China 53, 115, 164
    2008 Olympics xiv, xxv, 61
    Forbidden City 61
    jingpai 53
    Tiananmen Square protests 105

237

Tsinghua University 165
Beijing opera 114–15
Beijing World Park 135
benbangcai (cuisine) 179
Benjamin, Walter 34
Bergère, Marie-Claire xxiii, 113, 115
Berlin, Germany 8
    Television Tower xxiv
Berman, Marshall 31, 33, 34, 35,
    39–40
    All that is Solid Melts Into Air 31
Bethnal Green, London 185
Blade Runner 76
Blair, Anthony Charles Lynton "Tony"
    94
Bobos in Paradise 101
boulevards 33–4, 35
Boundary Estate, London 185
Bourgeois Utopia 143–4, 145
Boxer Rebellion 72
Bradbury, Ray xvii
Braudel, Fernand 59, 185
Brazil 189
Brick Expressionism 80, 82
Bridge 8, Shanghai 97–8
Bristol, United Kingdom 133
British Concession, Shanghai 116–17
Bronte, Charlotte xviii
Brook, Daniel xiii, 44
Brooking Institute 183
Brooks, David xxvi
Brown, John Seely 204
Brussels, Belgium 84
Bryant Park, New York 84
Budapest, Hungary 82
Buddhism 12–13, 109, 195
    Chan xxiii, 12–13
    gradualism and subitism 13
Bund, Shanghai xiii, 29, 54, 55, 57,
    73, 90, 120
Burroughs, William xvi

calendars xv–xvi, 69–71

California, United States xxvi, 64, 80,
    89, 94, 106, 143
Cambridge Water Town, Shanghai 139
Campanella, Thomas 22, 44, 57, 149,
    152
Canada xxiv, 124
Canaves, Sky 203
capitalism 59, 62, 191, 197, 198–9
*Capitalism with Chinese
    Characteristics* 58
Capitol Theatre, Shanghai 84
Caro, Robert 34, 35, 37
Carrier Corporation xviii
cars xi, 30, 39–41, 42–4, 141–3, 153
Carter, Howard 85
Cassidy, William 195
Castle of Otranto, The 74–5
Catherine the Great, Empress and
    Autocrat of All the Russias 59
Cato Institute on China and Economic
    Reform 57
CCTV (China Central Television) 203
cell-phones 141–2
censorship 7, 103, 105–6
central business districts (CBDs) 46,
    55, 132
Centre for Performing Arts, Shanghai
    30
Century Avenue, Shanghai 30, 43, 49,
    50
chai (拆) 148
Champs-Élysées 30, 31
Chan Buddhism xxiii, 12–13
Chang, Eileen 81
Chang, Leslie 168, 170
Chang Wonsuk 12, 63
Charpentier, Jean-Marie 30
Chen Duxiu 71
Chen Hangfeng 56, 87
Chen, Martha 189
Chen Yawei 41, 45, 46, 61–2
Chen Yifei 124

Chengdu, Sichuan 39
chengguan (city inspectors) 60, 184–5
chi ku (eat bitterness) 172
Chicago, Illinois 25
   1933 World's Fair (A Century of
      Progress) xix
   Tribune Tower 75
China
   1600–1046 BC Shang dynasty 72
   1046–256 BC Zhou dynasty 166
   221–206 BC Qin dynasty 63
   317–589 Six Dynasties 195
   618–907 Tang dynasty 195
   960–1279 Song dynasty 13, 203
   1368–1644 Ming dynasty 13, 131
   1644–1911 Qing dynasty 69–73,
      159, 195
   1850–1864 Taiping Rebellion 116
   1898 Hundred Days' Reform 69
   1898–1901 Boxer Rebellion 72
   1911–1949 Republican era xvi, 6,
      13, 70–1, 72, 73, 79–82, 102–3,
      159, 195, 208
   1915–1921 May Fourth Movement
      xvi, 6, 13, 70–1, 72, 73, 79–82,
      159, 208
   1927–1950 Civil War 116, 163
   1937–1945 Sino-Japanese War
      xxiii, 91–2, 122
   1949–1976 Mao Zedong era xxiii,
      122–3, 146, 148, 166–7, 195,
      196, 208
   1958–1961 Great Leap Forward 167
   1966–1971 Cultural Revolution 99,
      146, 148, 196, 208
   1976–1989 Deng Xiaoping era
      xxiii–xxiv, 195
   1989 Tiananmen Square protests
      105
   authoritarianism 4, 5, 7, 42–5, 58,
      103–6, 209
   banking system 194–8

baojia system 166
Buddhism xxiii, 12–13, 109, 195
censorship 103, 105–6
circular migration 174–9
Communist Party 47, 61, 63–4, 112,
   122
Confucianism 13, 69, 104, 109, 121,
   155, 171
'corpse walking' 171
corruption 64, 134, 148
and countdowns 11
cyberculture 104, 105–6, 168,
   203–5
decentralisation 47, 49, 149–51
diaspora 171
education system 7, 70, 103, 171–3
environmentalism 27–8, 92–3, 134,
   136–7
face, culture of 6, 54, 60–1
feng shui 30, 119, 136–7
film industry 207–8
forced relocations 147–9
GDP (gross domestic product) 27,
   41, 58, 194
generation gap 173–4
Grand Canal 163
guanxi (connections) 48, 182
hukou (household registration)
   system 166–9, 172, 174–7
innovation 103–6, 198–205
and intellectual property 103, 201–5
Kuomintang 91
land-leasing system 8, 47, 149–50
Mid-Autumn Festival (Zhongqiu
   Jie) 182
'Middle Kingdom' concept 135
migrant workers 2, 6, 8, 9–10, 50,
   58, 60, 87, 91, 148, 157, 164–79,
   182
modernity 3–4, 5, 13–14, 45, 80,
   159, 208–9
motorcycle industry 204

native place, importance of 171–2
poverty 163–6
property market 8, 149–50
R&D investment 205
shadow banking 194–8
shanzhai 201–5
soft power 102
south facing windows 30, 119, 136–7
Special Economic Zones (SEZ) xxiii–xxiv, 46, 55, 96, 135, 176, 201
State Council 168, 198
State Owned Enterprises (SOEs) 48, 96–7, 98, 147, 195
stoicism, culture of 173
Taoism 53, 62, 109
tax vouchers (*fapiao*) 186
time-consciousness xv–xvi, 11–13, 159–60, 208
urbanisation 10, 27, 43, 58, 133, 148, 150, 156, 158–60, 166–79
village communities 169–70
China Baptist Publication Society and Christian Literature Society Building 83
China Prophecy 19, 25
Chinese diaspora 171
Chinese New Year *see* Spring Festival
Choa, Chris 51
cholera 32
Chongming, Dongtan 134
Chongqing, China 113, 164, 204
Christensen, Clayton 200
Christian calendar xv
Chrysler Building, New York 75
Chunming Art Industrial Park 92–3
Churchill, Winston 132
Cities in Civilization 7–8, 88
Cixi, Empress Dowager of the Qing dynasty 70
Clark, Kenneth 77

Classical Aesthetics 77–8
clocks xv, 11, 70, 73
    water clock 11
co-operative loan societies 195
Cobb Fish and Chip Shop, The 133
Code 46 xxvi
Cohen, Jean-Louis 34
Cohn, Norman xvi
'collective walks' 39
Columbia Circle, Shanghai 83
commercialism 117–20
communism xxiii
Communist Party of China (CPC) 47, 63–4, 112, 122
    sixty-year anniversary 61
Confucianism 13, 69, 104, 109, 121, 155, 171
    antu zhongqian 171
Confucius 13
congestion and dispersion 139
Constructivism 85
'corpse walking' 171
corruption 64, 134, 148
cosmopolitanism 89, 115–17
    faux cosmopolitanism 131–9
Council on Tall Buildings and Urban Habitat 19
countdowns 11
Crabgrass Frontier 142
Craig, Thomas 200
creative class 93–4, 95, 101
creative clusters 88, 92–3, 97–102, 106–10
    failure of 99–102, 109–10
creative deficit 102–6
Creative Destruction 199
creative economy 7, 87–8, 90–110
creativity 12, 93, 102–10
crime 77, 152, 162, 164
Crimea 59
Crystal Palace, London xviii
Cubism 85

INDEX

cuisine in Shanghai 178
Culinary Nostalgia 179
Cultural Revolution 99, 146, 148, 196, 208
Cunningham, Maura xiv
cyberculture 104, 105–6, 168, 203–4
   hackers xx, 204
Cybernetic Culture Research Unit 185
cyberpunk xx–xxii, xxvi, 79, 204

da Vinci, Leonardo 105
Dalrymple, Theodore 40–1
Dalston, London 185
Dancing with Shackles On 106
danwei (work unit) system 49, 146–7, 167
Darwinian evolution 11
Davis, Mike 158
   Planet of Slums 160–1
De Soto, Hernando 190–4
   Mystery of Capital, The 190–1
   Other Path, The 191
Death and Life of Great American Cities, The 37–8, 161
decentralisation 23, 26, 47, 49, 141, 149–51
Debord, Guy 62
debrouillards 190
Deleuze, Gilles 79
'Democracity' exhibit xvii
den Hartog, Harry 134, 136, 137, 146
   Shanghai New Towns: Searching for Community and Identity in a Sprawling Metropolis 134
Deng Kunyen 90–3, 108–9
Deng Xiaoping xxiii–xxiv, 46, 55
Department for Culture, Media and Sport (DCMS) 94
Descartes, René 62
Detroit, Michigan 153
Devil's Road, The 80
Diamond Age, The 155–6

Ding Yi 92
Disneyfication effect 126, 156
disruptive technologies 199–205
Dongtan, Shanghai 134
Du Yuesheng 90
Dutch Town, Shanghai 134
DVDs 29, 60, 64

East China Normal University, Shanghai 183, 184
Economist, The xxv, 58, 169
EDAW 51
education 7, 70, 103, 171–3
Egypt 85
Eiffel Tower, Paris 84, 135
'800 Show' 88, 101
Einstein, Albert xvii
Eisenhower, Dwight David xii
'Electro the Motor Man' xviii
Embankment Building, Shanghai 165
environmentalism 27–8, 92–3, 134, 136–7
Erh Deke 124
eschatology xvi, xxiii, xxvi, 13
'Eskimo Igloo of Tomorrow' xviii
Europe
   mercantilism 192–3
   urbanisation 158, 161
Evangelical movement 145
Exhibition Centre, Qingpu 139
expressionism 6
   German expressionism 83

face, culture of 6, 54, 60–1
Facebook 142
Factory, The 100
Fallows, James *Postcards From Tomorrow Square* 54
Fan, C. Cindy 175, 177
Fan Wenzhao (Robert Fan) 84
fang nu (mortgage slave) 149
Fangualong, Shanghai 163

INDEX

fapiao (tax vouchers) 186
feng shui 30, 119, 136–7
Ferris, Hugh 76
financial crises
 Global Financial Crisis (2008/2009)
  xxv, 177, 189, 197
 Asian Financial Crisis (1997) 112
Financial Times xiv
First World Science Fiction conference
 xvii
Fisher, David xxv
Fisher, Mark xxvi
Fishman, Robert 21, 143, 151
 Bourgeois Utopia 143–4, 145
Fishman, Ted 139
Flintstones, The xx
Florence, Italy 8, 89, 135
Florida, Richard 93–4, 95
Forbidden City, Beijing 61
forced relocations 147–9
Ford Model T 142
foreign direct investment (FDI) 47,
 58, 60
Foreign Policy 9
Form in Gothic 77
Formula One 135
Fortune Magazine 19
Frafras 187–8
France
 Eiffel Tower 84, 135
 Île-de-France 131
 Paris xviii, 8, 21, 23, 30, 31, 32–4,
  35, 37, 39, 41, 55, 84, 89, 106,
  135, 208
 Versailles 131
French Concession, Shanghai 29, 82,
 97, 163, 165
Freud, Sigmund 80
Friedman, Milton 57
Friedman, Thomas 43, 199
Fudan University, Shanghai 106
Fuksas, Massimiliano 55

'Future of New China, The' xxiv
futurism xi–xv, xvi–xxvii, 2, 20, 72–3,
 85, 113, 114, 208
 collapse of faith in xiv, xx, xxvi
 cyberpunk xx–xxii, 79
 retrofuturism xiii, xx, xxii–xxvii,
  2, 209
Fuzhou Lu, Shanghai 29, 74

G'Five 202
gaige kaifang (reform and opening)
 xxiii–xxiv, 167
gaokao (college entrance examination)
 172–3
Gaoqiao, Shanghai 134
Garden Cities 139–41
Garden Cities of Tomorrow, The 139
Gate of Darkness 79, 81, 82
General Electric 108
General Motors xi–xii, xx, 30
Gensler xxv, 28, 51
Gensler, Art 28
geometry 31–2
Georges, Jean 183
Georgian Revival 82
German expressionism 83
Germany xv, 135–6
 Weimar Republic 8, 135
Gernsback Continuum, The xxi–xxii
Ghana 187–8
Ghost in the Shell xxv, 76
ghost malls 53
ghost towns 131–9
Gibson, William xxi–xxii, 79
 Gernsback Continuum, The xxi–xxii
 Ralph 124c41+ xxi
Giridharadas, Anand 13
Glaeser, Edward 25, 27, 37, 142
 Triumph of the City 35, 162–3
Global Language Monitor xxv
global population growth 169
Global Shanghai xxiii, xxvi

INDEX

Global Financial Crisis (2008/2009) xxv, 177, 189, 197

globalisation 3, 141–2

Goethe, Johann Wolfgang von 135

golden ages of cities 88–90, 105

Goldkorn, Jeremy 105

Goldwater, Barry xx

Gotham City 74, 76

Gothic Futurism 7, 74–85

gradualism 13

Grand Canal, China 163

Grand Theatre, Shanghai 82, 84

Granville Island, Vancouver 124

Great Depression xix

'Great Disruption, The' 200

Great Exhibition of 1851, London xviii

Great Leap Forward 167

Great Shanghai Industrial Heritage Revitalization Workshop, The 109

Great Wall of China 61

Greece xvi, 8, 89, 135

Green Gang 90

Green Metropolis 27

Greenwich Village, New York 40

Gregorian calendar xv, xvi, 69–71

Gregory XIII, Pope xv

Gropius, Walter 136

GDP (gross domestic product) 27, 41, 58, 194

Grosvenor House, Shanghai 84

Guan Songsheng 84

Guangdong Province, China xxiv, 45, 47, 116, 135, 164, 165, 168, 189, 176, 199, 201, 203

Guangxu, 11th Qing Emperor of China 69

Guangzhou, Guangdong 116, 164, 168, 189, 199

guanxi (connections) 48, 182

Guattari, Félix 79

Guizhou TV 203

gundilong (rolling earth dragons) 163

Guo Moruo 71

Gupte, Rupali 186–7

hackers xx, 204

Hagel, John 204

Hainan, China 47

haipai 7, 53, 70, 83, 111, 114–27

haipaicai (cuisine) 179

Hall, Peter 7–8, 32, 35, 37, 104–5, 139

   Cities in Civilization 88–90

Han Han 103

Han Haoyue 204

Hangzhou, Zhejiang 113

Hanna-Barbera xx

Harbin, Heilongjiang 82, 183

Harry Potter 132

Hart, Keith 187–8

Hart, Stuart 200

Hartley, John 93

Hassenpflug, Dieter 136

Haussmann, Georges-Eugène 23, 32–4, 35, 37, 39

hawkers 181–5

Hebei Province, China 176

Her xxvi

Hessler, Peter *Oracle Bones* 73

hippies xx

History of Future Cities, A xiii

Hitler, Adolf 135

HMA Architects and Designers 98

Höger, Fritz 83

Hollywood, Los Angeles 64, 80, 89, 94

Hong Kong 25, 44, 46, 47, 48, 57, 96, 116, 125, 155, 171

Hongqiao Lu, Shanghai 98

Hood, Raymond 75, 76, 84

Howard, Ebenezer xxv, 139–41, 146

   Garden Cities of Tomorrow, The 139

Hsia, Tsi-an

   Gate of Darkness 79, 81, 82

Hu Jieming 87

Hu Jintao 105
Hu Shih 71, 79
Huaihai Lu, Shanghai 98
Huang Fuxiang 45, 46, 55
Huang Ju, Shanghai 134
Huang Yu 201–3
Huang Yasheng 57–8
    *Capitalism with Chinese Character-
        istics* 58
Huangpu river 17, 41, 54, 90
Hubei Province, China 168
Hudec, László 80, 82–4
Hughes, Robert xxvi, 3
    Shock of the New, The xxvi
hukou (household registration) system
    10, 166–9, 172, 174–7
Hunan Province, China 157
Hundred Days' Reform 69
Huqiu Lu, Shanghai 83

Ian B (blogger) 185
IBM (International Business
    Machines) 200
Île-de-France 131
Imagine: How Creativity Works 101
Incomplete Café, Thames Town 133
India 203
    Mumbai 186–7
Indonesia 160
informal economy 181–205
    and clean up campaigns 183–6
    dualist approach 189–90
    legalist approach 190–4
    structuralists 190
    System D 190
innovation 103–6, 198–205
L'Institut d'aménagement et
    d'urbanisme de la région Île-de-
    France, Paris 55
intellectual property 103, 104, 182,
    199–205
International Labour Organization
    (ILO) 188

International Style xvii, 73, 76
Internet 104, 105–6, 141–2, 203–4
iPhone 104
iPhone Mini 202
Iraq War xxv
Italian Town, Shanghai 134
Ito Toyo 55

Jackson, Kenneth
    Crabgrass Frontier 142
Jacobs, Jane 6, 40, 94, 107
    *Death and Life of Great American
        Cities, The* 37–8, 161
Jacques, Martin xxvi, 3, 159
Jakarta, Indonesia 160
Jameson, Frederic 5, 62
    'Future City' 40
Japan xv, xix, xxiii, 18, 70, 204
    Sino-Japanese War xxiii, 91–2, 122
    Tokyo 19, 20, 26, 51
'Jasmine Revolution' 39
Jazz Age xxii
Jeanneret, Charles-Édouard *see* Le
    Corbusier
Jetsons, The xx
Jia Zhangke
    World, The 135
Jiading, Shanghai 135–8, 147, 149
Jiangnan shipyard xxv
Jiangsu Province, China 116, 203
Jianguo Lu, Shanghai 97
Jiangxi Lu, Shanghai 73
Jingan, Shanghai 88, 101
    Jingan Beishu 126
Jingling Lu, Shanghai 29
jingpai 53
Jinmao tower, Shanghai 1, 74
Jobs, Steve 104
John Hopkins University, Baltimore
    194
Johnson, Rian 208
journalism 70

Judeo-Christian tradition xvi

Kang Youwei 69
Keane, Michael 97
Khanna, Parag 9
King, Mel 162
Kirby, Andrew 143
knowledge economy 93
Knowledge, Innovation, Community
    (KIC) 106–7
Kohn Pedersen Fox (KPF) 19
Koolhaas, Rem 24, 76
    S, M, X, XL 40
Kruger, Frank 88
Kuhn, Philip
    Soul Stealers 171
Kunstler, Howard 139, 143
Kuo, Kaiser 105
Kuomintang 91

Lagos, Nigeria 160, 189, 199
land-leasing system 8, 47, 149–50
Land, Nick xiii, xv, xix, xx, xxiii, xxiv,
    4, 11, 84, 85, 111
    'Introductions to the Afterlife' 12
    'Neomodernity' 3
Lang, Fritz xxv, 76, 80, 83
    Metropolis xxi, xxv, 76, 83
lao jia (native town) 171
Laozi 53
Le Corbusier xxv, 1, 5, 17, 20–2, 23–4,
    26, 28, 30–2, 36, 40–1, 43, 83
    After Cubism 21
    City of Tomorrow and its Planning,
    The 30–2
    Purism 21
lean linear city xxv
Lee, Leo 70–1, 79, 80
Lee, Poy G. *see* Li Jinpei
Lehrer, Jonah 101–2
    Imagine: How Creativity Works 101
Letchworth, England 140

Lewis, Michael 74, 77
Li, David 202, 204–5
Li Jinpei 84
Li Keqiang 9
Li Peng 55
Liang Qichao xxiv, 69–71
Liang, Samuel
    Mapping Modernity in Shanghai
    121–2, 127
Liao Han-Teng 104
Lifestyle Ltd 98
lilongs 113–14, 116, 117, 120–7
Lin Yutang 70
Lincoln Center, New York 34
Liu, Alan 197
Liu, E.C. 127
Liu E 72
Liu Jiakun 139
Liu Jidong 91–2
Liu Na'ou 80
Liu Yichun 139
Lo, Vincent 44, 106–7, 111–12
Logan, John 146
Logon 88
London 8, 139, 185–6
    Bethnal Green 185
    Boundary Estate 185
    clean up campaigns 185–6
    Dalston 185
    Great Exhibition xviii
    Millennium Dome, Greenwich 94
    Old Nichol 185
    slums 185
    Victoria and Albert Museum 84
    Victorian era 139, 185
Looper xxvi, 207–9
Lovecraft, Howard Phillips "H. P."
    74–5
Low-Road spaces 102
Lu Hanchao 114, 117, 163, 175
Lu Xun 80–1
    Madman's Diary, A 81

True Story of Ah Q, The 81
Wild Grass 81
Lujiazui, Shanghai 1, 28, 30, 42, 44, 46, 48, 49, 50, 51, 55, 56, 57
Lujiazui Group 48
Luodian, Shanghai 134, 138
Lure of the Modern, The 71
Luwan, Shanghai 97, 138
Tianzifang 123–5
Luxembourg Gardens, Paris 35
Luxor, Egypt 85

M50, Shanghai 93, 101
Ma Qingyun 139
Ma, Kevin 201–3
mAAN (modern Asian, Architecture Network) 108–9
Macau 155
MADA s.p.a.m 139
Madman's Diary, A 81
Madonna 104
Malkki, Liisa 159
Manchester, England 144
Mandarin 11, 147, 196
Manhattan, New York 26, 27, 46, 84
Mantani Kenji 98
Mao Zedong xxiii, 148, 204
Mao, Isaac 205
Maoming Lu, Shanghai 104
Mapping Modernity in Shanghai 121, 127
market economy 59
markets (street) 181–5
Marx, Karl xxiii, 10, 170, 198
Marxism xvi
Marxist-Leninism 169
May Fourth Movement xvi, 6, 13, 70–1, 72, 73, 79–82, 159, 208
McGregor, Richard 63
McKinsey Global 9, 158
    McKinsey Quarterly 204
    'Preparing for China's Urban Billion' 27

McNeill, William 169
Mearns, Andrew 139
mechanisation 3
Mediatek 201
megalopoly 25
Memphis, Tennessee 89
mercantilism 192–3
Metropole Theatre, Shanghai 84
Metropolis xxi, xxv, 76, 83
Metropolis Now 9
Mexico City, Mexico 160
Mickey Mouse xvii
microfilm xix
Mid-Autumn Festival (Zhongqiu Jie) 182
migrant workers 2, 6, 8, 9–10, 50, 58, 60, 87, 91, 148, 157, 164–79, 182
    discrimination against 171–3, 175–7
Millennium Dome, Greenwich 94
Ming dynasty 13, 131
Minhang, Shanghai 146, 157
minimalist sculpture 18
minjian (popular lending) 194
Minsheng Art Museum, Shanghai 99
Modarres, Ali 143
modernism 40–1, 42–3, 73
Modernist Style 88
modernity xiv, xvii, xxii, 3–4, 5, 12, 13, 70, 74, 75, 145, 158–60, 208–9
    Western conception of 53–4, 80, 159–60
Moganshan Lu, Shanghai 92–3
Mok, Diana 141–2
Monster That is History, The 79
Montreal 1967 Expo xx
Moore Memorial Church, Shanghai 82
Mori Art Museum, Tokyo 20
Mori Akira 19
Mori Minoru 5, 17, 19–20, 22, 23, 26, 28, 51
Mori Taikichiro 19
Mori Trust 19

Moses, Robert 6, 23, 34–5, 36, 37, 40
motorcycle industry 204
Mou Zongsan 13
Moving Cities 112
'Ms. Drudge' and 'Ms. Modern' xviii
Mu Shiying 80
Mumbai, India 186–7
Mumford, Lewis 139, 142
Mystery of Capital, The 190–1

nail houses 148
Naipaul, Vidiadhar Surajprasad 161
Nanjing Lu, Shanghai 29, 30, 120
Nanjing, Jiangsu 203
nanotechnology 156
Napoleon III, Emperor of the French 32, 37, 39
National Geographic 9
Neo-Confucianism 13
neo-modernity 3, 5, 7, 11, 12, 73, 209
Netspeak 105–6
Neuromancer 76
Neuwirth, Robert 162, 166, 184, 189–90
   Stealth Nation 189
   System D 190
New Citizen Life 157
New Left xx
'new perceptionists' (*xin ganjuepai*) 80
New Urbanists 136
New York, United States 8, 9, 18, 23, 25, 26, 27, 34–5, 36, 37, 40, 75–6, 89, 160
   American Radiator building 84
   Bryant Park 84
   Chrysler Building 75
   Gothic Futurism 76
   Greenwich Village 40
   Lincoln Center 34
   Long Island 34
   Manhattan 26, 27, 46, 84
   September 11th attacks, New York 18

Skyscraper Museum 19, 76
Shea Stadium 34
United Nations Headquarters 34
Wall Street 94
West Chelsea 98
Woolworth Building 75
World Trade Center 46
New York 1939 World's Fair xii, xvii–xviii, xix
   'Democracity' exhibit xvii
   Electro the Motor Man xviii
   Eskimo Igloo of Tomorrow xviii
   Futurama pavilion xi–xii
   Ms. Drudge and Ms. Modern xviii
   Wondrous World of 1960 xii, xx
   Westinghouse pavilion xviii
New York Modern 76
New York Times 13, 43, 105
New Yorker, The 39
Nietzsche, Friedrich Wilhelm 4
Nigeria 160, 189, 199
Nightingale, Florence 132
1933 complex, Shanghai 99–100
No. 10 Steel Factory, Shanghai 98
nomadic culture 78
Normandie apartments, Shanghai 82
Novak, Matt xx

O'Connor, Justin 95
O'Neil, Dennis 76
Obama, Barack 203
Old City, Shanghai 181
Old Nichol, London 185
Olds, Kris 55, 56, 61
Olympic Games xviii
   1900 Paris Summer Olympics xviii
   1904 St Louis Summer Olympics xviii
   2008 Beijing Summer Olympics xiv, xxv, 61
Ong, Aihwa 47, 50, 62, 171
oracle bones 72

Oracle Bones 73
Oresteia xvi
Oriental Pearl Tower xxiv
Osnos, Evan 39
Other Path, The 191
Outlaws of the Marshes 201
Owen, David
   Green Metropolis 27
Ozenfant, Amédée 21

Paleofuture xx
Palmer and Turner 84
Pan, Lynn xxiii, 111, 114–15, 122, 127
Panyu Lu, Shanghai 82
Paraguay 189
Paramount Theatre, Shanghai 84
Paris, France xviii, 8, 21, 23, 30, 31,
   32–4, 35, 37, 39, 41, 55, 84, 89,
   106, 135, 208
   1832 cholera epidemic 33
   1900 Olympics xviii
   boulevards 33–4, 35
   Champs-Élysées 30, 31
   La Defense 55
   Eiffel Tower 84, 135
   L'Institut d'aménagement et
      d'urbanisme de la région Île-de-
      France 55
   Luxembourg Gardens 35
Paris Exposition: The International
   Exposition of Modern Industrial and
   Decorative Arts 84
Park Hotel, Shanghai 74, 82, 83
Parker, Richard Barry 140
Parris, Kristen 196
Peace Hotel, Shanghai 84
Pedersen, William 19, 26
pedestrian overpasses 43
penghu (straw huts) 163
People's Liberation Army (PLA) 48
People's Square, Shanghai xxiv, 82
'Perisphere' xvii

Perrault, Dominique 55
Peru 190–4
Pier One, Shanghai 82, 100
Pinkney, Cyrus 76
piracy 103, 104, 182, 199–205
Planet of Slums 160–1
Plato 31, 38
   cave allegory 62
Poe, Edgar Allan
   Devil's Road, The 80
Pol Pot 40
Poncellini, Luca 82, 83
population growth, global 169
Porter, Michael 94
Postcards From Tomorrow Square 54
Postrel, Virginia xiv, xxvi
Potemkin, Grigory 59
Potemkinism 57–9, 65
poverty 163–6
Power Broker, The 34
Prahalad, Coimbatore Krishnarao
   "C. K." 199
printing press 70
property market (China) 8
   speculative investment 149–50, 153,
      158
Pudong, Shanghai xxiv, 1, 5–6, 17,
   18, 22–3, 26, 28, 30, 41–51, 54–7,
   61–2, 73, 90, 111, 156
   backstreets 50
   emptiness of 5, 44
   foreign investment 48, 56
   free trade zone 47
   land leasing 47
   Lujiazui 1, 28, 30, 42, 44, 46, 48,
      49, 50, 51, 55, 56, 57
   and Potemkinism 5, 44, 57
   settlement of 49–50
   spectacle and deception 57
Pujiang, Shanghai 134
Purism 21
Putonghua see Mandarin 147

INDEX

Puxi 6–7, 17, 30, 42, 44, 49, 73, 90,
     114
  housing shortages 50
  Xintiandi 44, 97, 106, 111–114,
     123, 125, 127, 138

Qian Jun 194
Qian Meijun 194
Qin Hui 165, 174
Qin Shi Huang, Emperor of China 63
Qing dynasty 69–73, 159, 195
Qingpu, Shanghai 138–9, 152
Qiu Anxiong 87

Radisson Hotel, Shanghai xxiv
railways 141–2
Ralph 124c41+ xxi
Rebirth 87–8
Red Town, Shanghai 98
*Redevelopment and Preservation
   of Historic Lilong Housing in
   Shanghai, The* 123
Regulation of Land Use Rights 47
renao (热闹) 44, 152
retrofuturism xiii, xx, xxii–xxvii, 2,
     209
River at the Center of the World xxiv
roads 30, 39–41, 42–4, 141–3
Robards, Jason xix
Rogers, Richard 55
Roosevelt, Franklin Delano xviii
Roppongi Hills, Tokyo 20, 26
Roy, Ananya xiv, 8, 65, 161
Ruijin Lu, Shanghai 97
Russia 59

S, M, X, XL 40
Santa's Little Helpers' 56
Sao Paulo, Brazil 189
Saunders, Doug 9, 158, 163, 169
  Arrival Cities 176
Schiller, Friedrich 135

Schumacher, Fritz 83
Schumpeter, Joseph
  Socialism, Capitalism, Democracy
     198–9
Science and Technology Museum,
  Shanghai 30
Scott-Heron, Gil 87
Sculptural Development Department,
  Shanghai 98
Seattle 1962 World's Fair xxiv
Seattle Space Tower xxiv
Seed Studio 205
Seng Kuan xxiv, 48
Seoul Commune xxv
September 11th attacks, New York 18
shadow banking 194–8
shadow economy *see* informal
  economy
Shang dynasty 72
Shanghai
  '800 Show' 88, 101
  1933 complex 99–100
  1987 ferry disaster 42
  2006 pension scandal 134
  Ambrosia restaurant 82
  Anhua Lu 204
  Anting New Town 135–8
  Arts and Crafts Museum 82
  automobile boom xi, 153
  Baoshan 147
  Bridge 8 complex 97
  British Concession 116–17
  Bund xiii, 29, 54, 57, 73, 90, 120
  Cambridge Water Town 139
  Capitol Theatre 84
  Centre for Performing Arts 30
  Century Avenue 30, 43, 49, 50
  chengguan (city inspectors) 60,
     184–5
  Chunming Art Industrial Park 92–3
  clean-up campaigns 53–4, 57, 60,
     184

INDEX

'collective walks' 39
Columbia Circle 83
commercialism 117–20
congestion xi, 134, 146
cosmopolitanism 115–17
creative economy 7, 87–8, 90–110
crime 152, 164
cuisine 50, 178, 182–4
dragon head, as 45–6, 58
Dutch Town 134
DVD stores 64
East China Normal University 183, 184
Economic Commission 97
Embankment Building 165
Exhibition Centre, Qingpu 139
foreign investment 48, 56, 58, 60
free trade zone 47
French Concession 29, 82, 97, 163, 165
Fudan University 106
futurism xi–xv, xvi–xvii, xxii–xxvii, 2, 113, 114, 208
Fuzhou Lu 29, 30, 74
Gaoqiao 134
GDP (gross domestic product) 41
ghost malls 53
'golden age' xxii–xxiii, 2, 6, 89
Gothic Futurism 79–85
Grand Theatre 82, 84
Grosvenor House 84
growth model 58
haipai 7, 53, 70, 83, 111, 114–27
Hongqiao Lu 98
Huaihai Lu 98
Huqiu Lu 83
Incomplete Café, Thames Town 133
industrial heritage 87–8, 90–3, 96–102, 108–10, 147
Italian Town 134
Jiading 135–8, 147, 149
Jianguo Lu 97

Jiangxi Lu 73
Jingan 88, 101, 126
Jingling Lu 29
Jinmao tower 1, 74
Knowledge, Innovation, Community (KIC) 106–7
lilongs 113–14, 116, 117, 120–7
Lujiazui 1, 28, 30, 42, 44, 46, 48, 49, 50, 51, 55, 56, 57
Luodian 134, 138
Luwan 97, 123–5, 138
Maoming Lu 104
Metropole Theatre 84
migrant workers 2, 6, 8, 9–10, 50, 58, 60, 87, 91, 148, 157, 164–79, 182
Minhang 146, 157
modernism 42–3, 44, 73
and modernity 3–4, 5, 13–14, 45, 209
Moganshan Lu 92
Moore Memorial Church 82
Nanjing Lu 29, 30, 120
No. 10 Steel Factory 98
Normandie apartments 82
Oriental Pearl Tower xxiv
Panyu Lu 82
Paramount Theatre 84
Park Hotel 82, 83
Peace Hotel 84
pedestrian overpasses 43
People's Square xxiv, 1, 39, 82
Pier One 82, 100
pollution xi
and Potemkinism 57–9, 65
Pudong xxiv, 1, 5–6, 17, 18, 22–3, 26, 28, 30, 41–51, 54–7, 61–2, 73, 90, 111, 156
Pujiang 134
Puxi 6–7, 17, 30, 42, 44, 49, 73, 90
Qingpu 138–9, 152
Radisson Hotel xxiv

INDEX

Red Town 98
Ruijin Lu 97
Science and Technology Museum 30
Sculptural Development Department 98
Sculpture Space 98–9
shadow economy 181–6, 199
Shanghai Tower xxv, 1–2, 28, 51
shantytowns 163–6
shikumen 107, 113–14, 120, 123, 124, 125, 146, 181
Sihang Warehouse 91–2
Songjiang 131, 132, 134, 135, 147, 152
spectacle and deception 5, 44, 53–64
street food 50, 182–4
street life 50, 53–4, 60, 101, 181–5
street markets 181–5
suburbs 8–9, 131–9, 145–53, 156–8
Suzhou Creek 82, 87, 90–3, 163
Swedish Town 134, 138
Taikang Lu 124–5, 184
Thames Town 131–3, 134, 137–8
Tianzifang 123–5
tingzijian 119
Tongji University 106, 138
Union Building 82
Urban Cultural Bureau 98
Urban Planning Administration Bureau 137
Urban Planning Museum 1, 132
Westernisantion 53–4
World Financial Center (SWFC) 1, 5, 18–19, 24, 26, 51
Wu's House, Tongren Lu 82
Wujiang 146
Wujiaochang 106
Xiayu Kindergarten, Qingpu 139
Xinan Electrical Machine Plant 88
Xinchejian 204

Xintiandi 44, 97, 106, 111–114, 123, 125, 127, 138
Yanan Lu 104
Yangpu 106–7, 108
Yangshupu Lu 109
Yaoshuilong 163
Zhabei 91
Zhujiajiao 139, 151
Shanghai 2010 World Expo xi–xiv, xxiv–xxv, xxvi, 11, 27, 28, 53, 57, 64, 102, 148, 184
  Alsace Pavilion 28
  Canadian Pavilion 28
  China Pavilion 184
  Pavilion of the Future xxiv–xxv, 28
  Shanghai Automotive Industry Corporation-General Motors (SAIC-GM) pavilion xi–xii
  Shanghai City Pavilion 28
  Theme Pavilion 28
Shanghai Automotive Brake Company 97
Shanghai Automotive Industry Corporation-General Motors (SAIC-GM) xi–xii
Shanghai Creative Industries Corporation 99
Shanghai Economic Commission 97
Shanghai International Automobile City Property Management Co Ltd 135
Shanghai International Studies University 135
Shanghai Investment Commission 47
Shanghai Maker Faire 107
Shanghai Municipal Government (SMG) 48, 56, 93, 96–7, 99
Shanghai New Towns: Searching for Community and Identity in a Sprawling Metropolis 134
Shanghai Sculpture Space 98–9
Shanghai Star 57

INDEX

Shanghai Style *see haipai*

Shanghai Tower xxv, 1–2, 28, 51

Shanghai Urban Planning and Design Institute (SUPDI) 45, 46, 56

Shanghai World Financial Center (SWFC) 1, 5, 18–19, 24, 26, 51

Shanghaihua 147

shangyou zhengce, xiayou duice (policies above, counter-strategies below) 54

shantytowns 163–6

shanzhai 201–5

'Shanzhai: A Chinese Phenomenon' 201–3

sharism 205

Shea Stadium, New York 34

Shenbao 70

Shenzhen, Guangdong xxiv, 45, 47, 135, 165, 176, 201, 203

Shi Mengqi 203

Shi Yongjiang 201

Shi Zhecun 69, 80

Shih, Shu-mei 71, 79, 80

Shiji Dadao *see* Century Avenue

Shijiazhuang City, Hebei Province 176

shikumen 107, 113–14, 120, 123, 124, 125, 146, 181

Shirky, Clay 205

Shock of the New, The xxvi

Shui On Group 106, 127

Sichuan Province 39, 157

Sihang Warehouse 91–2

Silicon Valley, California xxvi, 94, 106

Singapore 47, 171

Six Dynasties (317–589) 195

siying (private lending) 194

Skype 142

Skyscraper Museum, Hong Kong 25

Skyscraper Museum, Manhattan 19
   New York Modern 76

skyscrapers 24–7, 55, 56, 75, 83–4

Sleeping Beauty xxiii

Slovakia 82

slums 139, 160–6, 185

Socialism, Capitalism, Democracy 198–9

Socialist Realism 146

Soleri, Paolo
   'Arcologies' 25
   'lean linear city' xxv

Song dynasty 13, 203

Songjiang, Shanghai 131, 132, 134, 135, 147, 152
   New City Construction and Development Company 131

Sony 200

Soul Stealers 171

South Africa 165

south facing windows 30, 119, 136–7

Special Economic Zones (SEZ) xxiii–xxiv, 46, 55, 96, 135, 176, 201

spectacle and deception 5, 44, 53–64

Specter, Michael xiii

speculative property investment 149–50, 153, 158

Speer, Albert 135

'Spirit of May 35th, The' 105

Spring Festival 9–10, 203

St Louis 1904 Olympics xviii

State Owned Enterprises (SOEs) 48, 96–7, 98, 147, 195

Stealth Nation 189

Stephenson, Neal 155–6, 179

Sterling, Bruce 79

Strangers in the City 171

Strawberry Hill, Twickenham 74

Streamline Moderne xvii, xxi, 82

street markets 181–5

street vendors 29, 50, 57, 60

streets 39–41

subitism 13

suburbs 8–9, 23, 131–53, 156–8

Summerson, John 23

Sun Jiwei 138

INDEX

Sun Xun 87
Sun Yat-sen 54, 70
Sun Zhigang 168
sustainable design 27–8, 136–7
Suzhou Creek, Shanghai 82, 82, 87,
  90–3, 163, 165
  'Suzhou Creek Rehabilitation Proj-
    ect, The' 92
  Suzhou Creek Warehouse, Shanghai
    91, 100, 108
Suzhou, Jiangsu 90
Sweden xv
Swedish Town, Shanghai 134, 138
Swislocki, Mark
  Culinary Nostalgia 179
System D 190

Taihu Lake, Suzhou 90
Taikang Lu, Shanghai 124–5, 184
Taiping Rebellion 116
Taiwan 171, 201
Taleb, Nicholas 107
Tang dynasty 195
Tao Ho 43
Taobao 182
Taoism 53, 62, 109
tax vouchers *see fapiao*
Thames Town, Shanghai 131–3, 134,
  137–8
  wedding photo industry 131, 133,
    137
Theogony xvi
Therborn, Goran 3
Things to Come xxi
Third World urbanisation 160–2,
  190–3, 199
Thompson, Benjamin 112
Thompson, James 139
Tiananmen Square protests 105
Tianzifang, Shanghai 123–5
Tide Players 152
Time 19

time-consciousness xv–xvi, 11–13,
  159–60, 208
  cyclical time 209
  linear time 208
tingzijian 119
Tokyo, Japan 19, 20, 26, 51
Tokyo University 204
Tong Le Fang, Shanghai 100
Tongji University, Shanghai 106, 138
Toronto CN Tower xxiv
traditionalism 75
traffic congestion xi, 134
Tribune Tower, Chicago 75
Triumph of the City 35, 162–3
True Story of Ah Q, The 81
'Trylon' xvii
Tsai, Kellee 194, 195, 196, 198
  Back Alley Banking 194
Tsai Wan-Lin
  *Redevelopment and Preservation
    of Historic Lilong Housing in
    Shanghai, The* 123
Tse, Edward 201–3
Tsinghua University, Beijing 165
Tudor Style 82, 83, 131
Turkey 135
Tuscany, Italy 112
Tutankhamun 85
Twickenham, England 74

UNESCO Asia Pacific heritage awards
  91
Union Building, Shanghai 82
United Kingdom xv, 48, 94, 99
  Atkins Consultancy 131, 137
  Bristol 133
  Cobb Fish and Chip Shop, The 133
  concessions in Shanghai 116–17
  Department for Culture, Media and
    Sport (DCMS) 94
  Factory, The 100
  Letchworth, Hertfordshire 140

London 8, 139, 185–6
Manchester 144
Millennium Dome, Greenwich 94
suburbs 144–5
Victorian era 75, 77, 139, 185
Welwyn, Hertfordshire 140
United Nations Headquarters, New
York 34
United States
California xxvi, 64, 80, 89, 94, 106,
143
Chicago, Illinois xix, 25, 75
Detroit, Michigan 153
Hollywood, Los Angeles 64, 80,
89, 94
New York 8, 9, 18, 19, 23, 25, 26,
27, 34–5, 36, 37, 40, 46, 75–6,
84, 89, 98, 160
Silicon Valley, California xxvi, 94,
106
suburbia 142–3, 151
urbanisation 158, 161
White House, Washington D.C. 135
University Avenue, Shanghai 107
Unwin, Raymond 140
urban architecture 4–5
Urban China in Transition 146
Urban Cultural Bureau, Shanghai 98
Urban Planning Administration Bureau
of Shanghai 137
urban planning
bottom-up emergence 38, 41, 48,
60, 90–3, 123–7
congestion and dispersion 139
Garden Cities 139–41
and geopolitics 39–40
and informal economy 183–7
roads 30, 39–41, 42–4, 141–3
top-down plans 30–7, 38, 39–41,
42–5, 47, 60, 92–3, 125, 126–7
Urban Planning Museum 1, 132
urban villages (cheng zhong cun); see
also shantytowns

Urbanatomy 114
Shanghai Expo Guide xix
urbanisation 5, 9, 10, 20–3, 27, 32, 36,
39, 43, 58, 133, 139, 148, 150, 156,
158–60, 166–79
congestion and dispersion 23–5, 139
environmental concerns 27–8
and informal economy 191
and slums 160–6
urbanism xiv, 5, 6, 9–10, 20, 22, 26,
32, 35, 36, 186
and anti-urbanism 38–41, 152, 161
New Urbanists 136
road-based 30, 39–41, 42–4, 141–3

Valley of the Kings, Egypt 85
van der Rohe, Mies 136
Vancouver, Canada 124
Versailles, Île-de-France 131
Vertical Garden Cities 25–7
Victoria and Albert Museum, London
84
Victorian era 75, 77, 139, 185
Victorian Style 131
Vietnam War xx
village communities 169–70
Volkswagen 135
von Hippel, Eric 205

Wakeman, Frederic 177
Wal-Mart xxvi, 199
Waldmeir, Patti xiv
Walkman 200
Wall Street Journal 203
Wall Street, New York 94
Walpole, Horace 74
Castle of Otranto, The 74–5
Wang, David 81
Monster That is History, The 79
Wang Fang 88
Wang, Gary 7, 104
Wang Jing

INDEX

'Global Reach of a New Discourse, The 103
Wang Meng 152
Wang Xiaolai 175
Wang Yirong 72
Wasserstrom, Jeff xxiii, xxiv, xxvi, xiv, 11, 73, 113
Global Shanghai xxiii, xxvi
water clock 11
Waters, Alice xxvi
Weber, Max 10, 77, 198
wedding photo industry 131, 133, 137
Weihei 696 art cluster 101
Weimar Germany 8, 135
Wells, Herbert George "H. G." 'Anticipations' 141
Welwyn, England 140
Wenzhou, Zhejiang 196–8, 199
West Chelsea, New York 98
Westernisation 53–4
Westinghouse pavilion xviii
'Westinghouse Time Capsule' xvii, xix
White House, Washington D.C. 135
Wikipedia xxiv
Wild Grass 81
Willis, Carol 76, 84
Winchester, Simon
River at the Center of the World xxvi
Winey, Dan 28
Wo Ju (Snail House) 149
Wong, Tony 97–8
Wood, Ben 44, 111–13, 127, 139
Wood, Ghislaine 84
Woolworth Building, New York 75
World Financial Center, Shanghai 1, 5
World Trade Center, New York 46
World War I xix, 82
World War II xix, xxiii, 91–2, 122
World, The 135
World's Fairs xii, xiii–xiv, xvii–xx, xxvi–xxvii
1851 Great Exhibition, London xviii

1933 Chicago World's Fair (A Century of Progress) xix
1939 New York World's Fair xii, xvii–xviii, xix
1962 Seattle World's Fair (Century 21 Exposition) xxiv
1964 New York World's Fair xix
1967 Montreal Expo xx
2010 Shanghai World Expo xi–xiv, xxiv–xxv, xxvi, 11, 27, 28, 53, 57, 64, 102, 148, 184
Worringer, Wilhelm
Form in Gothic 77
Wright, Frank Lloyd xxv, 25
Wu Jiang 137
Wu Jing Nuan 12
Wu Meisen 125
Wu Qidi 96
Wu's House, Tongren Lu 82
Wuhan, Hubei 113
Wujiang, Shanghai 146
Wujiaochang, Shanghai 106

Xi Jinping 9
Xi Yang Yang 148
Xiamen, Fujian xxiv, 39, 45, 47
xiaochi (snacks) 119
baozi 183, 184
bing 183, 184
xiaolongbao 50
Xiayu Kindergarten, Qingpu 139
Xin Gu 97
Xinan Electrical Machine Plant, Shanghai 88
Xinchejian, Shanghai 204
Xintiandi, Shanghai 44, 97, 106, 111–114, 123, 125, 127, 138
Xu Jilin 102–3, 115
Xu Xiaoping 104
Xu Zhen 92
Xue Song 92

Yager, Greg xiii

Yanan Lu, Shanghai 104
Yang Tingbao 84
Yang Yongliang 87
Yangpu, Shanghai 106–7, 108
Yangshupu Lu, Shanghai 109
Yangzi River 46, 156
yanzhidian (tobacco and paper stores) 119
Yaoshuilong, Shanghai 163
Ye, Juliet 203
Ye Longfei 47
Yijing 1, 12, 63, 69, 209
yin/yang 6, 63, 209
YouTube xii
Yu Hua 105, 148, 203–4
Yu Zhu 176
yuebing (mooncakes) 182
Yuyuan, Shanghai 181

Zha Jianying 152

Zhabei, Shanghai 91
Zhang, Li *Strangers in the City* 171
Zhao Qizheng 17, 22
Zhaojiabang, Shanghai 163, 165
Zhejiang Province 56, 58, 99, 116, 196–8, 199
Zhou Chong Xin 99
Zhou dynasty 166
Zhou, Kate 60
Zhou Tiehai 92, 99
Zhou Xinliang 125
Zhou Yixing 146
Zhu Rongji 55
Zhu Sheng 201
Zhuan Jun 84
Zhuangzi 62
Zhuhai, Guangdong 45
Zhujiajiao, Shanghai 139, 151
Zoroaster xvi